This volume identifies historical metrics as an important discipline within English studies, with significant questions about the composition and transmission of both alliterative and nonalliterative verse. The chronological range – Old English to the pre-Renaissance – covers a period of great linguistic and poetic change, at the end of which the formal foundations for English verse had been established.

Historical metrics and current issues within it are discussed from several distinctive perspectives, ranging from linguistics and generative metrics, through philological studies of individual texts and metrical problems, to the relationship between metrics and scholarly editing. That metrics involves interdisciplinary study gives the field an exciting breadth as well as a potential for controversy.

Issues in Old English are found in the chapters by Cable, Russom, McCully, and Obst, with a summary conspectus given by Stockwell. For early Middle English, Minkova's work on the *Ormulum* is of special importance to theories both of language and verseform, while alliterative texts are covered by Borroff, Matonis, and Osberg. Editorial practice, and its relationship to metrics, is discussed by Bunt and Duggan; and theories of Chaucerian metrics, including the origin of Chaucer's long line, are analysed by Youmans and Duffell. Cable's keynote introductory chapter outlines some of the main topics of this field of enquiry and indicates some of the ways in which significant questions may be asked, and may develop, within the discipline.

English historical metrics

English historical metrics

Edited by

C. B. McCully and J. J. Anderson

CAMBRIDGE
UNIVERSITY PRESS

Published by the Press Syndicate of the University of Cambridge
The Pitt Building, Trumpington Street, Cambridge CB2 1RP
40 West 20th Street, New York, NY 10011-4211, USA
10 Stamford Road, Oakleigh, Melbourne 3166, Australia

First published 1996

Printed in Great Britain at the University Press, Cambridge

A catalogue record for this book is available from the British Library

Library of Congress cataloguing in publication data

English historical metrics/edited by C. B. McCully and J. J. Anderson
        p.   cm.
ISBN 0 521 55464 0 (hardback)
1. English language – Old English, ca. 450–1100 – Versification.
2. English language – Middle English, 1100–1500 – Versification.
I. McCully, C. B.   II. Anderson, J. J.
PE253.E.E54   1996
829′.1–dc20   95–49017   CIP

ISBN 0 521 55464 0 hardback

Contents

Contributors

J. J. Anderson
Department of English and American Studies
Manchester University

Marie Borroff
Department of English, Yale University

Gerrit H. V. Bunt
formerly Department of English, University of Groningen

Tom Cable
Department of English, University of Texas at Austin

Martin J. Duffell
Department of Hispanic Studies, Queen Mary & Westfield
College, University of London

Hoyt N. Duggan
Department of English, University of Virginia

C. B. McCully
Department of English and American Studies
Manchester University

A. T. E. Matonis
College of Arts & Sciences, Temple University, Philadelphia

Donka Minkova
Department of English, University of California, Los Angeles

Wolfgang Obst
Philosophische Fakultät II, University of Augsburg

Richard Osberg
Department of English, Santa Clara University, California

Geoffrey Russom
Department of English, Brown University

Robert P. Stockwell
Department of Linguistics, University of California, Los Angeles

Gilbert Youmans
Department of English, University of Missouri–Columbia

Acknowledgements

Many people contributed to the making of this book. Chief among them are, of course, the speakers and participants at the First G.L. Brook Symposium, who ensured not only that the standard of presentation was exceptional but also that the questions and debates were conceptually rich, generating many further prosodic studies whose scope has by no means been exhausted. We also thank those of our colleagues who gave freely of their time and scholarship in both the symposium and its textual aftermath. In particular we thank Maxine Powell, whose secretarial and administrative skills did so much to facilitate the production of this text.

Manchester   C.B.M.
1995   J.J.A

Acknowledgements

1 Introduction

C. B. McCully and J. J. Anderson

In 1991, scholars from the United Kingdom, Europe, and America met in Manchester to participate in the First G. L. Brook Symposium. The theme of that inaugural event (the first in a series of biennial symposia) was English historical metrics, 'historical', for these purposes, being defined as the period including Old English (OE) and both the earlier and later phases of Middle English (ME, where early Middle English is abbreviated as eME).

Metrics – or 'prosody', to give the subject its older title – was chosen as a theme because of the vitality of recent approaches to the topic. Indeed, it could be argued that in few fields of linguistic or philological enquiry have more substantive gains been made during the last ten years. The vitality of the work has been given new impetus by the research into, and development of, nonlinear representations of stress and rhythm, beginning with the pioneering work of Liberman (1975), Liberman and Prince (1977), and, in work specific to metrics, Kiparsky (1977), whose seminal article on English poetic metres appeared, significantly, alongside Liberman and Prince's often-cited study in *Linguistic Inquiry* .

In this sense it is no accident that at least six of the contributors to this volume are linguists or have major research specialisms in linguistics. Russom, McCully, Minkova, and Youmans, for example, explicitly adopt nonlinear representations of poetic metre(s), and their analyses are 'generative' in the sense that they are rule-governed and predictive and that their results are reproducible from a constrained set of principles.

In a closely associated field, Obst and Stockwell reopen one of the most enduring debates in prosodic studies: if metrical systems describe (among other things) words moving through time, what role does temporal prosody play in the overall rhythmic organisation of a poem? Are time values abstracted from the analysis, or has temporal theory some more coercive role to play? Temporal theory itself – familiar to

1

prosodists from the late nineteenth century onwards, and familiar to OE scholars from the work of J.C.Pope (1942, 1966) – may be extended and deepened by being recast in a generative linguistic framework.

Nevertheless, it is one of the aims of the Brook Symposia to be cross-disciplinary, and other contributors here develop the insights of traditional philology, or of editorial practice, to specifically metrical fields. Borroff and Matonis, for example, are in dialogue about the structural and thematic relevance of alliteration to our understanding of ME texts. Osberg – both linguist and philologist – uses alliteration as a structural tool to uncover some of the principles underlying the metrical systems of the *Pearl* poet. And Bunt and Duggan are again in dialogue about the conservatism or otherwise of editorial procedures in ME: exactly what 'text' is the object of metrical analysis? How far can an authorial ur-text be legitimised? And what is the role played by the scribe(s) in the transmission of prosodic systems? In such questions, metrical analysis meets critical theory.

Cable, Duffell, and Youmans devote all or parts of their chapters to a careful reinterpretation of Chaucer's decasyllabic metre, arguing towards similar (although by no means identical) conclusions from different theoretical standpoints. One major conclusion, supported by Cable's contrasting of Chaucer and Shakespeare, by Youmans' assumption of a (nonlinear) binary hierarchy, and by Duffell's investigation of the historical origins of Chaucer's long line, appears to be that Chaucer wrote in a form of alternating decasyllabic metre whose internal consistency he himself invented – although this development had been anticipated by the earlier development of alternating metrical forms, and itself anticipates the later evolution of a verseform showing full-blown 'classical' foot structures, i.e. iambs, trochees, and the apparatus of traditional metrical description. This notion – the underlying contrast between 'alternating' and foot-based metres – may perhaps be a matter of degree (see especially the contribution by Youmans, who finds some examples of metrical structures in Chaucer which are characteristic of foot-based metres) rather than an absolute matter of kind. Perhaps, too, the contrast between alternating and foot-based might appear to be a self-evident truth, but set in the context of early English metrical systems, and supported by scholars working from different assumptions, it is a striking one. Yet as Duggan acknowledges, we currently lack any clear or definitive statement about when and how the 'classical foot' took on its coercive and prestigious role in English metrical systems. The work presented in this volume – by Youmans in particular – hints at some solutions to that difficult question.

Both perennial and entirely new questions are addressed here, and their scope explored. What is 'a metre'? What, in fact, is 'a line' (or a half-line)? Can metrical analysis provide one diagnostic for what Cable argues is the mental reality underlying poetic composition? Are early English metres really based (as many decades of scholarship have tended to assume) on the 'classical foot'? And if so, how can this be demonstrated? And if not, what other principles were obtaining? Did such principles apply throughout a particular poem ('homomorphic form', in Osberg's terms)? Or are some early English poems composed using a mixture of metrical systems ('heteromorphic form')? If such mixed systems exist, what is their history?

In conclusion, let us pick out one area where new work on metrics yields particularly exciting and challenging results. Minkova's paper on the regular (disastrously hypnotic, some would claim) metre of the *Ormulum* argues that the metrical structure is describable in terms of a nonlinear template. One might, of course, choose to describe Orm's metre without recourse to such a template (e.g. she says 'the septenarius consists of fifteen syllables, seven strong beats, weak syllables flanking each strong beat, and a strong caesura (= graphic line-break) after the eighth sylla-ble'), but Minkova shows precisely what descriptive gains may be made by adopting a nonlinear description. A linear display can be found in (1):

(1) Annd hé badd séttenn úpp o wrítt
     All mánnkinn fórr to lókenn . . .

The nonlinear template is captured in (2):

(2)

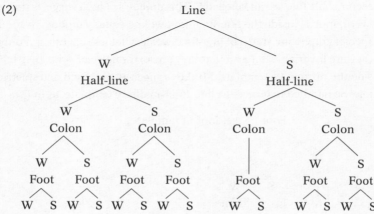

Minkova assumes – in common with most if not all contributors here, and in line with the vast majority of metrists of the last thirty years – that 'the language of poetry reflects adequately the phonology and prosody of the spoken language' and further that the 'metrical intuitions of the people who composed eME accentual-syllabic verse did not differ from the intuitions of poets of later time' (see Chapter 7). (The last assumption is familiar to historical linguists as the 'uniformitarian hypothesis'.) In other words, what bears a linguistic stress usually – although certainly not always – bears a metrical stress, i.e. matches a strong metrical position (a bottom-line S in (2)). Conversely, a weak (or weaker-than-strong) syllable usually – although again, not always – matches a metrical W. One of the advantages of a nonlinear template is that it allows a graphic identity to prosodic matching or mismatching; as Minkova puts it, 'the binary tree representation . . . adumbrates a difference between the positions in the line which is crucial in determining the validity of conclusions based on "mismatches" between prosody [in Minkova's terminology, linguistic stress] and metre [in Minkova's terminology, verse-specific structure]'.

With Minkova's example of Orm, let us outline some of the main features of this brand of metrical analysis. First, it is the case that Orm invariably ends the second half-line with a totally unstressed syllable (whose vowel is invariably written <e>). Yet in the template above, the second half-line ends with a W S foot; the final weak syllable is not incorporated in the overall design.

There are two reasons for this. First, notice that the final foot of the line is uniquely dominated by three S's: the foot itself, the colon, and the second half-line are all labelled S. This unique strength suggests that whatever happens inside the line-final foot will be equally unique. Second, the special graphemic status of line-final weak syllables suggests not only that they are invariable but also that they are 'extrametrical' – i.e. they fall outside the normative template. Minkova suggests that such extrametricality may be handled in terms of a line-final auxiliary template, as in (3):

(3)   Foot (= last foot of template)

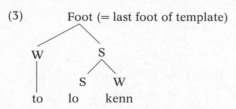

The extrametrical status of syllables such as <-kenn> is captured in the fact of their nesting within a final S; further, 'no level of stress other than absolute zero can be buried that deep down in the metrical hierarchy'; and further still, 'the weak metrical subposition cannot be filled with a lexical monosyllable, nor can it be filled by a disyllabic compound. Thus certain sequences distributed freely over other positions are disallowed from the last foot' (quoted material here is Minkova's; see Chapter 7, p. 104). So the assumption of hierarchy brings (at least) two descriptive gains: it predicts that whatever happens within the final foot will be somehow different to what is allowed elsewhere, and it predicts normative metrical structure line-finally through the existence of an auxiliary template – in effect, a metrical filter. The often-observed metrical tightness that holds in line-final positions (in this metre as in many others) is, then, a consequence of hierarchical organisation.

Turning to the opposite edge of the line (where there is an often-observed metrical looseness or lack of constraint), the initial W is norma-tively filled by a syllable which is either a clitic word (conjunction, preposition, auxiliary verb, adverb of degree . . .) or has a status lower than a clitic in the syntactic hierarchy (e.g. a verbal prefix such as ȝe-). This is another clearly defined metrical constraint: the initial W syllable of the line, traditionally called a syllable showing anacrusis to the first foot, is prosodically subordinate to the following syntactic constituent (the clitic host). Notice here, though, that, in contrast to what occurs line-finally, the constraint must invoke syntax (i.e. a clitic correspondence rule which defines the status of the W syllable in terms of reference to a clitic group); nor can the initial syllable be labelled extrametrical. These apparent facts may be captured by the template below:

(4)   Foot

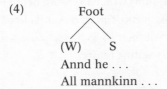

   (W)   S
   Annd he . . .
   All mannkinn . . .

Notice that the revised template makes the initial W optional. If it occurs, it will be a clitic or prefix; if it does not occur, prominence relations will be reversed 'from iambic to trochaic in the case of line-initial disyllabic words'. Stating the constraints on what occurs at the left edge of the line in terms of optionality (the template in (4)) and syntax (the clitic group) allows more freedom at the left than at the right edge of the line. As Minkova puts it, '[r]ight-edge extrametricality weighs down the foot, enriches it, and stipulates inflexible prominence relations . . . Left-edge clitic matching allows freedom and conformity with the stress patterns' (see further Chapter 7, p. 105).

Finally here the nonlinear template and its accompanying constraints allow a graphic realisation of typical statements about structure elsewhere in the line. It is commonly observed, for instance, that matching in the fifth foot (the first foot of the second half-line) is subject to the same constraints as the line-initial foot. The nonlinear template helps to explain why this might be so: the fifth foot is in the same relationship to its colon and half-line as is the first. Or again, matching in the fourth foot of the line is invariably regular. This foot is in the same relation to its colon and half-line as is the line-final foot, where constraint on matching is heavy (or even heavier).

As Minkova concludes, we conclude: this form of metrical analysis offers both conceptual richness and descriptive power. The understanding of pre-Chaucerian verse is enabled by postulating layered, rather than serial, representations (see also Russom and McCully, this volume). Formalising metrical constraints in terms of hierarchy and metrical/linguistic matching also allows a deeper understanding of synchronic word-stress patterning, especially the role played by secondary (word) stress in OE. Moreover, capturing apparent metrical facts in terms of a nonlinear template may offer unexpected evidence for segmental phonology: in Orm's metre, for example, the metrical structure of the line-final foot supports the view that the text is a reliable source of information about the weight of the fourteenth syllable.

If it seeks to investigate further the questions which the work of the First Brook Symposium has raised, and to raise further questions still about the nature of English rhythm and metres, then metrics as a discipline within English language studies is assured of an exciting future.

2 Clashing stress in the metres of Old, Middle, and Renaissance English

Thomas Cable

In his still standard edition of the Harley lyrics, G. L. Brook traced the origin of certain ME rhythms to the OE long line (Brook 1964: 18). Brook's observation served as a point of departure for the astute and subtle metrical analysis in Osberg (1984), which revealed the complexities of the traditions within which the lyrics were composed. Another Manchester scholar, J. P. Oakden, is the implicit point of departure for much of the analysis that follows (Oakden 1930, 1935). I intend to show that, although the earlier scholarship was helpful and clarifying, the actual developments are less straightforward and more complex. Yet there is a simplicity underlying the historical developments that is grounded in some of the best-known principles of recent theoretical phonology.

Let us begin with six lines of poetry containing the adjective *good* followed by a noun – two from OE, two from ME, and two from the Renaissance English of Shakespeare:[1]

(1)   x   x   / \ x
      þæt wæs gōd cyning   (*Beowulf* 11b)

     / (x) / \ x
      gōd gūðcyning (*Beowulf* 2563a)

                      ...x   x / (x) / x
      And he granted and hym gafe   with a goud wylle
                             (*Gawain* 1861b)

      x /   x /   x / x / x /
      A good man was ther of religioun   (*General Prologue* 477)

      x x /| (x)/ ...
      Like a good parent, did beget of him   (*Tempest* 1.2.94)

               ...x   / |\   /
      I will, my lord. God give your Grace good rest
                     (*Richard III* 1.4.75)

7

Because the monosyllabic adjective *good* (or *gōd* or *goud*), which is a likely candidate for metrical stress, is always followed by the stressed syllable of a noun, which is also a likely candidate for metrical stress, there is a clear possibility in each of these lines for clashing metrical stress. Yet three of the lines, one from each period, are scanned with the stresses separated by an x in parentheses. In the other three lines, one of the two potentially clashing syllables is scanned with less than full stress – either secondary stress, \, or lack of stress, x. In justifying these scansions, this chapter will sketch distinctly different metres for *Beowulf*, *Sir Gawain and the Green Knight*, Chaucer, and Shakespeare. The specific structures provide clues to the full metres, and the full metres in turn rationalise the analyses given to the specific structures. With a better understanding of the internal rhythmical mechanisms and their grounding in a stress-timed language (English of any period), we can describe more adequately how one metre develops into another either through misreading or through intentional modification.

Old English

The separate elements of OE metre – stress, quantity, alliteration, resolution and suspension of resolution, measures, breath groups, foot divisions, inferred pitch contours, etc. – are so highly regulated and interrelated that it is possible to start with one or two elements and either derive the others directly or specify them as natural corollaries. The interdependency of elements explains the multiplicity of theories that can begin at different points and accomplish more or less the same thing. The most widely used starting point is a set of stress patterns, as in the Five Types of Sievers (1885). Cable (1991) begins at yet another point – a count of syllables, four syllables to the half-line. In actuality, this is not radically different from the four-position base, which (along with the Five Types) goes back to Sievers' original theory and which Cable (1974) had restated with minor modifications.

Although not even a majority of half-lines in *Beowulf* literally have only four syllables (see Stockwell, this volume), there are advantages in starting with a count of syllables rather than with the more abstract count of positions. The main advantage is that otherwise the four positions must immediately be constrained so that the last two positions normally contain only one syllable or its resolved equivalent – as must also at least one of the first two positions. It is both theoretically more economical and intuitively more compelling to say that the half-line of OE normally contains four syllables (or the resolved equivalents) and then to allow an exception which specifies that a series of unstressed syllables can substitute for one of the first two syllables. The substituted series can consist of two, three, four, or five unstressed syllables. The effect of this statement and its exception is to remind one that if a half-line begins with a stretch of unstressed syllables, then one normally expects only one syllable (or the resolved equivalent) in each of the last three positions. Likewise, if the unstressed syllables are in second position (Type A), then the first, third, and fourth positions normally have only one syllable (or the resolved equivalent). Traditionally, this principle, to the extent that it has been recognised at all, has taken the form of one among many conditions and has been buried in the technicalities of the metre. In losing sight of it, one misses a central difference between the OE line and the ME alliterative long line. The ME first half-line, or a-verse (but significantly not the second half-line, or b-verse), routinely has two or more unstressed syllables before and after the first stress, as in the a-verse from the *Gawain* line cited above:

(2) x   x / x x x /
    And he granted and hym gafe

This pattern is unmetrical in the *Beowulf* metre, although it conforms to the usual handbook simplification (two stresses to the half-line and a variable number of unstressed syllables). Most Anglo-Saxonists would probably manage to identify the pattern as a variety of Type B; it is doubtful that many could take the next step and identify it as a metrical pattern that is disallowed in classical OE verse. Despite its absence in OE, it occurs everywhere in the a-verses of ME.

Starting with a very concrete count of syllables gives a salience to this difference between OE metre and ME metre that the more abstract 'position' or 'member' or *Glied* obscures. It also throws into sharp relief the possible readings when two stresses 'clash', the subject of this paper. Thus, Sievers' familiar Five Types of half-line labelled A through E can be seen to have four positions. The following verses from *Beowulf* are quite regular in having the stretch of unstressed syllables, if it occurs at all, in one of the first two positions:

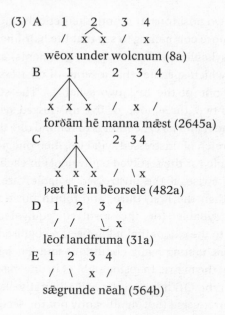

(3) A 1   2   3   4

wēox under wolcnum (8a)

B 1   2   3   4

forðām hē manna mǣst (2645a)

C 1   2 3 4

þæt hīe in bēorsele (482a)

D 1   2   3   4

lēof landfruma (31a)

E 1   2   3   4

sǣgrunde nēah (564b)

Three of the Five Types – C, D, and E – have the most typical pattern for clashing stress – a main stress and a secondary stress within a compound (*bēorsele, landfruma, sǣgrunde*). In addition, the example of Type D has clashing stress between two words (*lēof land-*). It is widely assumed that Types D and E are asymmetrical mirror images of each other (see also McCully, this volume), a relationship that seems especially clear when the verses are divided into feet, as in Sievers' system: D / | / \ x, E / \ x | /. For this reason, the two types are often taken together in discussion of secondary stress, clashing stress, and the use of the old poetic compounds.[2] Sometimes Type C is added to this grouping, in contrast with Types A and B, which have more evenly alternating stress (reminiscent of trochaic or dactylic and iambic or anapaestic metres respectively).

The count of syllables and the count of stresses interact in a complex way in a stress-timed language such as OE, ME, or Modern English. The difficulties of writing syllabic verse in Modern English are well known. With reference to experiments in syllabic metre by W. H. Auden, Marianne Moore, Yvor Winters, Alan Stephens, Thom Gunn, and Donald Hall, Fussell (1979: 7) notes that 'syllabism is not a natural measuring system in a language so Germanic and thus so accentual as English'. Fussell cites poems that begin syllabically and quietly enough, only to be overwhelmed by the stress accent: 'But in English, accent, like passion and murder, will out, and it will out the moment the poet, arrived at a climax, seizes all the techniques of prosodic reinforcement offered him by the conventions of the English language' (p. 8).

There are phonological reasons, however, for considering OE to be less stress-timed than Modern English – for example, the differences in the phonology of vocalic length and of reduced vowels in the two stages of the language (see McCully 1988: 369–74 and Cable 1991: 30–3). Still, on a spectrum, OE lies toward the stress-timed (or 'stress-based') end. Consequently, the considerations that Fussell describes in syllabic metres of Modern English apply to a certain extent to those of OE as well. In OE metre the problem is complicated by the allowance of a dip of two or more syllables (a 'strong dip'), which must be ended by a stressed syllable. Thus, the role of stress is built into the basically syllabic metre. Many of the technical rules regarding resolution, suspension of resolution, and secondary stress involve determining whether we have part of a multisyllabic dip or a syllable that counts as a position.

Let us think of two systems in tension – a syllable-count system and a system of periodicities delimited by stress. McCully (1988: 423–34; 1992) uses a 'bi-planar' model adapted from recent phonological theory to explain the traditional split in OE metrics between two-beat and four-beat theories. This analysis is both clarifying for the older problem and directly relevant to the problem at hand:

To the central issue, however, two-beat vs. four-beat . . . Such a definition is just what we expect if we claim that a four-beat reading is a bi-planar one: *gomban gyldan* and *þrym gefrunon* can both be interpreted as four-beat because each verse embodies two stresses . . . and four rhythmemes . . . Now we may give a definitive answer to the question 'two-beat or four-beat?' The answer is – both. One reading scans patterns of intensity, the other patterns of time-and-intensity. One is a monoplanar scansion, the other bi-planar. Notice also that a bi-planar model can be invoked in a monoplanar reading. The traditional constraint that an OE verse must contain at least four metri-cal positions can exemplify this, since these metrical positions must them-selves be constituted by rhythmemes. (McCully 1988: 432–33)

To this one can add, following Fussell (1979), that there is a potential for the system of periodicities of stress to overwhelm the system of syllable and quantity count (at least to modern ears).

These abstractions can be made concrete by reconsidering the rhythmical relationship of Types D and E. An understanding of how these two types are related will clarify the underlying principles of OE metre. I shall give five interrelated reasons for rejecting the idea that Types D and E are mirror images of each other: (i) the possibility of reading compounds with and without a pause, (ii) the contrasting distribution of short syllables in D and E, (iii) the contrasting distribution of secondary stress (v. tertiary stress) in D and E, (iv) the implications that expanded Type D* has for *metrical pause* and the lack of a corresponding structure in Type E, and (v) parallels in Modern English.

The first reason is simply a recognition of possible variant patterns; the next three reasons argue why one of these patterns is not only possible but plausible; the last reason is that the OE pattern is consistent with patterns of Modern English that have been studied in recent theoretical phonology.

(i) There are various ways of reciting verses of Types C, D, and E that are clearly distinct even to Modern English ears and more or less equally plausible. These variants primarily involve the placing of silent beats with respect to clashing stress. The present analysis departs from both McCully (1988) and Cable (1974) in the reading that is chosen. One is led to this choice through the technicalities of the arguments that follow. Thus, I would no longer read *eorl Bēowulfes* (795a) as both McCully (1988) and Cable (1974) read it, with a beat between the stresses of the two words:

(4) eorl Ø Bēowulfes

The key here is tertiary stress on the second syllable of *Bēowulfes*. If a syllable in that position bears secondary stress – as in, let us assume, *landfruma* – then the distributional evidence argues that the stresses 'back up' from the end of the verse and force a silent beat between the first two syllables (Cable 1991: 143):

(5) leof Ø landfruma

This reading is partly in accord with the elegant analysis in McCully (1988), which puts an additional silent beat between the first two elements of the compound:

(6) leof Ø land Ø fruma

McCully's (1988) reading is not only plausible but also probably the most natural one for modern Anglo-Saxonists, including myself: 'one two three-four'. The point to make here, however, and one that will be made again in the next section when we come to consider ME, is that this reading is not grammatically or phonologically necessary. It is a slower variant of the verse, which also has a faster variant without the silent beat in the compound – rhythmically 'one two-three-four'. Let us consider the reasons for the faster reading.

(ii) Except for a few Type A verses with secondary stress, suspension of resolution occurs almost exclusively in Types C and D.[3] For example:

(7) x   /   \ x   C
     in gēardagum (1b)

      /   /   \ x   D
     bāt bānlocan (742a)

The second elements of the compounds above, although they bear secondary phonological stress and presumably an intermediate level of metrical ictus, are short and are not resolved with the following syllable. The pattern with a short secondary stress occurs so rarely in Type E as to be questionable. Klaeber (1950: 279) lists five Type E verses of the pattern / \ x | / under 'Rare Rhythmical Types' but does not declare them unmetrical; similarly J. C. Pope (1966: 315) notes that the one example in the a-verse can be substantiated by several examples in the b-verse.[4] Cable (1974) also referred to the frequencies and norms of the Type E pattern without claiming an unmetrical classification. These empirical data form a textbook case for negotiating between the requirements of a consistent theory and the hard facts of exceptions to the theory. However, this is not the place to explore that metatheoretical topic (see Cable 1991). It will suffice to make the point that of the 446 Type E verses in *Beowulf* only half a dozen have the secondary stress on a short syllable; by contrast, of the 853 Type D verses in *Beowulf*, 506 have the secondary stress on a short syllable.[5] Clearly, some principle of metre must explain this difference in the frequency of short secondary stresses between these two types. Independently, Fulk (1992) and Cable (1991) have identified the determinative factor as the part of the half-line involved – whether near the beginning or near the end – and we have devised descriptive rules.[6] These descriptive rules, however, seem arbitrary and in need of some deeper rhythmical principle to be satisfying. Perhaps that deeper principle can now be found in the tension of the bi-planar model.

In the verse *mandryhtne bær* (2281b), there is a periodicity between *man-* and *bær* (as will be illustrated in (v) below). The strength of that periodicity also has the effect of subordinating *dryht-*, although not enough for it to be subsumed into the dip. A less weighty syllable – specifically one that is 'short' or 'light' (see note 3) – might well fold into the dip, giving the verse only three positions and making it unmetrical. Thus, short syllables are generally avoided in the second position of Type E. In a Type D verse, such as *lēof landfruma*, these dynamics do not operate. The first two syllables clash, adjustments are made in timing, and the last two syllables are free to be counted as syllables *and* as positions, without the pressure to be subordinated.

This explanation, then, can serve to answer a question that any adequate system of Old English metre should address: if D and E are mirror images, why can Type D have hundreds of verses of the form / / \ x (506 out of 853, or 59 per cent) while there are only a handful of Type E with a short secondary stress, / \ x / ?

(iii) Similarly, why are there almost no Type D verses with secondary stress (rather than tertiary stress or lack of stress) in the b-verse? The problem that this distribution poses has been discussed in Bliss (1967), Cable (1991), and Fulk (1992). Indeed, Type D verses with secondary stress occur in neither half-line with anything like the frequency of Type E verses with secondary stress. For example, *swīðferhþes sīð* (908a) would seem to be a reversible verse: *sīð swīðferhþes*. Yet there are surprisingly few unproblematic verses in *Beowulf* of this seemingly most ordinary pattern: two nouns or a noun and an adjective with four syllables, secondary stress on the compound, and no resolved stress or suspension of resolution.

The technical specifications just named are not excessive, because they describe what Anglo-Saxonists and general metrists think of as the most neutral Type D. There are many verses of the pattern *sīð Bēowulfes* (1971a), but there are also good reasons for considering that the compound has tertiary rather than secondary stress – as discussed extensively by Bliss and Fulk. In the part of the pattern where secondary stress is conventionally designated, Type D is overwhelmingly represented by derivational syllables such as *-ing-* and *-līc-*, by the medial

inflectional syllable of the present and past participle and the inflected
infinitive (-*end*- and -*en*-), by the second element of compound proper
names, and by the second syllable of weak verbs of class 2, all of which
arguably have tertiary stress or weak stress and not secondary stress
(although see also here McCully and Hogg 1990). To give three examples:

(8) /   /   \   x
    lindhæbbende (245a)

    / x   / \ x
    sele Hrōðgāres (826b)

    /   / \ x
    secg wīsade (208b)

Categorial distinctions between secondary stress and tertiary stress may
have the flavour of 1950s suprasegmental phonology, when combinations such as *elevator operator* were analysed at length. Actually, as early
as Sweet (1879), compounds with strong–strong stress sequences (*steel
pen*, *sponge-cake*, *town clock*) were contrasted with compounds with
strong–medium sequences (*snowball, rainbow, homeland*) and
with those with a strong–weak (*England, woodland, chairman*) along
with other patterns. Giegerich (1985: 122–4) makes use of Sweet's
groupings (and modifies them) in making the point that the familiar
bláckbìrd/blàck bírd contrast to illustrate stress in compound nouns
and in phrases oversimplifies the situation. Giegerich (p. 128) cites
Marchand (1969: 5) on 'semi-suffixes' (linguistic units that stand
midway between word and suffix) with examples from Modern English
(for example, *chairman*) that seem remarkably parallel to categories in
our problematic verses of OE (for example, *æþeling*). The point to make
is that the traditional systems of OE metre have not been fine-grained
enough in failing to distinguish among *heall heorudrēore* (487a), *feorh
æþelinges* (2424a), and *secg wīsade* (208b), the relevant stress patterns
of which (in third position, secondary stress, tertiary stress, and weak
stress respectively) have significantly different distributions (see Cable
1991: 137–51). Yet all three verses are scanned as Type D.

(iv) The fourth reason for not considering Types D and E to be mirror
images involves parallels between Type D verses with a posited pause
and Type D* verses in which the posited pause is filled by an actual syllable:

(9)   /   (x) / \ x   D
wearp   wælfȳre (2582a)
/   x   /   \   x   D*
rondas regnhearde (326a)

It is a parallel that I originally analysed in Cable (1974) and then re-examined in Cable (1991), with modifications necessitated by the Bliss–Fulk distinction between secondary stress and tertiary stress. There is no corresponding parallel in Type E, the pattern / x \ x / being unmetrical.

(v) Let us try to make sense of all these diverse facts in an expository way and then show that the main points of the story are well accommodated and illustrated by the device of the phonological grid. The story goes as follows. In Types A, B, and E, the two main stresses of the verse are spaced by at least one syllable. In Type D and in many verses of Type C the two main stresses of the verse actually clash. There are also patterns that might be considered clashing stress in Types A and E; for example, *gūðrinc goldwlanc* (1881a) and the first two syllables of any Type E. However, we shall see that these clashes are overridden or ameliorated by the fact just stated – that the two main stresses of the verse are spaced by at least one syllable. Some Type C verses, such as *ond gefrætwade* (96a), have traditionally been scanned with two stresses. Our revised taxonomy suggests that verses with weak stress or tertiary stress in third position have only one metrical stress. In accord with Bliss's idea of the 'light verse', there is no need in this instance to wrest an additional stress from among syllables that are unlikely candidates (see Bliss 1967: 6–23); the verse is metrical by virtue of conformity to requirements on the syllable-count and quantity plane. In the clashing-stress Types C and D, the way to alleviate the clash is not obvious. The most salient feature of these types is a kind of syncopation, a stressed beat followed immediately by another beat, slightly less stressed. Casting the problem in terms of the need to alleviate a stress clash is interesting in itself. It is the familiar way of discussing clashing stress in ordinary nonpoetic Modern English. The citation form of *thirteen* with stress on the second syllable is shifted to a pattern with stress on the first syllable when another stress immediately follows: *thirtéen*; cf. *thírteen mén*. Thus, the stress clash is alleviated. Bolinger (1962) analyses speakers' preferences for sequences such as 'mad and senseless slaughter' over 'senseless and mad slaughter' on the basis that in the first phrase the last two stresses are separated by an unstressed syllable, whereas in the second phrase they are not.

Suppose, however, that a certain degree of stress clash in OE poetry, while not *eurhythmic* according to the usual ideas of phonology (Liberman and Prince 1977; Hayes 1984; Visch 1989), is desirable. Suppose that the clashing stresses of Type D and of many traditional Type Cs serve exactly the purpose of sporadically interrupting the spaced patterns of Types A, B, and E. These syncopated interruptions keep the verse from settling into a predictable isochrony. Thus, contrary to a mensuralist theory such as J.C. Pope (1966), which equalises the measures by inserting stressed pauses, the point of the metre by the present view is to *avoid* such isochrony.

If the stress clash reaches a certain level, however, the usual means of alleviation kick in. For Type D with secondary stress on the compound, this means a spacer pause or a silent beat between the first two syllables of the verse:

(10)

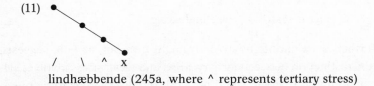

/ (x)/ \ x

gōd gūðcyning (2563a)

If the Type D verse has only tertiary stress on the compound, then successive subordination of each position left to right is possible:

(11)

/ \ ^ x

lindhæbbende (245a, where ^ represents tertiary stress)

A grid representation would contain four different column heights for 245a:

(12) x
      x   x
      x   x   x
      x   x   x   x
      lindhæbbende

For Type E, the initial grid might simply follow the usual workings of the Compound Stress Rule and the Nuclear Stress Rule in the familiar forms that they take in Modern English and in Modern German (although cf. here Maling 1971; McCully and Hogg 1994):

```
(13)                    x
             x          x
             x   x      x
             x   x   x  x
       Gūðbyrne scān (321b)
```

Gūðbyrne has the pattern of compound stress with heaviest stress on the left constituent and secondary stress on the right constituent; *scān*, being the rightmost stressed syllable in the phrase that forms the verse, takes phrasal (or Nuclear) stress, the heaviest stress in the verse.

While this representation is a plausible one for a Type E verse, it is not the only plausible representation. For example, if we take seriously the distinction between secondary stress and tertiary stress, and if we agree that the rules of grid construction have access to the syntactic information on which this distinction is based, then the three stressed columns in 321b might be increased by one level (in contrast to, say, *weallinde wæg*, 2464a, with tertiary stress):

```
(14)                    x
          x             x                   x
          x   x         x        x          x
          x   x         x        x   x      x
          x   x   x     x        x   x   x  x
        Gūðbyrne scān            weallinde wæg
```

On further examination, however, it might turn out, as Fulk suggests, that the distinction between tertiary stress and weak stress involves syllabic quantity, so that we would not wish the distinctions to be represented simply and directly on a stress grid. A bi-planar model would be especially useful here. The matter is an empirical one for future investigation (just as the question of the kind of information to which the rules of grid construction have access is a matter for further theoretical enquiry).

Either analysis would fit neatly with other facts. We can see the difference between *Gūðbyrne scān* or *weallinde wæg* and *rǣhte ongēan* (747b), a verse that is classified as unmetrical in many systems:

(15) x   x
      x   xx   x
      rǣhte ongēan

The two medial syllables are at the level of weak stress and are swallowed in the strong dip that is allowed in one of the first two positions. The verse thus has only three positions and must be marked as unmetrical.

The idea that the metrical form itself, once perceived and understood, exerts its own expectations and tilting effects brings us to the difference in *sound* between compounds in OE and ME metres. Let us turn directly to the ME alliterative long line to hear that difference. As sometimes happens in historical linguistics and historical metrics, the later development that a pattern undergoes clarifies the earlier pattern in a way that was not perceptible from simply focussing on the older form, no matter how intense that focus.

Middle English alliterative metre

Read in context and with attention to the patterns that emerge from grammatical and metrical analysis, the following two verses have significantly different rhythms. The first is from *Judith*, a poem in classical OE metre; the second is from *Sir Gawain and the Green Knight*, the style of which may be described as less strict than that of *Cleanness* but more strict than that of *Piers Plowman*:

(16) to his bedreste   (*Judith* 36a)
      on þe bed-syde   (*Gawain* 1193b)

Both verses have five syllables and a compound with *bed* preceded by two function words. It is *possible* to read the verses with the same rhythm, whatever the rhythm might be. One can imagine a selection of various rhythms that both the OE and the ME would fit. However, in context and in the light of metrical principles that have been argued for each tradition, the OE verse has the syncopated rhythm of clashing stress; the ME verse has a silent beat between its two stresses:

(17) þā ēadigan mægð   ofstum fetigan
      x x / \ x
      to his bedreste   bēagum gehlæste,
      hringum gehrodene   (*Judith* 35–7)

(18) And ho stepped stilly   and stel to his bedde,
Kest vp þe cortyn   and creped withinne,
                   x   x / (x)\ x
And set hir ful softly   on þe bed – syde   (*Gawain* 1191–3)

There is a similar contrast between the metrical pattern of the OE *gold-sele* and the ME *golde-hemmed*, from *Beowulf* and *Gawain* respectively:

(19) x x   /   \ x
to þǣm goldsele (*Beowulf* 1639a)

(20) x x / (x)\   x
þat is golde-hemmed (*Gawain* 2395b)

The *-e* on *golde* in the *Gawain* verse is purely scribal and has no historical justification. It happens to occur at the point where the metre requires a silent beat.

Silent beats between clashing stresses in ME have long been recognised by readers of the poetry. Tolkien and Gordon (1967: 149) divide three-stress verses into those 'with lifts all separated by dips', labelled (i), and those 'with two lifts clashing', labelled (ii). They give three examples of the second type from *Gawain*:

(21)   / /   /
smal sendal bisides (76a)
     /   /   /
þe borȝ brittened and brent (2a)
     /   /   /
were boun busked on hor blonkkez (1693a)

They write: 'In the (ii) types (with lifts clashing) there is a slight rhythmic pause in place of an unstressed element'. The present analysis simply follows the Tolkien–Gordon analysis and extends it to two-stress verses, including the relatively few verses with compound words. Tolkien and Gordon are not explicit about these patterns, but the drift of their discussion makes it logical to assume that they would read all of these clashing-stress patterns with a silent beat.

This reading is also in accord with the patterns assigned to compounds in Modern English by Giegerich (1985), who does something similar for Modern German, and by Hogg and McCully (1987). A debated issue of recent metrical phonology has been whether stress relationships are most adequately represented by trees, by grids, or by both. Giegerich's analysis is representative of a tree approach in its treatment of pauses: he attaches 'zero syllables', or silent beats, to monosyllabic lexical items (nonfunction words, or 'real' words, roughly nouns, verbs, and adjectives) within the lexicon and deletes them when the context requires no pause. The deletion is done by a rule of 'Defooting'. The analysis by Selkirk (1984) is representative of a grid approach, and it moves in the opposite direction: beats are not represented in the lexicon but are inserted where needed in context by rules with names such as 'Silent Demi-Beat Addition'. Either strategy, however, could be invoked to account for the difference that I have claimed between *to his bedreste* (an OE verse without a metrical pause) and *on þe bed-(Ø)syde* (a ME verse with a pause or silent beat within the compound).

It is important to understand, first, that both the reading with the silent beat and the reading without the silent beat are possible in both ME and OE and, second, that the evidence fairly clearly supports one reading for ME and the other reading for OE. The readings are optional in the same way that Modern English *three (Ø) blind (Ø) mice* can be spoken with the silent beats as indicated or without them. As Hogg and McCully (1987: 233–4) say of this phrase, 'it is arguably the case that zero syllables, identified as "pauses" or equated with lengthening phenomena, only have this status in speech uttered at a particularly slow tempo. At a "normal" tempo, and in connected speech, it seems undesirable for such zero syllables to remain non-phrase-finally.'

A worrisome feature of Giegerich's analysis is that although it easily allows both the slow and the fast readings for phrases such as *three blind mice* (with monosyllabic lexical items), the particular foot structure of his theory does not permit the fast option for certain compounds – specifically the deletion of the zero syllable in a pattern such as *good-(Ø) looking tutor*. His theory is left having to claim that this lack of optional deletion is desirable. Well-known contrastive examples argue otherwise, as in *a man-eating fish* and *a man eating fish*, represented by Selkirk (1984: 324–5, following Catford 1966) as follows:

(22) That was a | man-eating | fish
That was a | man ∧ eating | fish

(where <∧> symbolises pause). I shall assume that *man-eating fish*, *good-looking tutor*, and similar phrases can be spoken both with and without the silent beat.

Different modern readers give different interpretations to the ME patterns in question, depending on assumptions that they carry to the verse. One important problem of ME verse is of course the status of final *-e*. The assumption in Borroff (1986) that final *-e* was not sounded within the long line is compatible with her faster reading of the patterns we have been considering. (One assumption does not *entail* the other, but they are compatible.) Borroff's illustrative examples from Modern English are 'a *long* row to hoe' and 'a *hard* act to follow', in which the nouns *row* and *act* are subordinated to the adjectives *long* and *hard* respectively. She relates this pattern to the adjective-plus-noun configuration in *Gawain* 209, which she reads as follows:

(23)   C   c   C   C   C
A spetos sparþe to expoun in spelle, quoso myȝt

C represents a 'major chief syllable' and c a 'minor chief syllable' (and see Borroff 1962: Part II). The scansion that she gives 'finds its justification in the genius of the English language itself, which forbids the placement of primary stress on both components of such a sequence in a single phrase'. It is important to note, however, that the stress contours of 'a long row to hoe' and 'A spetos sparþe to expoun' are significantly different because of the additional weakly stressed syllables in the ME example – what Bolinger (1986) calls 'buffer syllables' between the stresses – even without counting the final *-e* on *sparþe*. A considerable part of metrical phonology of the past two decades has concerned the interaction of stressed and unstressed syllables. The final syllable *-poun* in 209a would receive phrasal stress by the Nuclear Stress Rule, and a plausible grid for the verse would be as follows:

(24)   x
              x   x
              x   x   x
        x   x x   x   x x   x
A spetos sparþe to expoun

Because the spacing of the stressed syllables allows more flexibility, it would also be plausible to reverse the relative stress on *spetos* and *sparþe*. This seven-syllable verse does not have the certainty of clashing stress that 'a long row to hoe' has. By my reading, the syllables would be spaced even further, because a good argument can be made for pronouncing the *-e* on *sparþe*. Furthermore, if *-poun* receives heavier stress

than the first syllable of *spetos*, the idea of primary stress and the statement that only four such stresses can occur in a line is not helpful (there
being a continuum of stresses). We are back to the question of how
many levels of ictus are metrically relevant.

All of this is to say that beyond a certain point the determination of
the reading is a problem of *literary metre* and not a strictly *phonological*
problem. A direct mapping of primary stress, or any other level of
phonological stress, onto metrical ictus will not give us the metrical
pattern. The problem with a dipodic reading of ME alliterative metre is
that the familiar dipodic metres are *regularly* dipodic – as in nursery
rhymes ('Pease porridge hot') and in verse by Rudyard Kipling,
W. S. Gilbert, and John Masefield. The regularities may be exceedingly
complex, as Stewart (1930: 77–91) has shown, but the complexities are
possible as variations because of an underlying template. The sporadic
occurrences of possibly dipodic verse in ME alliterative poetry do not
have reference to such a template.

The alternative to a four-stress reading with sporadic dipodic subordination is a sporadic lengthening of the line by a stress (producing a
five-stress line rather than the more normal four-stress line). One could
reasonably ask whether this departure from the norm is not as anomalous as the dipodic reading. In fact, it is easy to find in modern poetry
(especially poetry which has other characteristics of strong-stress
metre) the occasional extension of a line by an extra stress. Gardner
(1949: 115–17) compares *Piers Plowman* and T. S. Eliot's *Four Quartets*
on just this point. Tolkien and Gordon as revised by Davis (1967: 149)
write, 'Some poets, of whom the author of *Gawain* was one, often used
three lifts in the first half-line – though the third need not be of exactly
the same prominence as the other two.' One of their examples is the
verse we have been considering:

   /   /   /

a spetos sparþe to expoun

The extension of the whole line to five stresses is no more disruptive to
the metre than is a five-stress line from Eliot occurring in a predominantly four-stress passage; the scansion is Gardner's:

(25)   / / /   /   /

When the short day is brightest, with frost and fire

From all the technicalities of clashing stress, stress subordination, and temporal spacing, there emerges a picture of three rhythmical modes in *Sir Gawain and the Green Knight*: the mode of the a-verse, the mode of the b-verse, and the mode of the wheel (about which little will be said here; see Borroff 1962: chs. 5–6). These characteristic modes form a gradation of both speed and firmness, or of coerciveness. The a-verse is the slowest and least coercive. In it, all historically justified final -*e*'s are pronounced, and all lexically stressed items receive metrical ictus (nouns, adjectives, main verbs, lexical adverbs). Metrically stressed syllables that clash are separated by a metrical pause. The overall stress pattern of the a-verse is known only after these local dynamics have operated and after the whole a-verse (including syllables and pauses) has unfolded.

The b-verse has the full conservative syllable structure that the a-verse has (including etymological final -*e*), but it also has clear metrical constraints that shorten the verse and make it faster: there can be only two metrical stresses and only one strong dip (containing two or more syllables); and the verse should end on one and only one unstressed syllable. Thus, whereas the structure of the a-verse is not known until the end, certain facts can be anticipated about the rest of the b-verse when only one or two syllables have been read. The metre is firmer or more coercive in that the infrequent verses with more than two phonological stresses have unmistakable subordination of the middle stress:

(26)   /   /   /   /   x   /
        Of uche clene comly kynde   enclose seven makez
                                         (*Cleanness* 334)
                   /   /   /   x   /
        Thus þer stondes in stale   þe stif kyng hisseluen   (*Gawain* 107)
            /   /   /   x   /
        Al þe honour is your awen—   þe heȝe kyng yow ȝelde
                                         (*Gawain* 1038)

The subordinated stresses on *seven* and *kyng* are marked with x (as all the other unmarked syllables in these lines would be) to show that despite whatever phonological stress these syllables might bear, at the metrical level in Middle English alliterative verse the distinction is binary – ictus or nonictus.

The wheels of *Gawain* are generally shorter than the a-verses and longer than the b-verses of the long line, but the metre is faster, stricter, and more coercive than either (in promoting and demoting stresses and in causing final -*e* to be omitted when necessary for the metrical pattern). Rather than trying to justify these assertions about the metre of the wheels in *Gawain*, which must be the subject of a separate study, let us proceed to Chaucer's iambic pentameter, which has many of these same features.

Chaucer's alternating metre

Cable (1991) argued that what we traditionally think of as two different styles of the iambic pentameter – Chaucer's and Shakespeare's style – are actually two different metres. Chaucer's metre is a continuously alternating stress pattern from the beginning of the line to the end; Shakespeare's metrical line is divided into five rising feet. An abstract representation of the two metres using the notation of Jespersen (1913) makes the difference clear (although it is a representation contrary to Jespersen's argument, since he intended the alternating pattern to apply to *all* iambic pentameter in the Germanic languages):

(27) Chaucer   a/b\a/b\a/b\a/b\a/b
      Shakespeare   a/b a/b a/b a/b a/b

The letters a and b stand for syllables, and the diagonals show the direction of change of stress, whether rising or falling. Whatever the empirical and theoretical adequacy of these patterns may prove to be, it is worth noting a straightforward matter of simplicity before proceeding further. It is often said that the imposition of feet complicates metrical theory needlessly by introducing superfluous structure. Something like the continuously alternating pattern given for Chaucer is sometimes offered as a simpler system. Yet it should be clear that the use of the continuously alternating pattern introduces 80 per cent more structure than the five-foot line has, because the alternating pattern specifies the relationship between even and odd syllables (falling), whereas foot structure leaves that relationship indeterminate.

If the continuously alternating metre contains more structure than the foot metre does, it also forces Chaucer's verse into patterns that modern prosodists sometimes object to. Various pejorative terms are used to criticise this supposed misreading by those who prefer a more natural reading – 'wooden', 'mechanical', 'thumping'. Ten Brink (1901) is a favourite target. Indeed, if line 477 from the *General Prologue* is read as scanned at the beginning of this paper, there are obvious objections that one might raise via familiar phonological rules of Modern English:

(28) x /   x   /   x / x / x /
      A good man was ther of religioun

Why should *man*, a noun, be subordinated both to its attributive adjective *good* and to the copula that follows? Why should the preposition *of* receive metrical ictus? As it turns out, there are good reasons for concluding that the most prosaically neutral scansion to the ear of the twentieth-century reader was not the way Chaucer heard the rhythm or read the verse. The most persuasive reason is one that a paper on the subject cannot illustrate: simply to read a line like 477 in the context of several hundred lines by Chaucer and to hear the alternating stresses that the line naturally receives.

Metrists, of course, cannot do their work by telling readers to go and read the poetry (for, among other reasons, metrists would no longer have work to do). Thus, we must turn to the technical reasons for asserting that *man* is subordinated between *good* and *way* – or, more generally, that the line is continuously alternating from beginning to end. Here I would suggest that there are several diagnostic features which, when more fully explored than is possible here (for a discussion see Cable 1991), will argue for the regularly alternating scansion that many traditional metrists have assigned. These features include the relative infrequency of inverted first feet in Chaucer (compared with, say, Shakespeare); the higher ratio of unstressed syllables in a position of ictus to stressed syllables in a position of nonictus (again, in Chaucer than in Shakespeare), and the rarity in Chaucer of clear patterns of rising levels of stress over four syllables. We shall focus on this last feature, because it makes a telling contrast between patterns in Chaucer and patterns that have been fully discussed in Shakespeare, whose modulated foot verse will be the last variety we shall consider. In order to show what is generally missing in Chaucer, let us turn to Shakespeare.

Shakespeare's foot metre

Some lines of poetry are famous in metrical discussions for illustrating a particular point. Examples from Alexander Pope are especially popular for this purpose. So also are the first two lines of Shakespeare's Sonnet 30:

> When to the sessions of sweet silent thought
> I summon up remembrance of things past

Winters (1957: 91), Thompson (1961: 20), Wimsatt (1970: 775), and Woods (1985: 5–10) all cite these lines as examples of Shakespeare's highly varied metrical art – especially in comparison with the monotonously regular lines of mid-sixteenth-century poets such as George Gascoigne, Barnabe Googe, and George Turberville. Both Winters and Wimsatt identify the key pattern as stress rising through four levels; Wimsatt, in passing, uses that pattern to give a succinct justification for the concept of the *poetic foot*:

[I]n my own theory, which I have always considered mainly traditional, the preposition *of* in each line is a sufficient ictus of a foot (or a sufficiently strong syllable in an ictus position) because in each instance it is clearly stronger than the *preceding* syllable – *-sions, -brance* . . . [T]he adjective *sweet* (though it receives more stress than *of*) does indeed receive less stress than the first syllable of *silent* – just as in the second line, *things* receives more stress than *of* but less than *past* . . . In each of these lines then, we have an instance of a four-syllable stress sequence, two iambs, steadily rising, which is a characteristic tensional variant (but not a violation) in English iambic verse.

> 4   3   2   1   4   3   2   1
> *-sions of sweet si-;   -brance of things past;*
>   4   3   2   1
> *Hail! to thee, blithe spirit.* (1970: 775)

Wimsatt's insight is an important one because it provides a wedge for separating two metrical theories that overlap on the great majority of lines. For a certain minority pattern a theory of foot metre is more adequate than a theory of alternating metre, and thus the minority pattern is the key for deciding between the theories. Furthermore, once the diagnostic pattern is identified, we can see that it is far from being marginal in Shakespeare. Cable (1991) finds in Sonnet 104 four lines with four rising levels of stress, as in the sequence 'To me, fair friend'. The rarity of the pattern in Chaucer's poetry suggests that the more adequate description for that metre is a strict alternating pattern (although see too

Youmans, this volume). Thus, what is traditionally referred to as a single metre, the English iambic pentameter, appears to be two separate metres, which overlap on the majority of lines but diverge on a crucial minority.

With this concept of foot metre from Shakespeare we can describe the relevant patterns in the lines quoted at the beginning of this chapter, from *The Tempest* and from *Richard III*:

(29)   x   x   / | (x) /
    Like a good   parent, did beget of him   (*Tempest* 1.2.94)
                  x   / | \   /

    I will, my lord. God give your Grace good rest
                        (*Richard III* 1.4.75)

Good and *par-* bear clashing stresses separated by a silent beat, much as we have seen in Old and Middle English. Here the missing beat takes the place of the missing syllable in the second foot. The first foot is a tri-syllabic substitution, and thus the line as a whole contains the normal ten syllables.

Because comparisons are made only within feet, the metre does not specify that *good* is less heavily stressed than *Grace*. It seems likely, in fact, that it is, although if *your Grace* is taken as a conventional epithet, it is also possible for *good* to receive greater stress than *Grace*. It would still be the less heavily stressed syllable *within its own foot*, and the metre would not be disrupted. The flexibility of Shakespeare's highly modulated dramatic verse stems from technicalities such as this.

What links the examples of clashing stress from OE, ME, and the Renaissance is their reference to two basic patterns, both common in a stress-timed language – stress subordination and stress spacing. OE metre, ME alliterative metre, and Shakespeare's iambic pentameter all contain both patterns. Chaucer's alternating metre has frequent stress subordination, but it is less clear that it makes systematic use of stress spacing. Stress subordination and stress spacing are highly determined in the Old and Middle English alliterative metres, and the more we learn about those metres the more surely we can identify the appropriate contexts for each pattern. Because the foot metre of Shakespeare has an indeterminacy built into it (the relative stress between feet), there is always the possibility for more than one interpretation of stress within a still firm metrical scheme. We should understand, of course, that this flexibility of stress is characteristic not just of Shakespeare, who exploits the potential of the form to the fullest, but of a tradition of iambic pentameter that extends over the course of four centuries – beginning tentatively with Surrey and assuredly with Sidney, and continuing through Milton, Pope, Wordsworth, Tennyson, and many of the major poets of the twentieth century.

Notes

1 Lines cited from *Beowulf* are from Klaeber (1950). All verses of OE poetry are from *Beowulf* unless otherwise noted. Other sources are Dobbie (1953) for *Judith*; Tolkien and Gordon (1967) for *Sir Gawain and the Green Knight*; Anderson (1977) for *Cleanness*; Benson et al. (1987) for Chaucer; and Bevington et al. (1980) for Shakespeare.
2 See, for example, Cable (1974: 75–83) and McCully (1988: 492–527).
3 'Resolution' is the counting of a short stressed syllable and the following syllable as a single metrical unit. A 'short' (or 'light') syllable ends in a short vowel. (A 'long' or 'heavy' syllable has either a long vowel or, if the vowel is short, a closing consonant.) Resolution is not a process of elision but a mapping of two phonological units onto one metrical unit. 'Suspension of resolution' allows the short stressed syllable to bear metrical ictus without involving the following syllable. The precise contexts for suspension of resolution have never been clear.
4 In addition to the verses in *Beowulf* that Klaeber names (1584a, 463b, 623b, 783b, 2779b), Pope (1966: 370) cross-references 1009b.
5 These figures are tabulated from the catalogue in Pope (1966).
6 In Fulk (1992) it is the Rule of the Coda; in Cable (1991) it is the Antepenultimate Syllable Rule for Resolution.

3 Purely metrical replacements for Kuhn's laws

Geoffrey Russom

The word-foot theory (Russom 1987) employs the following principles to explain OE verse patterns:

(1) Metrical feet correspond to words.

(2) The verse (or half-line) consists of two readily identifiable feet.

A straightforward realisation of a verse pattern has two words, one for each foot. Below are two-word examples, taken from *Beowulf*, of the most important patterns:

(3a) gomban / gyldan 11a   Type A   [Sx/Sx]
'to yield tribute'

(3b) þonon / ȳð-geblond 1373a   Type B   [xx/Sxs]
'Thence tossing waves . . .'

(3c) on / wæl-bedde 964a   Type C   [x/Ssx]
'on the slaughter-bed'

(3d) lēof / land-fruma 31a   Type Da   [S/Ssx]
'beloved land-king'
hār / hilde-rinc 1307a   Type Db   [S/Sxs]
'old battle-warrior'

(3e) won-sǣlī / wer 105a   Type E   [Ssx/S]
'unlucky man'

Each example is identified according to the familiar Five Types system of Sievers (1885, 1893).[1] (Type Da includes the Sievers Types D1–3; Type Db is Sievers' Type D4.) To the right of the Sievers Type is the corresponding analysis in word-foot notation. In this notation, an upper-case S corresponds to a syllable with primary stress; a lower-case s corresponds to a syllable with secondary stress; and a lower-case x corresponds to a syllable with weaker than secondary stress. A slash marks the boundary between feet. There is a foot pattern for every type of native OE word, not only for stressed simplexes like *gomban* (3a), but also for compounds like *ȳð-geblond* (3b) and for unstressed words like *þonon* (3b) and *on* (3c).

Half-lines are often less straightforward than those in (3). Consider the following, for example:

(4a) geong in / geardum 13a   [Sx/Sx]
      'young in the courts'
(4b) (wið) ord ond / (wið) ecge 1549a [(x)Sx/(x)Sx]
      'with spear and with sword'
(4c) þanon / eft gewāt 123b   [xx/Sxs]
      'thence he went back'

Example (4a) has the same pattern as (3a), but in (4a) the unstressed word *in* substitutes for the unstressed syllable of the trochaic stressed word. Unstressed constituents may also appear as extrametrical syllables before the first or second foot of the verse. In example (4b), another variant of Type A, the extrametrical syllables are parenthesised and could be deleted without adverse metrical consequences. Like (4a), (4b) has a word group substituting for a trochaic word in the first foot. A somewhat different type of substitution occurs in the second foot of (4c), which contains two stressed words instead of the compound that appears in Type B verses like (3b).[2]

Here we will be concerned primarily with unstressed constituents, which may appear as feet (3b–c, 4c), as subparts of feet (4a–b), or as extrametrical syllables (4b). The metre of *Beowulf* could not have been appreciated during live performance if these three possibilities of scansion had to be weighed in each case. No such efforts were required, however. The metrical interpretation of a given unstressed constituent could almost always be predicted from its position in the verse. Some of the constraints on word order that facilitate scansion are discussed by Kuhn (1933), who explains them as archaic laws of particle movement still operative in poetry. I will show that Kuhn's laws can be captured as special cases of constraints on metrical ambiguity described in Russom (1987).

Kuhn divides unstressed constituents into two categories, *clitics* (*Satzteilpartikeln*) and *particles* (*Satzpartikeln*). A clitic is an unstressed constituent closely associated with some particular stressed word in a clause or sentence. Prepositions, articles, and possessive pronouns, for example, are closely associated with nouns and therefore count as clitics. OE unstressed prefixes are of course very closely associated with the following constituent, usually a verb. Kuhn (1933: 43 n. 92) treats such prefixes as clitic words. Particles are the more independent unstressed words within a clause. The conjunction *that*, for example, is not associated with any particular stressed word. Other words classified as particles by Kuhn are personal pronouns, sentential adverbs, auxiliary verbs, the copula, and finite main verbs that appear without alliteration near the beginning of the clause.

Kuhn proposed two laws to explain the relative placement of particles, clitics, and stressed words:

(5) First Law: Unstressed particles are grouped together before the first or second stressed word of the clause.[3]

(6) Second Law: Any unstressed constituents situated before the first stressed word of the clause must include a particle.

The force of these laws is most easily appreciated when we consider how they apply to Type B, as analysed by Sievers:

(7a) *þā Scyld / wearþ grim   [xS/xS]
      'Then Scyld became angry'
(7b) Ymb-ēo- / de þā 620a   [xS/xS]
      'She went around then'
(7c) Swā giō- / mor-mōd 2267a   [xS/xs]
      'Thus sad-hearted'

Sievers divides Type B into two identical feet with rising rhythm. He provides no purely metrical basis for distinguishing the verse-initial x positions of (7a–c) from their verse-medial x positions. Kuhn's first law (5) is therefore brought in to explain why we find nothing in *Beowulf* like (7a), with one particle (*þā*) before the first stressed word and another particle (*wearþ*) before the second stressed word. Moreover, there is usually a particle before the first stressed word of a clause-initial Type B verse, as predicted by Kuhn's second law (6). Verses like (7b), with a single clitic (*Ymb-*) before the first stress, occur much less frequently than do those like (7c), which has a particle (*Swā*) in that location.

The distinction between particles and clitics can be viewed as a distinction between more and less *wordlike* constituents. The least wordlike are unstressed prefixes. These are treated as words by the phonology but as word parts by the syntax (see Russom 1987: 8–11). During the OE period, most prefixes are transparently related to prepositions or adverbs, but the identity of the prefix as a word is often lost at a later date. In Modern English (MnE) *behold*, for example, the old prefix has no discernible relation to the cognate preposition *by* and is wholly incorporated into a simplex. Separable clitics such as prepositions are more likely to retain their identity as words. In some cases, however, a preposition can be incorporated into a simplex, as for example in MnE *today*, which descends from an OE prepositional phrase. The unstressed constituents most likely to survive as independent words are particles. Conjunctions like *that* have never been combined with stressed words to form simplexes.

Within the framework of the word-foot theory, Kuhn's laws can be replaced by the following principles:

(8a) Particles are more wordlike than clitics.

(8b) Unstressed prefixes are less wordlike than other clitics.

(9a) More-wordlike unstressed constituents work better as markers for light word-feet (x or xx).

(9b) Less-wordlike unstressed constituents work better as substitutes for word parts like inflectional endings or as extrametrical syllables.

Three types of unstressed constituents are distinguished in (8), which I propose as a refinement of Kuhn's two-way distinction between particles and clitics. In (9), I obtain the effects of Kuhn's laws (and other effects) with stylistic preferences that favour assignment of unstressed constituents to their most appropriate metrical roles.

As analysed within Sievers' theory, the Type B verse *þā Scyld / wearþ grim* (7a) has the foot boundary in a natural location, between subject and predicate. It is hard to see why such verses should be rejected in favour of verses like *Swā giō- / mor-mōd* (7c), with the foot boundary inside a simplex.[4] No such problems arise in the word-foot analysis of Type B:

(10a) *þā / Scyld wearþ grim   [x/Sxs]
      'Then Scyld became angry'
(10b) Ymb- / ēode þā 620a   [x/Sxs]
      'Then she went around'

(10c) Swā / giōmor-mōd 2267a   [x/Sxs]
       'Thus sad-hearted'
(10d) þanon / eft gewāt 123b   [xx/Sxs]
       'thence he went back'
(10e) ge- / seted ond gesǣd 1696a   [x/Sxxs]⁵
       'set down and stated'

The problematic (7c) has now become (10c), a straightforward realisation of a two-word verse pattern. From the perspective of the word-foot
theory, (10c) is obviously less complex than (10a), which substitutes a
group of three words for a compound. According to principle (9b), the
least-wordlike unstressed constituents make the best substitutes for
word parts. Since the verse-medial x positions of Type B correspond to
word parts, we would expect these x positions to be occupied by prefixes
or other clitics rather than by particles such as *wearþ* in (10a). According
to principle (9a), particles excluded from verse-medial position will be
especially welcome at the beginning of the verse because they make the
best markers for light feet. The word-foot theory, then, provides two
purely metrical reasons for placement of particles before the first stress
in Type B. Kuhn's first law is no longer required to explain why particles
occurring in this type are always grouped together by the *Beowulf* poet.⁶
This theory makes some additional predictions of its own about Type B
variants with an unstressed constituent inside the second foot. *Beowulf*
contains somewhat more than three hundred of these.⁷ In about four of
every five cases, the unstressed constituent between the stresses is a
prefix, as in example (10d).⁸ Such a stylistic preference cannot be
explained by Kuhn's laws, which make no distinction between prefixes
and other clitics. According to principle (9b), on the other hand, the
less-wordlike prefixes are superior to nonprefixal clitics as substitutes
for word parts.

    Kuhn's second law (6) predicts that any clitic appearing before the
first stress of a clause-initial Type B verse will be accompanied by a particle. The prediction fails in (10b) and six similar cases (34a, 1408a,
1870a, 2345a, 2516a, 3156a; cf. also 652a). In these a prefix is *isolated* as
the only unstressed constituent before the first stressed word of the
verse. The second law allows isolated prefixes to occur freely when the
verse is not clause-initial (see Kendall 1983: 19). This happens, however,
in only one Type B verse (10e). Variants like (10b), which the second law
rejects, actually outnumber the supposedly normal variants like (10e).

Our stylistic preference (9a), on the other hand, identifies both (10b) and (10e) as complex verses that use the least appropriate kind of constituent for their light feet. From this point of view, the rarity of verses like (10e) comes as no surprise. Because the purely metrical (9a) assigns no special status to clause-initial prefixes, it is not embarrassed by the distributional asymmetry in the small sample of eight irregularities.

Unstressed constituents sometimes appear as extrametrical syllables at the beginning of a Type A or D verse, where they are said to stand in *anacrusis*:

(11a) (Ā)rās þā / (se) rīca 399a   [(x)Sx/(x)Sx]
       'The mighty one arose then'
(11b) (ofer-)wearp / (þā) wērig-mōd 1543a   [(xx)S/(x)Sxs]
       'the weary-minded one stumbled then'
(11c) (Hū) lomp ēow / (on) lāde 1987a   [(x)Sx/(x)Sx]
       'How did it go for you on your journey'
(11d) (gē æt) hām gē / (on) herge 1248a   [(xx)Sx/(x)Sx]
       'both at home and in the army'

Note that if the verse-initial constituents are interpreted as light feet, (11a–d) will have three feet, in violation of principle (2), which defines a verse as a pair of feet. Anacrusis is not a high-frequency phenomenon, occurring somewhat fewer than ninety times in *Beowulf*; but it cannot be ignored. The word-foot theory must explain how verses like (11a–d) could be identified as legitimate two-foot patterns.

Anacrusis is characteristic of the on-verse (or a-verse), the first of two verses linked by alliteration within the long line. In the second half of the line, called the off-verse (or b-verse), anacrusis is much rarer. There are only eight clear cases in *Beowulf*, all examples of Type A (93b, 666b, 1223b, 1504b, 1773b, 1877b, 2247b, 2592b). As it turns out, the metrical roles of verse-initial unstressed constituents are signalled by especially strict adherence to principles (9a–b) in on-verses. The following procedure will yield the correct metrical interpretation in the vast majority of cases:

(12)(a) Assume that an unstressed constituent at the beginning of a verse marks a light foot unless
    (b) the constituent is an isolated prefix and the verse appears in the first half of the line.

This procedure is, I think, simple enough to be learned intuitively, without explicit instruction or awareness (see Jakobson 1963 on unconscious command of metrical rules).

Under conditions specified in (12b), the audience will assume (unconsciously) that the isolated prefix stands in anacrusis, and two feet will be expected to follow. On-verses (11a–b) show the normal type of anacrusis. On-verses like (11c–d), with nonprefixal constituents in anacrusis, occur quite infrequently. I found only five others in *Beowulf* (25a, 107a, 1549a, 1563a, 2093a). With anacrusis confined largely to isolated prefixes, it is not surprising to find particles grouped together after the first stressed word of a Type A or D verse, the only other location available. Thus principles (9a–b) do the work of Kuhn's first law (5) in these as well. It seems best to regard the seven verses like (11c–d), for which procedure (12) will not work, as complex rather than unmetrical. In such cases, evidently, the audience could 'guess again' about the roles of verse-initial constituents, performing a second intuitive scansion before accepting or rejecting the verse. This effort of 'second-guessing' was so seldom required that it might have proved stimulating rather than oppressive (see Russom 1987: 148–9).

Recall that in Type B the effect of Kuhn's second law (6) is obtained when principle (9a) discourages employment of isolated prefixes as light feet. Now that the concept of anacrusis has been introduced, we are ready to deal with Type C:

(13a) ge- / rūmlīcor 139a   [x/Ssx]
       'farther away'
(13b) ge- / būn hæfdon 117b   [x/Ssx]
       'they had settled in'

Procedure (12b) will yield the wrong assumption about the isolated prefix of (13a), and such on-verses are rare, as expected. I found five others in *Beowulf* (424a, 659a, 1034a, 1073a, 2766a). There are fifty-nine Type C off-verses in which an isolated prefix constitutes a foot; but forty-seven of these are like (13b), which consists of a prefixed nonfinite verb and its auxiliary, no doubt an indispensable type of formulaic pattern.[9] Such complex but useful verses pose no major problems of scansion, because their isolated prefixes will be correctly interpreted as feet by procedure (12a). It is not surprising to find that deviation from principle (9a) occurs with significant frequency only in the second half of the line. Grouping of particles in Type C can be explained quite independently of the first law. Constraints on enjambement block assignment of unstressed words to verse-final x positions in this type, leaving only one location in which particles can occur (see Russom 1987: 26).

The permissible extent of anacrusis testifies to its intimate association with prefixes. OE prefixes usually have one syllable, sometimes two. Anacrusis usually consists of one syllable, sometimes two, never more. Verses like (11c–d) would appear, then, to be secondary developments resulting from substitution of nonprefixal syllables for the syllables of isolated prefixes. On this hypothesis, the most complex type of anacrusis would consist of two nonprefixal syllables. As it turns out, verses like (11d) are extremely rare. There are no others in *Beowulf*. Once the association is made between prefixes and anacrusis, interpretation of verses like the following becomes straightforward:

(14) in hyra / gryre-geatwum 324a   [(x)xx/Ssx]
‘in their warlike armour’

A string of three unstressed syllables like *in hyra* cannot substitute for the syllables of a prefix, because there are no OE trisyllabic prefixes. If anacrusis is expected to conform to the pattern of a prefix, *in hyra* will never be interpreted as anacrusis. In (14), the extrametrical word actually facilitates scansion, providing an unambiguous marker for the light foot.[10]

Kuhn's second law (6) has nothing to say about the vast majority of Type A and D verses in *Beowulf*. It applies only to thirty-five clause-initial verses of these types that happen to have anacrusis.[11] Consider the following examples:

(15a) (Ge-)syhð / sorh-cearig 2455a   [(x)S/Ssx]
‘He sees sorrowfully’
(15b) (Tō) lang / (ys tō) reccenne 2093a   [(x)S/(xx)Ssx]
‘It is too long to narrate’
(15c) (Hē ge-) fēng þā / fetel-hilt 1563a   [(xx)Sx/Ss]
‘He took the ring-adorned hilts’

The second law predicts that anacrusis in verses like these will include a particle. In thirty-two of the thirty-five crucial cases, however, the anacrusis consists of an isolated prefix, as in (15a). In (15b), the element in anacrusis is a nonprefixal clitic. Kuhn's laws make the correct prediction only about (15c).[12]

Some of Kuhn's adherents note that violations of the second law in Types A and D tend to involve clause-initial finite verbs, and suggest that such verbs should be regarded as unstressed particles even when they alliterate, as for example in (15a).[13] It would be more accurate to say that the violations tend to involve isolated unstressed prefixes because of independently necessary constraints on anacrusis.[14] Unstressed prefixes are characteristic of verbs, and nonfinite verbs normally appear near the end of the clause in OE, as in other Germanic languages.[15] The only type of prefixed word that will occur very often clause-initially is the finite verb. When Kuhn's adherents set aside exceptions with finite verbs, then, they set aside the major type of exception likely to be encountered.[16] As amended, the second law applies in Types A and D only to those clause-initial verses with anacrusis that have a nominal or adjectival form as the first alliterating word. There is only one on-verse in this exclusive set (15b). Its unstressed verse-initial word is predicted to be a particle, but *Tō* is obviously proclitic to *lang*. The second law remains vulnerable to refutation even after a good deal of its empirical content has been removed.[17]

Extrametrical constituents appear after the first stress in Types A, D, and E:

(16a) þrāge / (ge-)þolode 87a   [Sx/(x)Sx]
       'he suffered hardship'
(16b) brond / (nē) beado-mēcas 1454a   [S/(x)Ssx]
       'brand nor battle-swords'
(16c) Niht-weorce / (ge-)feh 827b   [Ssx/(x)S]
       'He rejoiced in his night's work'

The parenthesised constituents are not very problematic, because they cannot be confused with verse-initial light feet. The poet still shows considerable respect, however, for principle (9b), which identifies the unstressed prefix as the least disruptive kind of extrametrical constituent. *Beowulf* has a large sample of Type A1 verses like (16a), about 675 in all. About three of every five extrametrical constituents appearing before the second foot in this type are unstressed prefixes. Example (16b) represents Type D. In this type, which usually has a compound noun or adjective in the second foot, prefixes will not often occur verse-medially, and other extrametrical constituents will be avoided as usual. I could find no more than 28 Type D verses with an extrametrical constituent before the second foot.[18] Type E has only about half the frequency of Type D, but 41 Type E verses have an extrametrical constituent before the second foot, and in 37 cases this constituent is an unstressed prefix.[19] A typical example is (16c), with a prefixed verb in final position. Kuhn's laws, which make no distinction between prefixes and other clitics, cannot explain why nonprefixal clitics are so unwelcome as extrametrical syllables in verse-medial position. There is nothing much to say about grouping of particles in Type E, because this type never has anacrusis (see Russom 1987: 34). Any unstressed particles in a Type E verse will appear before the second foot, the only available location.

We have seen that Kuhn's laws make the wrong prediction about a number of verses. The counterexamples would be less damaging if the laws applied in a wide variety of crucial cases. Only in Types B and C, however, do the laws perform significant work, and this work is rendered unnecessary by the word-foot theory, at least within the domain of the verse. Kuhn may make some interesting predictions about larger units of poetic discourse. I suspect, however, that apparent successes of this kind will also turn out to result from independently necessary metrical or syntactic rules.[20] We all owe a great deal to Kuhn, of course, for discovering that Old English poets imposed special restrictions on the placement of unstressed constituents. His observations have a value quite independent of his laws and deserve the attention they have received.[21]

Notes

1 Examples and frequency counts are taken from *Beowulf*. The edition cited is Klaeber (1950). I have added hyphens in compound words for expository convenience.

2 For a general account of such substitutions, which are subject to a number of constraints, see Russom (1987: 14–19, 83–92).

3 The particles may be separated by a clitic but not by a stressed word. Particles appearing late in the clause are not governed by the first law, since Kuhn (1933: 10) regards these as stressed. I propose metrical reformulations only for (5–6), which govern the order of unstressed constituents. The rules assigning stress to function words look like purely linguistic rules, and it would be desirable to treat them separately (cf. Russom 1987: 101–15).

4 A survey of work on Germanic metres (see See 1967: 5) points out that most Type B verses have the foot boundary in an unnatural location when divided according to Sievers' theory.

5 The two short syllables connected by an arc are equivalent to one long syllable by resolution (see Russom 1987: 44–6). Verse (10e) is a long Type B variant with a second foot of the form Sxxs (corresponding to long compounds like *sibbe-ge-driht*).

6 I have space here to consider placement of unstressed constituents only within the domain of the half-line. See Mitchell (1985: sect. 3947) for criticism of attempts to apply Kuhn's laws within larger domains.

7 When the number of verses is large, I do not supply exact counts, which would involve us in subtleties of preferred scansion. Such efforts would be wasted here because we are dealing with gross discrepancies that would emerge from any reasonable tally.

8 Cable (1974: 32–44) points out that the constituents typically employed as extrametrical syllables are prefixes and the negative function word *ne*. I have therefore counted *ne* as a prefix. The identity of *ne* as a word seems quite weak. Incorporation has already taken place in OE forms like *næs* 'wasn't' (from *ne wæs*). If *ne* is prefixal, (9a) predicts that it will not often appear in isolation as a light foot. *Beowulf* contains only three verses in which this happens: 511a (Type B), 2263b (Type C), and 3016b (Type C).

9 The twelve other verses are 288b, 304b, 526b, 562b, 922b, 997b, 1395b, 1412b, 1595b, 2497b, 2569b, and 2740b.

10 An extrametrical constituent is almost obligatory in subtype A3, which has the pattern xx/Sx (see Russom 1987: 35–6). Without a third unstressed syllable to mark its light foot, an xx/Sx verse might well be rejected as incomplete, since it would look like the first foot in a Type A pattern with anacrusis [(xx)Sx/Sx].

11 94a, 109a, 217a, 234a, 399a, 723a, 758a, 1027a, 1125a, 1169a, 1384a, 1390a, 1518a, 1537a, 1543a, 1545a, 1557a, 1563a, 1665a, 1711a, 1758a, 1977a, 1987a, 2044a, 2093a, 2367a, 2455a, 2529a, 2538a, 2628a, 2697a, 2705a, 2756a, 2936a, 3141a. The count includes all verses favourable to Kuhn's laws but omits some that may or may not be clause-initial, e.g. 2252a, 2640a, 2681a. Adjacent verse-initial prefixes are counted as an isolated double prefix in 1027a, 1711a, and 2628a.

12 The second law makes the correct prediction about *Hū lomp ēow on lāde* (11c), but this violates the first law because it has particles (*Hū, ēow*) in two locations.

13 The alliterating verb would then supply the necessary particle before the first stress. See Bliss (1967: 12–21), Lucas (1987: 152), and Kendall (1983: 8). Others have argued for some degree of stress on finite main verbs appearing early in the clause, e.g. Cosmos (1976), Obst (1987: 33–5), and Russom (1987: 103–7). The evidence presented here does not of course tell

against stylistic analyses that draw on Kuhn's observations while remaining agnostic about the proper formulation of his laws (e.g. Donoghue 1987a).

14 The bias against use of nonprefixal constituents for anacrusis applies to all verses, not just to clause-initial verses. Verses like (15b) are rare because of this bias, not because of Kuhn's laws. McCully and Hogg (1990: 326) also represent the unstressed prefix as the paradigmatic extrametrical constituent, though their theory of OE verseform is in other respects quite different from that adopted here.

15 Nonfinite forms are characteristic of subordinate clauses, where verbs are normally placed late, in prose as in poetry (see Kuhn 1933: 51–2).

16 This ad hoc procedure is not comparable to Sievers' decontraction of contract forms in positions where the metre requires it (*pace* Lucas 1987: 152). Sievers' procedure is legitimate because the contract monosyllables selected for special treatment are vastly outnumbered by ordinary monosyllables that could (but do not) appear in the same positions.

17 The second law does make the correct prediction about the handful of clause-initial off-verses with anacrusis, all five of which have a monosyllabic particle before the first stress (93b, 666b, 1223b, 2247b, 2592b). From our point of view there should be no strong bias towards prefixal anacrusis in such cases, since procedure (12b) does not distinguish prefixes from clitics or particles in the off-verse. See Donoghue (1987b) for an excellent discussion of the data within Bliss's framework.

18 Da (includes Sievers' Types D1–3): 356a, 473a, 612a, 723a, 896a, 1027a, 1162a, 1323b, 1454a, 1724b, 1727a, 1790a, 1863a, 1997b, 2093a, 2471a, 2562a, 2628a, 2751a, 2756a, 2863b, 2936a; Db (Sievers' Type D4): 1114a, 1531a, 1539a, 1543a, 2367a, 3077a, 3084a. Some of these might be analysed as 'expanded D' patterns of the form Sx/Ssx, Sx/Sxs, or Sx/Sxxs with an unstressed constituent inside the first foot.

19 Type E with extrametrical prefix: 256a, 455a, 476a, 650a, 654a, 658a, 697a, 775a, 877a, 911a, 1498a, 1681a, 1723a, 2608a; 5b, 14b, 17b, 118b, 610b, 667b, 688b, 690b, 827b, 884b, 999b, 1241b, 1483b, 1562b, 1624b, 1760b, 1920b, 2037b, 2426b, 2489b, 2583b, 2703b, 2765b. With extrametrical clitic or particle: 183b, 186b, 603b, 2882b. The unstressed prefix is also strongly preferred within the first foot of Type E as a substitute for the unstressed syllable of a compound. Of 73 Type E verses with an unstressed constituent in the first foot, 64 are like *sǣ-bāt ge- / sǣt*, 633a.

20 Recent work has sought to explain some of Kuhn's observations in purely syntactic terms and others in purely metrical terms, abandoning the mixed concept of verse grammar. See Stockwell and Minkova (1989), Blockley and Cable (1990).

21 I owe thanks to Bruce Mitchell for useful advice.

4 Domain-end phenomena and metrical templates in Old English verse

C. B. McCully

One of the most basic problems for any prosodic analysis lies in determining metrical constituents. Simply using the term 'metrical constituent', however, is problematic. What constituents are intended, and how is it possible to prove either their integrity, their boundaries, or their function in OE poetry? Phonemic segments, syllables, and 'feet' (however feet are to be defined; see here McCully and Hogg 1990 and, for a different interpretation, Russom 1987) are of course properly and necessarily included in metrical analysis, but attention must also be given to further and larger constituents. In OE, these larger constituents are, transparently, the half-line or verse, and the long line itself. Again, simply using terms such as 'half-line' and 'line' commits one to the notion that there are such metre-specific constituents, specified domains within which a poet's metrical skills (repetition, parallelism, variation, and so on) are employed. One of the basic issues of metrics, then – for the poet as well as the reader/hearer – is metrical constituency and metrical domain. In this respect it is salutary to heed Shippey's comment (1972: 102) that 'we have no evidence that Anglo-Saxons even knew what a "line" of their own poetry was'. Perhaps this is unduly pessimistic, but it seems worth while to enquire once again as to the constituency of verses and lines and the principles such assumed constituency might entail. How do we know – how can we infer – where half-lines begin and end?

There are several possible answers. One is to relate the structure of OE verses and lines to syntactic organisation. It is immediately apparent, after all, that many OE verses are self-contained syntactic units; yet this is not invariably the case. A verse such as *Beowulf* 8a, *wēox under wolcnum* ('prospered under clouds'; since all citations are from *Beowulf*, the text will appear as Beo. unless otherwise indicated), or 8b, *weorðmyndum þāh* ('thrived in glories'), can certainly be analysed as phrasally self-contained and appositional, yet there are very many other verses which cannot be so analysed; 12a, *þǣm eafera wæs*, or 24b, *lofdǣdum sceal*, or 30a, *þenden wordum wēold* cannot be analysed as self-contained. So it seems reasonable to suppose that we cannot seek for a wholly syntactic definition of the verse. Further, if we were to define metrical constituency through a syntax common to both poetry and prose we would have neatly side-stepped the apparent fact that verses are *metre-specific* constituents. This is not of course to deny that syntax has some extremely telling things to say, via Kuhn's laws (and see Russom, this volume), about what kind of syntactic entity can function as a metrical lift. And yet about the larger and seemingly more simple issue, the issue of metrical domain and how this is to be determined, purely syntactic information seems insufficient.

Another possibility is to analyse metrical constituency through alliterative patterning. Alliteration is governed by rules (see here Suzuki 1985; McCully 1988, 1992) which are sensitive not only to the structure of half-lines but to the structure of the long line as well. It is quite possible, however, that the rules governing alliteration are sensitive to structures which have already been generated from syllable weight, stress, and metrical constraints. On the current view, alliterative patterning is really a post hoc stylisation, a decorative ornament which takes previously assigned structure as its basis and point of departure. (For later verse, the same would hold true of rhyme; see below.) There are many who would disagree with this view (e.g. Hoover 1985), and it is certainly undeniable that a great deal can be inferred from alliterative structure (see here McCully and Hogg 1994 on later alliterative writing in ME). On the other hand, it is not insignificant that the most elegant phonological analysis of OE alliteration (Suzuki 1985) posits that alliteration depends on an (apparently universal) association convention which matches initial syllable nodes within an obligatory directional parameter (a right-to-left parameter in OE). That is, a theory of the syllable, and of syllabic concatenation, is logically prior to a theory of alliteration. Further, the selection of what Sievers and others termed the *Hauptstab* – the alliteration originator, the first stave of the b-verse – is governed by higher-level S W labelling. The first stave of the b-verse is the strongest of the verse, and alliterative matching spreads from it into the staves within the a-verse; alliteration cannot spread to the final stave of the b-verse, since the association convention linking segments does not permit this, because to link rightwards would be to cross the originating morpheme. In other words, and given logically prior structures such as syllables and nonlinear node-labelling, alliteration spreads 'backwards' from the b-verse. Notice also that on this theory it is redundant to have a metrical rule stipulating that 'a weak constituent of a weak constituent may never alliterate' (cf. Russom 1987: 73), since constraints on alliteration may be more elegantly confined to the possibilities allowed by logically prior structures. Putting these points together, one has a picture of OE alliteration as in (1):

(1) Alliterative matching in OE

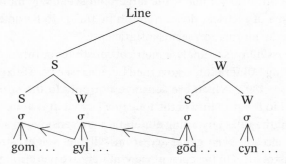

('gomban gyldan;   þæt wæs gōd cyning', Beo. 11)

If this view of alliterative matching is correct, then it is impossible to use alliteration itself as a defining machinery for verse constituency: long-line structure, half-line structure, and lifted syllables have already been assigned, and alliteration begins, as it were, where stress leaves off. Cable (1991: 227) supports this view, arguing that alliteration in OE is 'a superficial feature'. It is possible that alliteration is to OE verse what rhyme and its many manifestations are to later English verse: superficial stylisations, rather than constitutive or generative principles of underlying metrics.

A third way in which we can go in search of OE verse constituency is to see the verse not primarily as a piece of syntactic structure, nor as a piece of alliterative geography, but as a finite artefact whose structure is constrained by metre-specific rules. One such rule, and the one focussed on here, is a domain-final rule, a rule which demarcates verses as metrical constituents. It is, crudely, a rule which encodes metrical expectations by constraining how half-lines may end.

Rules of this kind are familiar from many kinds of verse in many different languages. In the later English tradition, for example, one thinks of structures such as the ballad stanza; see (2a):

(2a) Line-end constraints (i)

> A slúmber díd my spírit séal
> I hád no húman féars (/)
> She séemed a thíng that cóuld not féel
> The tóuch of éarthly yéars (/)

These lines (see also Attridge 1982) may be analysed as underlying four-beat structures, where the metrically salient pause (symbolised here by the parenthesised slash) in lines 2 and 4 functions to reinforce rhyme as a domain-end marker. Another example can be found under (2b), where the salient pauses again function as domain-end markers, reinforcing not only the stanzaic schema but also emphasising the striking duple symmetry of the stanza:

(2b) Line-end constraints (ii)

> The fáir breeze bléw, the whíte foam fléw,
> The fúrrow fóllowed frée (/)
> Wé were the fírst that éver búrst
> Ínto that sílent séa (/)

Having introduced the notion of metrically salient pauses, I would not wish to introduce them anywhere in the verse line in order to legitimise a predetermined metrical pattern. Unlike, for example, Abercrombie 1965, I conceive of such pauses as typically functioning as line-end or domain-end markers; such markers occur very characteristically when the number of realised beats in the line is odd, i.e. three or five. Their appearance in English verse, then, is arguably governed by metre-specific principles (McCully 1988 embodies such principles in the Multiple Condition).

As well as these fairly crude domain-final constraints in English, it is also worth noting the quantitative hexameter's final and inevitable cadence. In the Latin tradition, it is precisely this place in the line – the domain-final position – where quantity and stress are in an isomorphic relation (see Allen 1973; McCully 1991):

(2c) Line-end constraints (iii) (relevant structure boldened)

Tityre, tu patulae recubans sub **tégmine fági** (stress)

.... | – – | – ∪ ∪|– – (quantity)

The line-final dactyl and spondee are entirely characteristic. Interestingly, something rather similar happens in English 'quantitative' translations, e.g. of the same line, where syllabic quantities (or supposed quantities; see McCully 1991) reinforce stress-patterning at the line end. (2d) is Webbe's translation:

(2d) Line-end constraints (iv) (relevant structure boldened)

Tityrus, happilie thou lyste tumbling **únder a béech-tree**

.... | – ∪ ∪| – –

Note that elsewhere in the line, almost invariably in Latin but less frequently in Englished versions, stress and quantity have no such reinforcing relationship; they are typically in tension. It is only at the end of the metrical domain where they are in such a cardinal isomorphic relation. That relation functions as a domain-end marker.

Examples may be multiplied almost indefinitely. Jakobson (1987: 75) notes that Russian binary verseforms end predictably – the last downbeat in the line always carries a word stress; he also notes Efik riddles, where 'in each hemistich . . . the last three of the four syllables present an identical tonemic pattern: lhhl/hhhl/lhhl/hhhl' (p. 74); or, turning again to more familiar data, Duffell (1991 and this volume) has argued convincingly that the invention of the 'pentameter' (the inverted commas are explored in Cable, Youmans, and Duffell, this volume) in both Romance and English verse traditions depends crucially on poets' eliminating line-end triple-time closures, so that alternating patterns became the metrical norm: in Duffell's view, Chaucer, for example, 'by his virtual elimination of triple-time closes which are a source of variety in Italian *X(I)*s, invented the iambic pentameter' (1991: II, 460). And, as Cable has recently shown, ME alliterative verse, especially that written in the West Midlands, has a normative structure for its b-verses whereby they obligatorily end on one, and only one, unstressed syllable, unlike the a-verse, which may end on up to two unstressed syllables (Cable 1991: 92ff.).

There is evidence in plenty, then – and evidence, moreover, drawn from poetries with different structures (stress-based, quantitative, tonemic) – that domain-final constraints are defining devices. This may be a metrical universal. After all, metrical verse is metrical (as opposed to merely being rhythmical) because it is composed in constituents (verses or lines) whose identity depends on final constraints of the kind outlined above. This is certainly no new view. Omond (1907), for example, argued that the only structural distinction between poetry and prose was the existence of a metre-specific constituent, namely, the line – but neither Omond nor many later scholars have had much to say about the specifics of line endings. Those specifics, as both Duffell (1991) and Cable (1991) have shown, relate to the genesis or maintenance of particular forms of poetry as well as to line-internal particulars. Prosodists overlook such constraints at their peril. In particular, it seems that domain-final constraints must be included in any statement of specific Verse Design (Jakobson 1987), since '[t]he verse design *determines the invariant features* of the verse instances and *sets up the limits* of variations' (p. 78 [my emphasis]).

If this reconstruction is correct, as the evidence overwhelmingly suggests, then clearly we should expect OE poetry to exhibit domain-final constraints, of a kind to be determined. The traditional view, drawn from Sievers 1885, is restated in Strang (1970: 326):

As in later English, [in OE verse] there is more than one feature which acts as a line-end marker. The end of a half-line is always determinate in syllabic structure; if it is occupied by a lift this goes without saying, but if it is occupied by a drop there is the special restriction that the drop must there be monosyllabic.

What may demarcate OE verses, then, is a special relationship between stress and syllable(s) which functions only at the verse end. Verses, that is, may end on a lift; on a resolved lift; or on a lift or resolved lift where that is followed by one, and only one, unstressed syllable. Some familiar examples demonstrate that such a set of constraints is well-founded; see (3):

(3) Traditional verse-final constraints in OE

Him ðā Scyld gewāt   26a (end = one lift)
tō gescæphwīle   26b (end = lift + monosyllabic drop)
to brimes faroðe   28b (end = resolved lift + monosyllabic drop)
þær wæs mādma fela   36a (end = resolved lift)

The traditional theory is, in effect, that OE verses may end in one of these four ways – or actually two ways, if the term *lift* covers both stressed syllables and resolved stressed syllables (see also McCully 1992). It is a useful theory of demarcation. There are, however, a number of problems with it.

First, the theory depends on resolution. Resolution is traditionally held to be a metre-specific device of equivalence, whereby two syllables, the first of which is stressed and light (i.e. contains a nonbranching Rhyme), are analysed as in some sense as heavy as one stressed syllable (i.e. a syllable containing a branching Rhyme). But why should this be so? If resolution is metre-specific, is poetic structure being massaged for the sake of a theory of Verse Design? Or is there support for resolution in the phonology of nonpoetic language?

Second, the traditional theory lends itself to what is essentially a static view of the verse – the verse as a series of positions, the last of which is demarcative. On the other hand, it may be the case that metre, and particularly the construction of a metre, is not static but dynamic, in the sense that the occurrence of a particular kind of entity at the verse end helps to determine what the other constituents of that half-line will be. If, for example, the verse ends in a monosyllabic fully stressed lift, then, in the tradtional terms of the *Typentheorie*, the whole verse must be a B type or an E type. Similarly, if the verse ends on a lift followed by mono-syllabic drop, then the entire half-line must be either C or A. And again, if the verse ends on a secondary-stressed lift, or secondary stress followed by a monosyllabic drop, then that verse must be one of the two varieties of Type D. Local choices, that is, are less casual than they first appear: placement of particular syllable–lift configurations verse-finally has not merely a demarcative but also, apparently, a dynamic function. Given a theory of constituency and domain, metrical structure itself may turn out to be a finite-state concept, in the sense of Chomsky (1957: 18ff.). This view gains support, paradoxically, from the most traditional views of metre(s), and OE metre in particular, when this last is viewed as a set of consecutive positions, or slots. If the first slot is filled by a stretch of two or more unstressed syllables, for example, then this (as Cable 1991 convincingly shows) has implications for what material can fill other (drop) positions in the same verse; conversely, if the initial slot is filled with a lift, this also has consequences for the type and frequency of those metrical entities that can appear elsewhere. The dynamism entailed by such a model suggests, then, that OE verses are not merely a set of positions but also a network of relationships, themselves governed by abstract rules and constraints which spread over the half-line domain.

A third and final problem with the traditional view of verse-final constraint is of a more technical kind and is related to verses like those seen here:

(4) hlyn swysode   611b
    fēond treddode   725b

    ymbsittendra 9b
    lindhæbbende 245a

There is a large class of verses of this kind, where the penultimate syllable is either a medial derivational syllable or an inflectional participial one (Cable 1991: 138; Campbell 1959: 34). On the traditional view, syllables such as *-od-* and *-end-* are analysed as secondarily stressed. But the suspicion must be that this analysis is circular. Are such syllables analysed as stress-bearing because they are required to be so in order that verse-final constraints are met? Or is there some more principled analysis?

Recently, both Russom (1987) and Cable (1991) have argued that verses of the kind seen in (4) should be analysed as ending on two unstressed syllables, or where the penult carries tertiary stress. Russom derives his theory (see also this volume) from the concept of the foot (the 'word foot' in Russom), and how foot structure matches word structure. On how feet and words are matched, Russom writes that '[e]very foot boundary must coincide with a word boundary', noting that the internal boundaries of compounded forms count as 'word boundaries' for these purposes (1987: 15). Thus, on Russom's theory, a word such as *bealdode* 'he encouraged' is analysed as one Sxx foot co-extensive with the three syllables of the word, and *sǣ-mannes* 'sailor's' is analysed as Ssx, two feet, where the first is monosyllabic and co-extensive with the initial monosyllable, and where the second is disyllabic and co-extensive with *mannes*.

Cable, on the other hand, derives his 1991 analysis from a careful reinterpretation of Bliss's (1967) findings on tertiary stress (and see Fulk 1992). Cable's arguments, though, bear more on the distribution of half-lines containing problematic 'less-stressed' syllables than on the phonology that might lie behind assignation of primary, secondary, and weak stress.

As the last paragraph indicates, it is possible that both Russom and Cable are wrong in their analysis of verse-final structures, especially the structure of the last two syllables – the crucial topic here. This is so for linguistic reasons. As McCully and Hogg (1990) demonstrate, words like those seen in (4) are handled by stress-assignment rules whose parameters are left-to-right and whose operation is cyclic. The form of the Old English Stress Rule (OESR) is given in (5):

(5) OESR
Assign maximally binary S W feet from left to right, where S must contain branching or be dominated by a branching foot at the left edge of the domain (McCully and Hogg 1990: 333)

Working cyclically on the examples in (4), the OESR works to erect the crucial structures as follows:

(6)

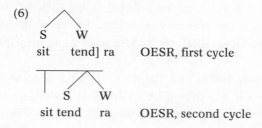

S   W
sit   tend] ra   OESR, first cycle

S   W
sit tend   ra   OESR, second cycle

The same derivation is obtained for words containing medial *-od-*, whose vowel was certainly historically long (Campbell 1959: 332–3), and as such is capable of bearing stress, since the S assigned by the OESR must contain branching (i.e. be assigned to a heavy syllable) non-root-initially. Nor, contra Russom, is there any phonological (as opposed to verse-specific) reason for assuming that metrical feet are always co-extensive with word boundaries. In sum, then, there are phonological reasons for doubting both Cable's and Russom's analysis of how the problematic verses of (4) end, especially since the traditional theory of verse-final constraint seems to be supported by phonological procedures which, it will be recalled, seem to imply some degree of stress on penultimate heavy syllables in examples such as those in (6). Notwithstanding this, however, Cable's reworking of the distributional evidence still remains to be explained.

To return to the problems with the traditional analysis of verse-final constraint. One has been discussed, but two – the role of resolution and the constructive role of such constraint – remain. In what follows, building on the idea that OE verse may not be composed of static sets of positions but rather of constituents whose sub-structures have implications elsewhere in the half-line domain, I offer a conception of verse-final structure which is itself linked with the structure of the overall verse. One way of handling such a conception is through a metrical template.

Templates are familiar from work in e.g. syllable theory (Selkirk 1984; Giegerich 1985) and stress phonology (Hayes 1982; Hogg and McCully 1987) as well as in metrics (Hayes 1983; Minkova, this volume). In verse-specific terms, templates, themselves necessarily abstract, encode the notion of underlying structure: they embody Jakobson's notion of Verse Design. The familiar string of S W positions underlying descriptions of the pentameter line (see e.g. Kiparsky 1977) can, for instance, be taken as a (relatively crude) template, as could the array of longs and shorts governing Latin quantitative metrical patterning. As far as OE is concerned, it seems worth while to search for an abstract template which is both descriptive and generative, that is, allows all and only relevant half-line patterns to be constructed, and which sets the limits of their metrical variation(s) – variations which include, of course, how verses may end.

The metrical structure of D- and E-type verses in *Beowulf* may, for example, be analysed through one metrical template. D- and E-type verses may be taken together, not (as McCully 1988 claimed, a claim rebutted in Cable 1991) because these types are simple reversals or mirror images of one another but because the template which apparently generates them is distinct from the template which generates Types A–C. Further, although the mirror-image argument is far from adequate (it cannot handle the different distribution of the relevant types, for example), it does seem to be apparent that at the kernel of each D- or E-type verse is a compound or quasi-compound constituent, one where secondary stress is retained as a crucial structural feature of composition. The similarity of such structural features is at least suggestive. And there is also the apparent fact that the notion of expanded dip is only applicable to Types A–C; it plays no role in Types D and E. Last, in the historical development of English metres, it is erstwhile Types D and E which are lost post-Conquest (as Cable 1981 demonstrates). This loss is related both to the morphology and the phonology of secondary stress, but it is surely significant that such linguistic change impacted on Types D and E and not on other types whose potential included the potential for secondary stress (e.g. A-type verses such as *gūð-rinc gold-wlanc*). If Types D and E are lost together, it is not so much as speech patterns that they are lost but as possible representatives of an underlying metrical system. Since it is the job of metrical templates to generate such an underlying system, it seems reasonable to include D- and E-type verses in one template, especially where such a template is observationally adequate.

In constructing such a template, a first question to answer – given the network, outlined above, of relationships within the verse – is how to symbolise verse-final lifts and drops. As it turns out, the nonlinear notation for such verse-final structures links with the general symbolism for what constitutes a lift in OE poetry. Aligning morae with syllables, and aligning syllables with S W prominence, one arrives at the following description:

(7)   L(ift)

S   W
α

Conditions: 1. L may be nonbranching (= stressed monosyllable)
           2. α may branch S W where that string is resolved

Such a fragment will describe lexical monosyllables; resolved bisyllables such as *guma*; nonresolved bisyllables such as *gyldan* or *Wealdend*; or trisyllables whose first two syllables are resolved (*æþeling, gumena*). Notice that if (7) is allowed to stand in verse-final position, it captures some of the ideas discussed earlier: if verses end weakly, then they may end on one, and only one, monosyllabic drop.

A further way of expanding the analysis is to think of (7) in terms of moric enumeration. If one thinks of the possible disposition of syllables in verse-final position in OE, there are four possible minimal arrays of morae, syllable, and stress, as seen in (8), where syllabic rhyme structure is the key:

(8a)   ‾‾‾‾‾‾‾

       m   m   (Weard, mann, sǣ)

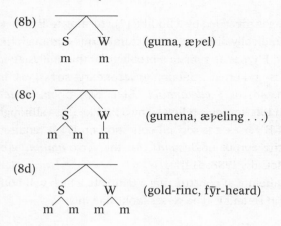

(8b)   S   W   (guma, æþel)
        m   m

(8c)   S   W   (gumena, æþeling . . .)
      m m   m

(8d)   S   W   (gold-rinc, fȳr-heard)
      m m m m

This range of moric possibilities maps neatly onto the structure seen in (7). In terms of verse-final strings, it is the structures seen in (8) that typically occur. Oddities in the pattern, such as (8d), which does not map easily onto (7), are handled by a metrical filter (familiar from Cable 1974; see also McCully 1988) which essentially states that for any syllable to be lifted, that syllable must be immediately adjacent to some lesser-stressed syllable. Under the terms of such a filter, the final W of (8d) cannot qualify as a metrical lift (in this context, a secondary stress), since it is not adjacent to a weaker syllable. It is thus equivalent – despite the heaviness of its Rhyme – to a mere weak stress. Notice also that the moric tier seen in (8) also allows for the possibility that final segments in OE are extrametrical (although cf. McCully and Hogg 1990): notably, lifts are isomorphic with linguistic stresses in that they have minimally bimoric Rhymes, whereas no such relationship holds for W syllables, which are typically monomoric – especially if the final segment of W syllables is analysed as extrametrical (see also Giegerich 1985, 1986).

With this background, we can proceed to initiate a template for D- and E-type verses in *Beowulf* (although of course such a template can and should be applicable to the widest possible range of data). In the most straightforward kind of D verse, for example, the kernel of the verse contains a compound or other derivative morpheme, as in *unhǣlo* (*wiht unhǣlo*, Beo. 120b) or *Scyldinga* (*weard Scyldinga*) or *āngengea* (*atol āngengea*, Beo. 165a). This kernel is in each case preceded by a lift like (7). Then there are so-called D2 verses, such as *Heort innanweard* (Beo. 991b). Here, too, the kernel contains a secondary stress, and again in each case this string is preceded by a lift like (7). Turning to E verses, matters do not seem radically different in structural terms (although the distributions of D and E types do remain a problem for this analysis): in such verses, there is a kernel containing secondary stress, as in *weorðmyndum* (Beo. 8b) or *Scedelandum* (Beo. 19b) or *murnende* (Beo. 50a), and again this kernel is followed by a lift like (7) – although note that in terms of E verses, the second condition on (7) is required only once in the entire corpus of *Beowulf* (for the verse *hordmāðum hælepa*, 1198a; see McCully 1988: 519).

The first tentative attempt at constructing a template which will both generate and constrain D- and E-type verses looks like this:

(9)

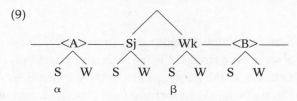

Conditions: 1. <A, B> may be nonbranching
2. α, β may branch S W where that string is resolved
3. Sj may be nonbranching, or may branch S W where that string is resolved, but if so, Wk must also branch. Where Sj branches S W = non-resolved, Wk must be nonbranching

The string Sj–Wk represents what I have here called the kernel structure. This structure is either preceded by a lift (the <A> expansion) or followed by one (the <B>). Where <A> is realised, a variety of D-type verse is also realised. Where <B> is realised, a variety of E is realised. Conditions (1) and (2) simply state what kinds of branching or non-branching feet may occur. Condition (3) is slightly more interesting in that it makes structure in one part of the verse dependent on what structures occur elsewhere – but recall that we already have two ways of legitimising this kind of dynamism: the form of the OESR itself, whose iterations across words are strictly cyclic and quantitative; and the general issue of the interrelatedness, perhaps even the finite-state nature, of metrical stringing itself; see the discussion above. Placement, type, and position, that is, are not merely local phenomena; their domain is the half-line or the verse itself.

Under (9), notice also how verses may end. They may end either under the Wk node (D types) or under the <B> expansion (E types). In both cases, the template captures the traditional view: depending on the structures that occur elsewhere, verses may end on a monosyllabic lift or on a branching foot containing one, and only one, weak syllable.

We should briefly run through what verses are generated by the crude template in (9). Take a normal D1 verse, say, *weard Scyldinga*. Here <A> is nonbranching, as permitted; Sj is also nonbranching: it dominates the syllable *Scyld-*; and since this is so, Wk must branch. It does so, to dominate the string *-inga*. Now take a D2 verse, say, *Heort innan-weard*. Here again <A> is nonbranching. Sj, however, branches, to dominate *innan-*; since this is so, Wk is nonbranching, dominating the lexeme *-weard*. Now take some simple E verses, ignoring the <A> expansion. Take *weorðmyndum þāh*. Here Sj is nonbranching, as permitted, but Wk must now branch. It does so, to dominate *-myndum*. And finally, <B> is nonbranching, as permitted.

Clearly, the template in (9) represents a crude first effort, and more tinkering – with the conditions, rather than with the overall structure – is required in order to generate and constrain a wider range of verses (and see the various different templates in McCully 1988). In order to handle more complex material, it seems necessary to revise the template to the structure seen below:

(10)

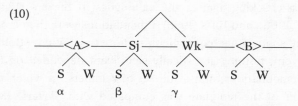

Conditions: 1. <A, B> may be nonbranching
2. α, β, γ, may branch S W where that string is resolved, but where γ branches, β may not branch
3. Sj may be nonbranching, or branch S W where that string is resolved, but if so, Wk must also branch. Where Sj branches S W = nonresolved, Wk must be nonbranching
4. <A, B> may be prefixed
5. Wk does not alliterate

This template and its accompanying conditions seem to account adequately and straightforwardly not only for simple examples of D and E verses but also for some more complicated cases. As a test, take an E verse such as *wīgheafolan bær* ('he bore the helmet', Beo. 2661b). Here resolution is found under the Wk node (under the γ symbol), and Sj is nonbranching, as permitted, while the rest of the verse patterns as required. To take a more complex example still, *fæderæðelum onfōn* ('he inherited paternal rank', Beo. 911a). Once more there is a resolved string under the Wk node, and Sj branches, again as permitted (notice that β does not branch). What is not permitted, apparently, is the presence of two resolved bisyllabic strings in the embedded kernel: Condition (2) is designed to meet this prohibition. Similarly, the presence of Condition (4) is designed to handle verses such as *fæst-rǣdne gepōht* ('firmly resolved thought', Beo. 610b) where a final foot is prefixed. Occasionally in E verses, prefixes of this kind slot into the preceding W node of the Wk foot; nor is this surprising, since OE was a stress-based language, and as in all stress-based languages, weak syllables tend to attach under enclisis to a preceding stressed syllable (and see here Suphi 1985, 1988): compare here a verse such as *wudurēc astāh* ('the woodsmoke ascended', Beo. 3144b, emended by Kemble).

What remains is to check the power of the template seen in (10) against text. Taking Klaeber's 1950 edition of *Beowulf* as the base text, the corpus was scanned. The procedure involved extracting matching verses and cross-checking against the catalogues in Sievers (1885), J.C.Pope (1942, 1966), and Bliss (1958). Emendations were then cross-checked against some other convenient edition (e.g. Wrenn/Bolton 1973). In the event, nothing statistically significant depended on the cross-check of emendations, and a full set of numbers, in which the generative power of the template was compared with Sievers' 1885 tabulation, can be found under (11):

(11) Statistics A

        Sievers

        2nd verse D types 403

        1st verse   D types 454

        Total   857

        2nd verse E types 334

        1st verse   E types 138

        Total: 472

        Combined total D and E (Sievers): 1,329

        Total verses matching template: 1,374

I believe the count is accurate to within 1 per cent. Nevertheless, it is still puzzling that the template developed here records more verses as D or E – puzzling because this may mean that the template is underdetermined. The discrepancy, however, is accounted for by the fact that Sievers catalogued verses such as *folcstede frætwan* as A types (on the grounds that the post-initial syllable was short; see Sievers 1885: 278), whereas the template generates such verses as a variety of E. (Notably, Sievers himself noted that these verses could 'theoretically' be classified as E types.) Sievers counted 59 of such subtypes. If one strips 59 from 1,374 (the original total verses accounted for by the template), one arrives at the figure 1,315.

This seems to be a fairly striking and remarkable result. One hundred years separate Sievers' analysis from the analysis sketched here, and different phonological machinery is involved in each case. Nevertheless, the results suggest that there is an immediate theoretical validity to Sievers' analysis, if not to his *Typentheorie*, which, as many commentators have noted, is impeachable on other grounds.

To sum up, we may claim that an analysis of OE verseform which includes interrelatedness among its generative principles has some advantages over analyses which see verses as static entities whose constituents are merely local (one thinks, in particular, of Sievers' and Bliss's notions of 'the foot'). At the same time, the template-based analysis captures analytic and practical similarities between metrical approaches. Built in the first instance out of one significant piece of metrical structure – the end of the half-line – a template-based analysis also captures regularities of constituency and allows a consistency of approach in which linguistic constituents such as syllables and feet are more or less isomorphic with constituents of metre (the 'less isomorphic' cases being handled by metrical filter). On the other hand, the cost in such an analysis is three fold. (a) How relevant is 'tertiary stress' (cf. Cable 1991 and Fulk 1992)? (b) How is the different distribution of Types D and E (and their subtypes) to be handled in template theory? (c) The template sketched above is predicated on the assumption that D and E types are not discrete entities but are in some sense mirror images. The template in (10), however, generates verses such as *hilderinc hār* (cf. the normative D, *hār hilderinc*), and as Cable (1991) shows, such verses rarely (if ever) occur in *Beowulf*. Such nonoccurrence of course harms the mirror-image assumption, and it may be that some deeper supplementary principles (e.g. 'rhythmemes' (see McCully 1992), or even scriptist, graphic constraints) are required in order to curb the generative power of such a template. (On the other hand, it may be possible to include a further condition on the template so that 'where <B> is nonbranching, Wk must branch' – this would be a prohibition against domain-final clashing stress, and would also bar verses such as the hypothetically possible / x \ /.) Still, the initial findings of the theory outlined here are at least striking, and further progress may be possible within its parameters. There may be yet more surprising facts at the end of the line.

5   Can Old English rhythm be reconstructed?

Wolfgang Obst

In this chapter I should like to argue that rhythmicality of a text is often not more than a plausible assumption on the part of the reader, an assumption which cannot be proved empirically. What can, however, be discovered and regarded as empirically valid are metrical restrictions, distributional regularities in the text which exceed the normal distributional properties of the language. Concerning the rhythm of *Beowulf*, however, we can go a step further. Here the distributional properties are such that they in fact not only allow a rhythmic interpretation but seem to rule out a nonrhythmic one.

This chapter has two main sections. In the first, I shall deal with general principles concerning rhythm; the second will be dedicated to the rhythm of *Beowulf*. Each section will consist of two parts. In the first part of the first section I shall give a definition of 'rhythm' and introduce four types of rhythm. In the second part of the first section I shall talk about the problem of reconstructing rhythmic language. In the second section I shall in its first part reexamine the distributional evidence in *Beowulf* concerning its rhythm. In its second part I shall try to show that a nonrhythmic interpretation of these data can be ruled out.

1. General principles

1.1. Types of rhythm

'Rhythm', as I want to use the word in this paper, is simply the division of a stretch of time into isochronous segments by regularly recurring acoustic events such as prominent beats of a drum against silence or against less-prominent beats, as prominent syllables in an utterance against less-prominent ones (or silence), as prominent notes of a melody

59

against less-prominent ones, or as the drops of a dripping tap against silence. In short, I shall regard 'rhythm' and 'isochrony' as roughly synonymous, knowing that other users of the word do not.

There are four types of rhythm, which are characterised by the presence or absence of two features: rhythm can be measured or unmeasured, and rhythm can be patterned or unpatterned. By combining these features we get the following types:

1. − measured, − patterned
2. − measured, + patterned
3. + measured, − patterned
4. + measured, + patterned

Patterning results from a consciousness of the number of beats in a bar and the number of bars in a line; measuring results from a consciousness of the duration of the beats in a bar.

The following fragment from Wulfstan's *Sermo Lupi ad Anglos* (Bethurum 1971: 261) is an example of a piece of rhythmic language which is neither measured nor patterned (an exclamation mark represents a silent beat):

(1) / ! forðam mid / micclum / earnungum / ! we ge-
    / earnodon þa / yrmða / ! þe us / on- / sittað /

The rhythm of this sentence comes about by keeping the distances between the stressed syllables equal. The number of syllables in these units (bars) is irrelevant. There are units of one, two, three, and four syllables in an irregular sequence. The beats in these units do not follow a regular numeric pattern; the resulting rhythm is unpatterned. The beats are automatically stretched or shrunk according to the number of syllables which happen to fill a particular bar. All the syllables in one particular bar count as equal; that is, their duration is not measured deliberately but is automatically determined by their number in that particular bar.

As examples of unmeasured but patterned rhythmic language we can take most verses which are written in one of the traditional English verseforms. A very simple and regular pattern is found in lines like the following from Pope's *Essay on Criticism* (Butt 1961: 249, vv.88–9):

(2) Those / RULES of / old *dis-* / *cover'd* / not *de-* / *vis'd*
    Are / *Nature* / still, but / *Nature* / *Metho-* / *diz'd*

Each bar contains two syllables, which count as equal in duration, one stressed, one unstressed. The unstressed syllable of the last bar forms the upbeat of the following line.

There are, of course, more complicated patterns, as e.g. the transposition of the classical Alcaic ode into a corresponding German rhythmic form by Friedrich Hölderlin in his poem *Vanini* (Beissner 1946: 262):

(3) Doch / die du / lebend / liebtest, die / dich em- / pfieng,
        o / oo / oo / ooo / oo / o
  Den / Sterben- / den, die / heil'ge Na- / tur ver- / gißt
        o / oo / oo / ooo / oo / o
  Der / Menschen / Thun und / deine / Feinde
        o / oo / oo / oo / oo
  / Kehrten, wie / du, in den / alten / Frieden. /
        / ooo / ooo / oo / oo /

  But / she you / loved in / life and who / then re- / ceived
  You / dying, / holy / Nature in / time for- / gets
  Man's / deeds, and / all your / foes de- / parted,
  / Passing like / you into / peace and / silence. /

In this poem bars with two and three beats are permitted only in specified positions. They cannot be exchanged without destroying the intended metrical pattern of stressed and unstressed beats.

I shall now talk about measured rhythm. Measured rhythm in English is found mainly in connection with music. There is unpatterned and patterned measured rhythm.

As unpatterned measured rhythm we may regard the musical setting of a prose text as we find it in Thomas Tomkins' anthem *When David heard that Absalom was slain* (alto ɪ):

(4)

  When Da-　vid　heard　that　Ab-salom　was　slain

In this type of rhythm, syllables within a bar do not count as equal but are alotted a certain artificial duration, here in accordance with the requirements of the harmony. The length of a syllable is not determined by its natural duration in speech and by the number of syllables in the bar but by artificial deliberations of the composer. We could therefore call measured rhythm 'artificial', whereas unmeasured rhythm we could call 'natural'.

Measured rhythm, too, can follow certain rhythmic patterns. In the following example every stressed syllable is allotted twice the duration of an unstressed one:

(5) ♩ / ○ ♫ / ○ ♫ / ○ ♩ / ○

The Lord's my shep-   herd I'll not want

Here, too, mensuration is something artificial, something additional to the language. In ordinary nonrhythmic language we are indifferent to the length of the syllables.

Mensuration is not something which is only found in connection with music. There are rudimentary forms of measurement also in some kinds of poetry. A nursery rhyme like *Goosey, goosey, gander* does not scan as

(6a) / goosey / goosey / gander /

but as

(6b) / goosey / goosey / gan- / der

We give the syllable *gan-* twice the length of the other syllables, and this we do against the normal pronunciation, accepting an unnatural stress on the second syllable *-der* (see here also McCully 1988, Part I, chs. 1 and 3).

Another case of measurement in poetry can be seen in our poem by Hölderlin. Here Andreas Heusler would have measured the three-beat bars not with three equal beats but with the first beat being twice as long as the second and third. The last line in his interpretation would read:

(7a) / ○ . . / ○ . . / ○○ / ○○ /

instead of

(7b) / ○○○ / ○○○ / ○○ / ○○ /

1.2. The reconstruction of rhythm

It will be obvious that the different types of rhythm I have just described pose different problems concerning their reconstruction. As rhythm is an acoustic phenomenon, its existence is bound to the time of its performance and to the memory of those who have heard the performance. As soon as the oral tradition which keeps rhythm alive is interrupted, rhythm is lost – unless we are provided with written conventions for its preservation, as we are in musical notation. Apart from very few genres such as nursery rhymes and church hymns, rhythms in English are transmitted not orally but in the written medium. Here rhythm has to be reconstructed by the reader.

How can one pick up rhythm from a written text? The answer is that one can pick it up whenever the distributional evidence suggests that there is something to be picked up, even if this has not been intended by the author.

A reader has the ability to construct rhythm even where none has been intended by the author. The following sentence from the *Guardian Weekly* (24 March 1991, p. 23) makes perfect rhythmic prose for somebody who, like me, is looking for it:

(8a) / ! He / now pre- / sents an / exhi- / bition /
        / ! de- / voted to / various / stages /
        / ! of the con- / struction /
        / ! of Sir / Christopher / Wren's /
        / master- / piece. /

What we have to do, when we understand or misunderstand a text as rhythmic, is to keep the stretches of time between stressed syllables equal. This can easily be done when the number of unstressed syllables between the stressed ones does not vary too much. A text which, intentionally or unintentionally, has this feature is potentially rhythmic, has the potential to arouse the reader's readiness to put rhythm to it. With most readers this readiness will, of course, only be triggered by the addition of various poetic conventions. But basically it is dependent on the recurrence of a stressed syllable after a relatively constant number of unstressed syllables. It is this readiness to construct a rhythm from the data which an author who creates a rhythmic text has to rely on.

If the author had a particular rhythm in mind, it is very difficult to identify it when there is no recurring pattern. Rhythmic prose can be manipulated by the reader in many ways, for example by introducing rests for lacking stressed syllables, or by suppressing or bringing out medium stress. In the sentence I took from the newspaper, one could suppress the secondary accent on *ex-* in *exhibition* and read

(8b) / ! He / now pre- / sents an exhi- / bition

Or we could drop a rest and read

(8c) exhi- / bition de- / voted to / various / stages

We could put a stress on *of* and read

(8d) / of the con- / struction

It seems that talking about the reconstruction of rhythm makes sense only when a recurring rhythmic pattern is involved. One can then establish the pattern from unambiguous cases and apply it to ambiguous ones. Thus, in our poem by Hölderlin we can decide that the last syllable of *Sterbenden*, *-den*, which is unstressed in ordinary speech, is used here as if it were stressed. It is the pattern as we have abstracted it from other stanzas that tells us that *-den* is used here to fill a metrical lift.

There are, however, cases where, instead of rhythmically disambiguating the text by a pattern we have already abstracted, we collect evidence for a rival pattern. The following quatrain from one of Shakespeare's sonnets (31) is a case in point (Evans 1974: 1755):

(9a) How / many a / holy / and ob- / sequious / tear
       Hath / dear re- / ligious / love stol'n / from mine / eye
       As / interest / of the / dead, which / now ap- / pear
       But / things re- / mov'd that / hidden / in [thee] / lie.

We are used to believing that we can expect ten syllables per line (neglecting licences). We are further used to believing that there is the rhythmic pattern of a two-beat bar (an iambic line is rhythmically a line of two-beat bars beginning with an upbeat). And we are used to believing that there can be deviations from the pattern, which are licences of individual realisation, such as the stress on *stol'n*, where the pattern demands an unstressed syllable, and the lack of stress on *from*, where the pattern demands stress. We can bend the language so that it fits the rhythmic pattern, and can enjoy the tension between the expected pattern and its violation.

But our approach can be quite different. Instead of basing the reconstruction of the rhythmic pattern of this text on our knowledge of literary and rhetorical tradition, we might alternatively base it on the linguistic facts. We then preserve the natural stresses of the language and construct a more natural rhythmic pattern:

(9b) How / many a / holy / ! and ob- / sequious / tear
       Hath / dear re- / ligious / love / stol'n from mine / eye
       As / interest / ! of the / dead, which / now ap- / pear
       But / things re- / mov'd that / hidden in / [thee] / lie.

In this pattern we do not expect five two-beat bars per line, but five bars of either one, two, or three beats, provided the number of syllables per line does not exceed ten. This is the pattern Shakespeare's language authenticates; it is not just a singular licence. If licences are frequent enough, they have become a pattern themselves.

Which of the two patterns Shakespeare had in mind, the more natural one or the more abstract iambic one, or both, we do not know (although see also Cable 1991 and this volume). What we know is that the natural use of the language, the distributional data, suggests the latter rhythmic pattern, not the former one.

So far we have discussed unmeasured language, and it was the possibility of relying on the natural linguistic stresses which enabled us to provide a rhythmic interpretation of the texts involved and possibly discover a rhythmic pattern. This possibility of relying on the natural use of the language is no longer there when we have to deal with measured rhythm. Language which is distorted by temporal mensuration normally no longer gives a clue to its rhythm. That means that measured rhythm can only be transmitted by special notational conventions.

There are, however, exceptions where measurement can be deduced from distributional linguistic evidence, as e.g. in the *Ormulum* (see Minkova, this volume). Orm is thought to have written his work in verses of seven bars, as can be seen in the following lines (Bennett and Smithers 1966: 175, vv. 13–14):

(10a) Annd / he badd / settenn / upp o / writt
       All / mannkinn / forr to / lokenn

If we have a closer look at Orm's septenarius, however, we discover that it is in fact something quite different, not

(10b) o / oo / oo / oo / o
       o / oo / oo / oo /

but

(10c) o / oo / oo / oo / o
       o / oo / oo / o / o

Instead of seven bars, we have eight bars, the seventh of which has only one syllable and has to be measured twice as long as other (stressed) syllables, although linguistically it is not different from those syllables, so that it would certainly have been possible to fill its bar, like the other bars, with the two syllables which are available, and thus to keep the language natural.

How can we prove the eight-bar interpretation against the evidence provided by the stress rules? According to Bennett and Smithers (p. 361), we do not find all the types of syllables on the first beat in the seventh bar which we find in all the other bars. Whereas in the other bars we find words of the types *inne*, *swellten*, *tǣlenn*, and *sune*, we do not find *sune* in the seventh bar. In *sune* the syllable *su-* ends in a short vowel, whereas in the other words the first syllable ends in a consonant or long vowel. One must look for a reason why a syllable such as *su-* cannot appear in this position. A possible explanation is that in this position a syllable had to be stretched over the whole bar, and that a syllable ending on a short vowel could not be overstretched in this way.

Measurement plays only a minor part in poetry. I have introduced the concept in this paper because it was applied by some scholars (Heusler, J.C. Pope) in metrical research in *Beowulf* by their use of mensurating notational systems.

2. Reconstructing the rhythm of Beowulf

2.1. The distributional evidence

What we have always known is that there are very complicated metrical restrictions in *Beowulf* which are not found in the ordinary OE language. What has to be worked out is how these restrictions came about. Are they determined by a simple rhythmic structure, or do they have to be explained quite differently? There have been several attempts to put rhythm to the verses, most notably that of J.C. Pope (1942), but as I have tried to show, this can easily be done to any text in which the number of unstressed syllables between the stressed ones does not vary too much. Thus, an attempt to make *Beowulf* rhythmic without any further empirical foundation is no more than a meaningless postulation (see also Stockwell, this volume). To use a mensurating notation for this postulated rhythm adds more problems. It either presupposes another postulate, namely that the rhythm of *Beowulf* was measured, a postulate for which there is no evidence, or it is applied negligently because one is not aware of its mensural implications. It is therefore advisable not to side with the so-called timers in *Beowulf* metrics, but rather with the so-called stressers. This means one has to start by reexamining the distributional evidence.

In classifying the verses of *Beowulf* linguistically, taking into consideration the number and different types of syllables, the kinds of stress, the position of stressed syllables in the verse, and the position of word boundaries, I find 309 metrical types which belong to the bulk of 96 per cent of the verses (that is, of 5,736 verses). The remaining 4 per cent of the verses (238), which are irregular, belong to a group of another 126 subtypes, different from the first group. All the 309 regular subtypes can be imagined as being generated by quite a simple calculus:

(11) I $\qquad$ $O \quad o_n \quad O \quad o$

II $\qquad$ $\left. \begin{array}{c} o_m \\ \\ O(o_l) \end{array} \right\} \left\{ \begin{array}{c} O \quad \underline{o}_n \quad O \quad \underline{o} \end{array} \right\}$

III

IV $\qquad$ $o_k \qquad\qquad O \quad o$

o = unstressed syllable

o_n etc. = one or more unstressed syllables

O = stressed syllable (primary, secondary, or enclitic tertiary stress), short and therefore covered by an unstressed syllable (resolution) or long

Underlining: one of the two positions or both have to remain unfilled

The formula must be read in the following way: a core verse (Type I) has four positions: strong, weak, strong, weak. The first weak position can have more than one unstressed syllable (n). The core can have a prefix (Type II/III). In this case at least one of the two weak positions of the core has to be silent in compensation for the prefix. The prefix is either a weak position (Type II), normally filled with two or three, rarely with one or more than three syllables (m). Or it is a sequence of strong + weak (Type III), where weak normally remains silent or contains one unstressed syllable, rarely more (the <l> subscript in III).

Of all the verses in *Beowulf*, 91.3 per cent correspond to the types I–III. There is a fourth type of comparatively little importance, to which only 4.7 per cent of the verses correspond. This type consists of only one strong position preceded and followed by a weak position. The statistical norm for the number of unstressed syllables in the preceding weak position is (k) 4.

So far I have established only a metrical pattern, not a rhythmic pattern. With my formula I have only arranged the verse types of *Beowulf* in a hierarchy of classes:

(12)

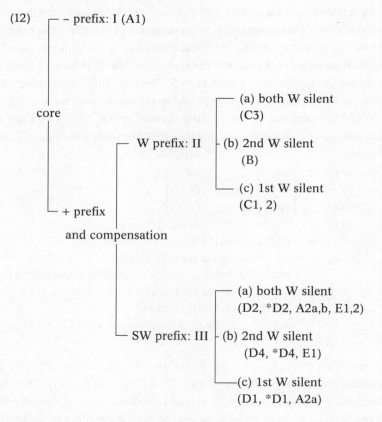

All the verse types can be further subclassified according to the number of syllables in weak positions, to word boundaries, and to resolution.

Is it possible to establish criteria according to which one classificational system is better than another? Can we say that Sievers' system is wrong? I would like to claim for my system that it is more consistent than Sievers'. The same criteria are applied to all verse types in the same order, which cannot be said for Sievers' classification. I should like to claim that my system is less prejudiced by premature interpretation (such as ignoring the third stressed position in D and E) and therefore less prone to unjustified subsumptions (A2,3 as A, C3 as C). The consequence of these improvements is that I can construct a simple initial formula (not in Magoun's sense, of course) which generates all the different subtypes.

I know that this metrical pattern is primarily a linguistic construct, my personal way of classifying the data as they have been visible to me. There may be more data than I have been able to see. And it would be incautious to assume that this was necessarily what the poet had in mind. But perhaps it is a calculus he could have had in mind (perhaps with a few modifications), and if he had, it would have generated the same distributional results.

There are two conditions a generative metrical calculus has to fulfil in order to be a plausible hypothesis about the poet's own metrical concepts: (a) it has to account for all the distributional characteristics of the poem, and (b) it has to be simple enough to be imagined as having been applied by the brains of an Anglo-Saxon community. That is, it must be adequate to the data and psychologically plausible.

2.2. The rhythmic interpretation of the distributional pattern

Undeniably, it is also possible to put rhythm to my classificational construct. We would only have to imagine the temporal distance between strong positions to be equal, and we would get the rhythmic pattern of (13):

$$
\begin{array}{lll}
(13) \quad \text{I} & &
\begin{matrix} /\,O & o_n\,/\,O\,o\,/ \\ /\,O & /\,O \;\; / \end{matrix} \\
\text{II} & \left\{ \begin{matrix} /\,! & o_m\,/ \\ & \end{matrix} \right\} & \left\{ \begin{matrix} /\,O & o_n\,/\,O \;\; / \\ & \end{matrix} \right\} \\
\text{III} & \left. /\,O(o_l)\,/ \right\} & \begin{matrix} /\,O & /\,O\,o\,/ \end{matrix} \\
\text{IV} & /\,!\,o_k\,/\,O\,o\,/ &
\end{array}
$$

The result of this interpretation would be an example of unmeasured but patterned rhythm, the pattern being a little more complicated than most of the patterns of modern poetry but not too complicated to be still within human rhythmic capability. It would have, I think, the psychological plausibility we expect. But without any further justifying evidence, this rhythmic interpretation would be nothing more than a subjective, albeit rhythmic, construct.

Can we provide more evidence? I think we can. There are distributional restrictions which can be taken as excluding a nonrhythmic interpretation of *Beowulf*. The verse types on which my argument is based are (1) the type represented by *gúðrînc mónig* (838b), and (2) the type represented by *brẽostnêt brõden* (1548a).

My argument hinges on the syllables with secondary stress (*-rînc* and *-nêt*). Sievers would have subsumed both types under A (*fóldan scẽatas*, 96b). He would have said that each verse had two lifts, and that both *-rînc* and *-nêt* did not represent a lift, but a secondary lift. In *mónig*, he would have argued, we have a shortened lift, because this lift contains only the short syllable *mó-*, whereas *-nig* has to fill the following dip, the last of the four positions every verse must have according to Sievers' preconception.

Evidence is against Sievers. There is no need for the assumption that every verse should have four positions. His treatment of *mónig* is highly implausible. If there is resolution in OE poetry, it must be due to general psychological reactions towards syllables ending in a short vowel. It is very improbable that this reaction should take place in some lifts but not in others of the same kind. Therefore, *mónig* cannot be metrically equivalent to *scẽatas*. On the other hand, *gúðrînc* and *brẽostnêt* cannot be equivalent to *fóldan*. The type *brẽostnêt brõden* is almost entirely restricted to on-lines (= a-verses), whereas *fóldan scẽatas* is not; and *gúðrînc mónig* is a regular verse, whereas its counterpart without a secondary stress is not. From this evidence it must be concluded that these verses cannot be classified as A and that their secondary stress is not a feature which makes them just slightly deviant from ordinary A-type verses, but a feature which is essential to their independent existence.

It is the independence of these verse types, and the indispensability of their secondary stress, which provides an argument for rhythm in *Beowulf*. If the syllable with secondary stress does not replace an unstressed syllable, its relative stress must have been perceived by the user of the language. There are two possible hypotheses to interpret this fact.

Either

The *Beowulf* poet used two audible levels of metrical dip, a light dip as in *fóldan scéatas*, and a heavy dip as in *bréostnêt bróden*. This seems very unlikely. One can easily imagine two audible levels of metrical lifts, as in

(14) / óoôo / óoôo /

but not of metrical dips. A dip as an unstressed position is psychologically a position of weakness, of audible insignificance. A differentiation of stress levels in this position would be very unlikely. Therefore the second hypothesis is more plausible:

Or

The syllable with secondary stress fills a metrical lift, not a dip, unlike the unstressed syllable. This means that we have a sequence of three lifts. The question now is how a syllable with secondary stress between two syllables with more stress can be marked as a metrical lift and not automatically become a metrical dip. This, as far as I can see, is possible only in isochronous units. If the time stretch between the lifts is equal, no difficulty arises in recognising a lift, even if it is surrounded by syllables which have a higher stress.

If this analysis is correct, distributional evidence suggests that *Beowulf* was a rhythmic poem. We are no longer in a position where rhythm can only be postulated but where a nonrhythmic interpretation can be ruled out by evidence.

We have evidence for a metrical pattern, and we have evidence in favour of its rhythmic interpretation, but we do not have evidence that this rhythmic pattern was in any way mensurated. Therefore I am not inclined to use a musical notation to represent this rhythm, as did Heusler (1925–9) and J. C. Pope (1942, 1966). I think that it is due to this mensurating overinterpretation that the approach of the timers met with so much scepticism from the stressers.

In my book on the rhythm of *Beowulf* (Obst 1987) I pretended to be a member of the stressing denomination, one who in the end converts to the somewhat purified beliefs of the timers, guided by the light of distributional evidence. I now confess that I did this because of the missionary effect I thought such an attitude might have. In fact, I have always been a timer, an academic grandchild of Heusler's. I have always believed in the rhythm of *Beowulf*, and my aim has been to find the real one. I became convinced that, if this could be done at all, it could only be done by completing the work of the stressers and by collecting more distributional data.

6 On recent theories of metrics and rhythm in 'Beowulf'

Robert P. Stockwell

Introduction[1]

The years between 1987 and 1991 were good ones for Old English metrics, with four major new books on the topic published (Russom and Obst in 1987, Cable and Creed in 1991).[2] But some old issues remain, especially the chronometric conflict. My purposes here are those not of a player but of a spectator trying to understand and explicate this rather esoteric literature. These four books provide four theories, and of course Sievers (1893) is taken as a reference theory.[3] These four new theories fall into two groups: those which don't insist on keeping time and those which do. In the first group are Cable and Russom; in the second, Obst and Creed.

(1) Cable (1991 and this volume) is Cable's most recent refinement of Sievers (1893), the benchmark achronometric theory.

(2) Russom (1987 and this volume) is a word-based theory of metre which is characterised by its author (p.6) as 'quite compatible with the rhythmical interpretations of Pope (1942) and Creed (1966)' – and, I shall assume, Creed (1990). By declaration, then, Russom is not against chronometric scansions. But in fact his scansions do not favour isochronous readings of one particular variety (say, Pope's or Creed's) rather than another (say, Obst's), or even suggest isochrony in general. Further, Cable has said that his own (nonisochronous) theory 'is compatible with major aspects of Geoffrey Russom's word-foot theory of Old English metre' (this volume). Though not obvious on the surface, it will become clear that the systems of scansion of Cable and Russom share a great deal.

(3) Obst (1987 and this volume) provides a new solution to the clashing-stress problem. This problem arises when two strong, or strong and secondary, stresses occur next to each other without a dip between

73

them. Obst's solution conflicts dramatically with Cable's. Part of Obst's solution (a carefully constrained use of silent beats) is also explicit in Creed's theory, as it was in J. C. Pope (1942) (though in Pope's presentation – and all others of this type – there was a fundamental error, discussed below, which has not been noted before). It was originally proposed, without any constraints, in Heusler (1925–9). But most of Obst's theory is quite incompatible with Creed, Pope, and Heusler. Though chronometric, Obst (unlike other chronometrists) characterises the limits on the number of unstressed syllables in the dips, the weak positions, of each verse as tightly as Cable does. The slack he allows is in the number of feet per verse. This innovation – allowing more than two feet per verse – is extremely controversial: the interesting question to be examined is how solid is the justification for this radical manoeuvre.

(4) Creed (1990) is the most recent version of the Heusler–Pope chronometric theory. I shall examine Creed's arguments from the point of view of how they improve on Pope, if they do. It will turn out that the weakest point in Pope's argument, a barely discernible crack in his foundations, has become a chasm.

Definitions and notational conventions

No two of these theories are couched in exactly the same technical vocabulary, nor do they use identical (or even similar) notation systems to represent their scansions of verses or lines. I shall, without apology or further justification, change all their notations to conform to the following system, most similar to Russom's but not identical to any:

An exclamation point (!) will represent an empty beat, either strong or weak as needed to fill out a foot. When it replaces a strong beat, it is equivalent to the concept recognised under labels such as 'musical rest-pulse',[4] 'silent beat', 'silent ictus'. When it replaces a weak beat, it is equivalent to 'zero syllable' (e.g. in Lass 1987 or Giegerich 1985). Though in my opinion the question is not whether such an entity is needed in order to read *Beowulf* rhythmically, but where and how often, I will not represent empty beats in scansions which are quoted from Cable or Russom, since empty beats are not built into their theories of Beowulfian scansion. However, Cable has much that is interesting to say about how and where such beats would be manifested in the rhythmic realisation of his scansion, and I will use this notation in that connection.

I will represent three levels of stress on syllables: namely, S, s, and w (for 'strong', 'secondary', and 'weak'). These are equivalent in the traditional terminology to 'lift', 'half-lift', and 'dip' or 'drop'. All syllabic positions (not necessarily occupied by syllables, because an empty beat can appear instead of a syllable) in my metrical scansions are therefore dominated by one of four symbols – !, S, s, w. Though a difference possibly existed between 'tertiary' and 'weak' stress in Old English, I will not represent it in scansions. Intermediate between strong and weak, that is, I will recognise only the single half-lift level, generally the second element of a compound noun. I will collapse 'tertiary' with weak, to this extent oversimplifying these theories.[5]

S must dominate two morae (as in all the early Germanic languages).[6] There are three possibilities for this to occur (using the appropriate Greek alphabet letters for 'syllable' and 'mora'; F stands for 'foot', the higher prosodic unit into which syllables are rhythmically grouped; V for 'vowel', C for 'consonant'):

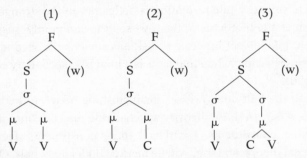

The first is simply a word containing a long vowel or long diphthong in the stressed (or only) syllable, as in, say, *gōd* or *ōþer*. The second is a word containing a short vowel (or short diphthong) in the stressed syllable followed by a tautosyllabic consonant, as in *word* or *worda*. The third is a 'resolved stress', 'resolved beat', or simply 'resolution'. Here the foot begins with a stressed syllable containing a short vowel followed by at least a second syllable, as in *lofu* or *hevene*. The second syllable may be heavy or light. In either case it is resolved into the light stressed syllable, making it heavy. That is, these two are functionally equivalent:

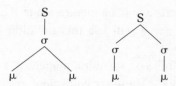

Resolution is a consequence of the Germanic rule that a single mora is not heavy enough to carry the stress alone (i.e. to form, by itself, the left branch of a foot). This rule is very familiar to everyone who has been taught to scan OE verse, but perhaps some further clarification will not be unwelcome.

It is important to realise that resolution is not a fact merely about Germanic metrics in general and OE metrics in particular. It is carried into the metrics from the general phonological rules of the language.[7]

My metrical notation for resolution, as described above, is S^w – not the same as S w – and this is my way of saying, 'This raised w is not the same as an ordinary w, though it is pronounced the same; rather it is an unstressed syllable which merely makes the S heavy and does not count as occupying a position of its own.' It is also necessary to allow for s w in the same sense: that is, both lifts and half-lifts must have full bimoric left-branch weight. While resolution is obligatory in the strongest positions, such as the first ictus of the a-verse, it is commonly 'suspended' (i.e. fails to take place) in weaker positions such as the second foot of the b-verse, especially when that ictus is a linguistic secondary stress, as in componds.

I will call the half-line a 'verse', distinguishing between the 'a-verse' and the 'b-verse'. In those theories which divide the verse into immediately smaller constituents, I will call these constituents 'feet' as in phonological theory, and they will be marked off by diagonals. Obst distinguishes also the clitic group, the next higher cluster. Though I believe it is correct to make this distinction in order to enrich the phrasing specifications (e.g. caesurae), it plays no role in relating his theory to more familiar ones, and I shall ignore it here.[8]

The metrical constituents of feet are 'positions', usually occupied by one or more syllables but often also by silent beats.[9] Positions can be defined independently of feet, as in Cable's theory (1991: 39), where a position 'is identified locally as a change of ictus from the preceding position', i.e. a dip or a lift. Cable's theory thus does not have constituents intermediate between verses and positions, and it explicitly disallows foot boundaries. To show equivalences between theories which do and do not include foot boundaries, I will in the appropriate instances add empty beats to indicate the rhythmic effects of the foot boundaries.

In abstract formulas which summarise a large number of actual scansions, I will need to introduce a few ad hoc symbols not needed in scansions themselves.

Cable (1991)

This theory is significantly different from that of Cable (1974).[10] Since the differences represent Cable's own revisions and improvements of his earlier theory (which he viewed as a refinement of Sievers' reference theory), I shall not deal with the earlier work.

Cable develops his theory along three parameters: syllable-counting, strong stress (including alliteration), and quantity (syllable weight). Since all theories acknowledge alliteration on at least one stressed syllable per verse as the functional equivalent of rhyme, combining a pair of verses into a cohesive unit, nothing more needs saying about this parameter. As for syllable-counting, Cable's intention is quite different from the syllable-count limitations in Romance verse or later English verse, as syllable-counting is understood in 'octosyllabic' or 'decasyllabic' verse (see too Duffell's comments about the $X(I)$, this volume). Rather he counts positions, which are prototypically represented by one syllable each.

But this is true only prototypically. Allowing resolution (i.e. not counting the weak syllables that are resolved into the stressed syllable, which is to say, counting $S^W = S$), Cable finds 3,037 verses with four syllables (of more than 6,000). Some adjustment is necessary in order for the four-syllable principle to be of much value. If one took the four-syllable claim literally, disallowing resolution, the number would drop by about half (to 1,675, by my count). That is, the syllable-count claim is literally true of about one-fourth of the verses in *Beowulf*. If we both allow resolution (thus deleting many counterexamples from the surface claim) and agree to ignore certain prefixes (treating them as 'invisible' or 'extrametrical'), the covered percentage rises above half, but only slightly. Syllable-counting, in the sense in which it is true of Romance verse or later English verse, is not really a property of early Germanic verse.

Given a forced choice between 'stressers' and 'timers', Cable is a stresser: i.e. his theory is not strictly chronometric. His theory is the latest in a line which starts with Sievers and includes A.J.Bliss as its leading prior expositor. But, unlike Bliss, Cable tries to make the account explanatory in the sense that the Sievers taxonomy falls out naturally from (i.e. is an epiphenomenon of) a few rather general principles, and in the sense that these principles are at least imaginably something which a scop could 'know' intuitively.

What Cable does is turn on its head the standard constraint on verse endings. This familiar constraint is stated by McCully (this volume) as follows: '[V]erses may end on a lift; on a resolved lift; or on one of these where they are followed by one, and only one, unstressed syllable'; that is, S(w) or S^W (w). Cable's theory takes that limitation on verse-ending unstressed syllables as the norm for all weak positions and then allows limited expansions in one of the first two positions. His theory has four requirements that a verse in *Beowulf* must not violate in order for the metrist to claim that the verse 'fits' the metric template:

(a) A verse must have four positions (as Sievers claimed); no more, no less. Prototypically, there is one syllable for each position, plus an additional syllable to raise the mora count to two or more whenever the stressed syllable is light – i.e. resolution.

(b) One of the first two positions can be expanded with unstressed syllables.[11] This expansion is extrametrical, in the sense that the verse is metrically well formed whether or not the additional syllables are present.

(c) Unstressable prefixes like *ge-*, *be-*, *on-*, and the negative particle *ne* usually count for nothing. They are nearly always extrametrical and invisible to the metrical template.[12]

(d) Resolution in a verse-final lift is disallowed if it follows a heavy stressed syllable (i.e. the antepenultimate syllable of the verse). This guarantees that there will be four positions in verses like 120a, *wonsceaft wera* (S w S w). To anticipate a difference between Cable and Obst, the latter always requires resolution; his scansion of 120a is $S/s/S^W$. His argument on this point cannot be taken lightly (see his paper in this volume). It is simply that resolution is a linguistic phenomenon having psychological reality; the association of syllable weight to stress (and therefore to lifts) cannot be turned off and on as a metrical convenience.

The key to Cable's system is the expanded dip.[13] It is 'the feature that accounts for the strong-stress feel of Old English poetry' (1991: 28). The fact that the expanded dip is variable and unpredictable in length, particularly in the first foot ('the first half-verse' (ibid.) – Cable does not sanction the concept 'foot', which would avoid this awkward usage), is taken to explain why the view could have arisen that OE verse was characterised by 'strong-stress metre'. Pure strong-stress metre would have temporally equally spaced strong stresses, with unlimited weak syllables scattered between them. In *Beowulf*, Cable's view is that the scattering of weak syllables is wholly constrained to a single expanded dip.[14] *Beowulf* may therefore be viewed as partially strong-stress metre and partially syllable-counting.

But even allowing 'partial strong-stress metre' as a characterisation entails temporal regularity. It assumes a high degree of chronometric scansion above and beyond the natural-language reading. Specifically it requires an imposition by the metre of greater temporal regularity than would occur in natural speech, in two areas: (a) rapid pacing of the expanded dips; and (b) minimisation of clashing strong and/or secondary stresses either by division into feet (which entails temporal separation) or by demoting one member of a clashing pair (which entails temporal joining). Both adjustments also occur in ordinary speech, both modern and ancient, of course.[15] The rhythm of verse is optimised to the extent that violations of isochrony are eliminated with greater regularity and consistency than they would be in ordinary speech.

No one disagrees, as far as I can determine, about the necessity for rapid pacing of expanded dips in a performance of *Beowulf* (though there is some disagreement about what gets included in the dips, mainly a controversy about finite verbs early in the verse). The disagreement comes over the manner, and the contexts, in which minimisation of clashing stress[16] must have taken place, and from it emerges what appear to be the major divergences between theories.

Cable views all clashes of the type S s (e.g. *gēardagum*) as requiring 'subordination' of the second syllable to the first. I have been unable to grasp what 'subordination' means here. That is, he scans 542a as indicated:

S s w   S
flōdȳþum feor

rather than with demotion:

> S w w   S
> flōdȳþum feor

He adduces various considerations, such as syllable length, to conclude that 'the contour is not so much a a drop from a peak to a valley, as from a peak to a foothill' (1991: 33). But the reason he cannot demote the second syllable in 542a has nothing to do with peaks or foothills or clashes: if he demotes it he will have a three-position verse, which (with good reason) he believes would be a violation of the most fundamental constraint of all.

By comparison, Obst scans the same verse

> S /s w / S
> flōdȳþum feor

which appears the same as Cable's scansion until the implications of the foot boundaries sink in: namely, the fact that there are three feet, and the general rule/perception that the initial (filled or empty) positions of feet are equally spaced from each other. That is, for Obst it's a lift whether it's a mountain or a foothill. Cable allows the retardation effects – the 'empty beat' sense – of monosyllabic feet only in verses of Sievers' Type D1. He scans 2582a thus:

> S ! S s w
> wearp   wælfȳre

Obst's scansion is

> S / S /s w
> wearp wælfȳre

which without the foot boundaries (to determine the pacing) would be equivalent to

> S ! S ! s w

in a system lacking foot grouping. I do not fully grasp Cable's reasons for rejecting the empty-beat strategy of reconciling clashing stresses except in this single verse type. He declares these other three verse types to be nonclashing, though they are at least superficially good candidates for clash resolution:

Type C – wS / Sw, as in *Maldon* 41a on flōt fēran
Type D4 – S / Sws, as in *Beo.* 1306a hār hilderinc
Type E – Ssw / S, as in *Beo.* 2115a andlangne dæg

Instead, I think it will be more enlightening to turn to Obst and see why he claims that these *also* require pacing adjustments to reduce the clash. Then I will return to Cable.

Obst (1987)

I will examine first his argument for assigning stress-clash status to those examples which Cable denies.[17] The argument is summarised by Obst (this volume), but I re-present it here in a simple-minded fashion which helps me, as very much of an outsider to these subtle issues, to understand it better.

Consider three verses from *Beowulf*, plus a nonce verse made up to clarify this point:

S w   S w
foldan scēatas (96b)
S s   S^W
gūðrinc monig (838b)
S   s   S w
brēostnêt brōden (1548a)
S   w S^W
*healde monig

For Cable these are all of the same type (Sievers' A, and readily generated by his rules), except that my nonce verse would be blocked by Cable's antepenultimate condition ((d) above): that is, everyone agrees that the nonce verse is impossible, but for strikingly different reasons. For Obst the nonexistence of S w S^W proves that the secondary stress of *gūðrinc monig* (838b) is essential to its viability as a verse, from which it follows that it cannot be demoted (cannot count as weak and therefore cannot count as an A type, cannot be subordinated to the left-adjacent S). Furthermore, the type seen in *brēostnêt brōden* (1548a) is confined, overwhelmingly, to the a-verse, which is not at all true of the type seen in *foldan scēatas* (96b). But if the secondary stress in 838b and 1548a is not demoted metrically, then it must be a lift. Since a lift can't exist *between* two lifts (the primary stresses of these verses) unless all three are paced isochronously (i.e. three feet), it follows that secondary stresses count as lifts. In the calculation of metrical feet, a foothill is as good as a mountain if there's a valley adjacent.

A consequence of Obst's analysis is that many verses have three feet, and the traditional 'two lifts per verse' restriction goes by the board. A very small number of verses must be treated as exceptions even with this restriction gone.[18] However, it is *not* the case that Cable's (and Sievers') 'four position' restriction is entirely surrendered. This is immediately obvious in Obst's Type I (discussed above), and though it becomes less obvious as one proceeds through his four types, in fact the restrictions on his types almost match Cable's – with a very few exceptions noted below, and except in the rhythmic interpretation already discussed above. I shall now examine Obst's four basic types, which are not at all similar to Sievers' Five Types, though they cover the same set of possible verses.

Type I. Sw. / Sw

'S' (throughout these formulas) includes 'S^w' (i.e., resolution). The period after the first w means 'iterate the w freely', i.e. expand the dip (the expansion is limited in fact but not in principle). Obviously there's nothing new to discuss here; it's universally familiar and agreed upon.

Type II. ! w. / Sw / Sw

Throughout these formulas, underlining the dips (including an iterable one) means that at least one must remain unfilled and that both may. Except when they are both unfilled, the result is four positions – but *both* of the first two dips may be expanded, as in 504a:

> w w S w w   S
> æfre mǣrða þon mā

The vast majority of the examples which appear superficially to have double expansions are eliminated by Cable's principle (c) above, which makes *ne* and prefixes like *ge-*, *for-*, etc. invisible to the scansion, as in 52b, where *on-* is extrametrical:

> w w   S w   S
> hwā þǣm hlæste onfēng

The number of legitimate counterexamples is probably small enough to ignore. Of the single subtype seen in 504a (two syllables in each dip, no prefixes or instances of *ne* to discount), I find only nine more examples.[19] Of the more complex types with longer iterations in either dip, there are very few examples like 487b (three plus two legitimate syllables in the first two dips):

> w ww S   w wS
> āhte ic holdra þȳ lǣs

The only verses which appear superficially to be of greater complexity are all allowed by the extrametricality of unstressable prefixes and *ne*, such as 1460b:

> w www S w w S
> nǣfre hit æt hilde ne swāc

Obst must allow more than a single expanded dip in his scansion only because he disallows extrametricality. In regard to characterisation of the dips, Obst's theory would mesh precisely with Cable's and Russom's if he used the notion of extrametricality as they do.

Returning to the Type II formula to consider the consequences of leaving the second and third dips both unfilled, we no longer have four positions: we have

> w. / S / S

Up to this point it has been possible to negotiate compatibility between Cable and Obst's Types I and II without calling upon foot structure (bowing, as it were, to Cable's preference). Now, however, foot structure must be added or the theories declared to be incompatible in this category. If foot structure is added to Cable's theory, a rhythmic reading can be assigned to the type

> w. S S,

namely

> ! w / S / S

(with the pacing entailed by the foot structure). There are three feet and four positions (counting the empty beat as one). If we are unwilling to do this, then we have a conflict: to work for Cable, a verse like 512b requires bisyllabic reading of the contracted vowel:

w w w   S   S(w)
þā git on sund rēon

and a verse like 794b requires textual emendation to work (for *genehost* read *genehhost*, which makes the first stressed syllable heavy):

w   w S   w   S(ᵂ)
þær genehost brægd

But the vast majority of Obst's Type II examples of the type

w. S S

in fact have a resolved final S; i.e. they are of the type

w. S S(w)

and they would all fall under Cable's stricture against resolution when the antepenultimate syllable is heavy (traditional 'suspension of resolution'). Thus, given this issue about resolution of the verse-final foot, which seems to require that one theory or the other must yield, the attempted reconciliation fails.

Type III: S(w). / S$\underline{w}$ / S$\underline{w}$

As with Type I, there are four positions except when all three weak positions are zeroed out. To exemplify those which are compatible with Cable's four positions, differing only on the rhythmical interpretation of the foot boundaries (which follow from the number of lifts):

S   / S   w/S
Fyrst forð gewāt (210a)
Sᵂ / S w   w/S
Hafa nū ond geheald (658a)
S/ S /s   w
wīs wēlþungen (1927a)

There are, contrary to Obst's formula, no examples where all three weak positions are unfilled, unless we disallow resolution verse-finally (agreeing with Cable; but Obst never allows this reading). Thus,

S   s   S   w [Cable] v. S / S / Sᵂ [Obst]
heard hēr cumen (376a)

The large number of examples of this type – about two hundred – suggest that Cable may be right about verse-final resolution.[20] The other possible exceptions to this generalisation involve contracted verbs, as in 820a:

> S /s / S
> feorsēoc flēon

I can characterise Obst's final type, but I can't compare his treatment with Cable's, since Cable does not deal with A3 verses in his 1991 theory. Obst considers them lightly, attaching little importance to their exceptionality (they occur in only 4.7 per cent of the verses in *Beowulf*). He suggests, interestingly, that 'they may have been derived by a . . . process of compensation [for the long dip]' of the type seen in all the other formulas where a prefixed dip empties one or both of the dips in the core feet. At any rate, they fall under Obst's final type:

> Type IV. ! w. / Sw

A typical example:

> w www /S w
> þæt hine on ylde (22a)

The distinguishing features of Obst's theory are clear by now, I believe. It is strongly chronometric, but it does not have certain defects of older chronometric theories which will be pointed out below. It will now be useful to move on to Creed.

Creed (1990)

Before taking up what I view as the substance and mildly interesting serious content of this book, I should say up front that the time and effort devoted to the computational testing of his metrical theory and the extended presentation of it here seem to me to have been misguided. And since I am not writing a review, I shall forgo expressing my annoyance with his ad hoc terminology made up for reference to familiar and reasonably well-defined notions (e.g. 'HC's', or 'halfline constituents', for 'feet'; 'Fine Parts' for 'positions'). Nor is one happy to find that his entire corpus is *Beo.* 1–315 and 2946–3053. This leads to distortions like a long discussion (pp. 154–5) of *Beo.* 193,

S   s^W   S   s   S   s   w   S
nȳdwracu nīþgrim, nihtbealwa mæst

as though this heavy line presented a general problem; but in fact only two other lines of this weight appear in *Beowulf*.[21] *Any* scansion of it in the terms suitable for most lines is going to be indefensible on any principled basis. It is best to place it in a category of exceptions and forget it.

Having now vented a bit of spleen, I turn to the virtues of this theory. It is a hermeneutic reconstruction of Kemble's (1833, rev. 1835) intuitive basis for lineation, with the entailment that to the extent that Kemble was right (i.e., virtually always, by later consensus), his implicit theory of scansion, putatively made explicit by Creed, is also correct. Creed's 'grid' or 'great net' columnation of foot and measure equivalence from line to line is chronometric, like the musical notation of J.C.Pope (1942). Here is how it works.

Establish a grid (which I represent in a notational variant, a tree) onto which each line is mapped:

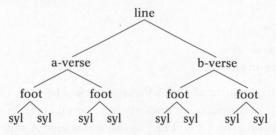

For 'syl' read 'position which is prototypically a single syllable'. There are, then, eight columns, grouped as shown. A nice trochaic line is organised in the obvious way, with the alliterative head initiating the b-verse:

S   w / S   w / S   w / S w
gōd mid Gēatum Grendles dæda (195)

All lines are forced into this grid, allowing empty beats to fill out the grid and maintain isochrony. The pivotal syllable is the alliterating head of the b-verse. It is assigned to the third foot if it is not preceded by unstressed syllables which cannot be assigned to the second foot, and to the fourth foot if there are such syllables. Pope made this same mistake: it entirely destroys rhythmic isochrony, because it forces two lifts into a single foot:[22]

w w w ww /S w /w/ S^W   S^ww

hī hyne þā ætbǣron tō brimes faroðe (28)

To see why this scansion is a mistake, perhaps it would be helpful to begin by looking at the line that led Pope to his surprising conclusions – what would be called 'the initial impulse', if vowel shifts were being discussed.[23] I do not mark the various single and double accents that Pope uses above the words because they are devices for overriding the system (like marking an accent on the off-beat, which would otherwise be weaker than the on-beat). One should not resort to override marking until it is clear what the neutral values are.

(1) *Beo.* 6–7 (Pope 39)

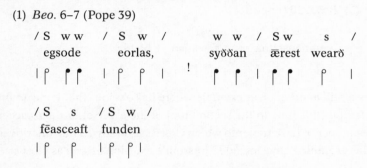

The revelation that came to Pope is thus reported (1942: 49):

Without knowing what I was doing [in a practice reading], I had substituted a rest for the first beat of a B-verse . . . How natural it sounded! – perhaps too natural for such an ancient poem. There was a natural pause after *eorlas*, hence a good opportunity to measure this pause and make a rest out of it . . . the alliteration, moreover, was signalized by primary accent, though this belonged to the second measure instead of the first.

This was the idea of the empty beat. Pope was, I believe, correct in principle, but his example is one where his implementation of the principle gives the wrong rhythm. By treating the first beat of the b-verse as empty, coupled with the assumption that a normal line has only four feet,[24] Pope is forced to accelerate startlingly (in fact, to double the tempo) in the final foot. The normal musical interpretation is given in (2), with the first foot of the b-verse after a short air space indicated by the exclamation point (because it is in fact a short rest). But note that this rhythmic interpretation demands five feet, as Obst would have it; or else a foot must be allowed to straddle the a- and b-verses:

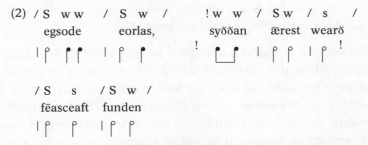

(2) / S w w   / S w /   ! w w / S w / s   /
   egsode   eorlas,   syððan ærest wearð

/ S   s   / S w /
fēasceaft funden

This is exactly the same reading that Pope uses (1942: 58) when the off-verse begins with a weak verbal prefix:

(3) *Beo.* 220 (Pope 58)

/ S w / S w /   (w) S^w / S w /
wundenstefna   gewaden   hæfde

Here is still another clear example where it is obvious that Pope doubles the tempo (this time in the second foot of the a-verse) in the unacceptable manner of (1), a trap into which Creed has followed him uncritically. In this example I have included Russom's scansion as well as Obst's:

(4) *Beo.* 15 (Pope 165)

/   w w / S   s w / S w / S w   / (Russom)
/ ! w w / S   s w / S w / S w   / (Creed)
/ ! w w / S /   s w / S w / S w   / (Obst)

      þē hīe ær   drugon aldor   (lē)ase

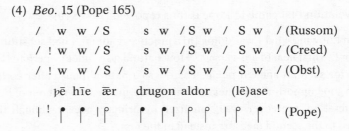

                                                ! (Pope)

We can now return to *Beo.* 28 and Creed's scansion of it:

    w w w w ww / S w /w/ S^W S^{ww}
    hī hyne þā ætbǣron tō brimes faroðe

It turns out, from this example and a few others, that Creed's stacking of parallel constituents in the grid leads him into Pope's rhythmic fallacy even in lines where Pope himself avoided it.[25] Note the last foot in Creed's scansion of *Beo.* 28 shown above, and compare it with Pope's:

    w w w w ww / S w w / S^W / S^W w
    hī hyne þā ætbǣron tō brimes faroðe

I suspect there are problems with a 'verse-straddling' foot like Pope's, but it is surely better than doubling the tempo in the last foot.

Up until this point, I had thought of Creed as an updated and perhaps better defended version of Pope's chronometric scansion. In that view, if I still maintained it, Creed might have felt I was doing him an injustice. However, on the argument outlined above, I conclude that Creed has actually done Pope an injustice, and that Pope's rhythmic sense, though off at times, was in a significant range of instances more reliable than Creed's. It is now apparent that foot divisions are assigned more rigidly, more formulaically, with less musical sense, by Creed than by Pope. I believe it is obvious that Pope was using essentially the same criteria for assigning up-beats, down-beats, rests, and foot and measure boundaries that are used by Creed (and, by Creed's logic, also by Kemble). That is because the filling-out of musical measures of equivalent beat content must have required Pope to make the same kinds of grid comparisons which Creed makes. After all, the essence of musical measures written in the same time notation is that you can stack them one on top of the other and always come out even, as well as determine exactly where the points of correspondence are – beat one, beat two, etc.

But musical measures that stipulate some fixed and invariant number of isochronous beats (four) of the type used by Pope and Creed are too much of a strait-jacket for the verse of *Beowulf*. This fact is the main reason many scholars prefer either an achronometric reading of OE verse types, however the types themselves are formulated, or a different kind of chronometric one like Obst's.

Russom (1987)

Russom's theory that every foot must correspond to the syllabic structure and stress pattern of some OE word is enormously appealing.[26] Ignoring prefixes (or setting them aside as separate 'function words'), only two kinds of feet must be considered: those beginning with a stressed syllable, and those containing only unstressed syllables. Sievers' Types B and C are eliminated from the inventory.

After Russom thinks further about the problems of matching his metrical system to the rhythmic values of Pope and Creed, I am not sure he will conclude that his theory of metre is in fact compatible with

Pope's and Creed's theories of rhythm, as he claims (1987: 6). Russom's theory provides exactly twenty-five possible foot pairings to generate well-formed verses (1987: 20–3). For every S in his pairings, the possibility of S^W exists, raising the total to seventy-five. Similarly for s^W (of which there are seventeen), raising the total to ninety-two. Russom assigns a fair number of weak syllables to extrametricality (indicated by parentheses in the scansons): e.g. Type A1 with anacrusis:

> (w w) S w / S w

For example:

> (w w) S w/(w) S w
> gē æt hām gē on herge (1248a)

He even allows verse-internal extrametrical syllables other than verbal prefixes (the latter would be allowed also by Cable):

> (w w) S / (w) S   s w
> ne ge-frægn / ic frēond-līcor (1027a)

With Obst's theory it is possible to make a direct conversion from metrical structure to rhythmic pattern. This is not possible with Russom's theory because of the extrametrical syllables. Consider verse 1027a above. Without the extrametrical syllables, it is a standard D1 and would be scanned by Obst this way:

> S / S / s w

But including the extrametrical syllables in the scansion makes 1027a wildly exceptional – in fact the only one of its type:

> w w / S^W w / S / s w

For Cable this verse is rather straightforward. The first two syllables are extrametrical. The final syllable of *-frægn* can arguably be ignored (as it is, in fact, in Russom's scansion). What remains for Cable, as for Russom, is a standard D1.

In fact, all of the 'allowable foot pairings' of Russom (1987: 20–3) turn out to scan properly in Cable's system even without the foot boundaries. A few examples, with the first scansion by Russom, the second by me following Cable's rules, are:

on fēonda geweald (808a)   w / Swws – wSwS[27]
ofer hronrāde (10a)   ww / Ssw – wwSsw[28]
sīde sǣnæssas (223a)   Sw / Ssw – SwSsw[29]
fēond mancynnes (164b)   S / Ssw – SSsw[30]

The scansions of Russom and Cable converge quite remarkably, especially given their totally divergent initial assumptions. Cable can add a
substantial element of psychological reality to his theory by adopting the
word-based foot; he would also gain, by that same move, a natural
explanation of the one stress clash which he accepts independently
(namely, any S / S).

Conclusions

Even though Russom has metrical feet and Cable does not, their scansions turn out to be very much alike, principally because they both allow
substantial numbers of extrametrical syllables to be ignored. Obst's
scansions take in all syllables and assign them a consistent isochronic
rhythmic interpretation, at a certain cost in the resulting complexity and
loss of conceptual elegance. The rigidity of the frame by means of which
Creed and, earlier, Pope achieve isochrony is not compatible, pace
Russom, with any other theory and has serious internal inconsistencies.

Notes

1 I have no doubt that the errors which remain after their many helpful crit-
   icisms are still awesome, either because I didn't take their advice or didn't
   understand it, but I remain very grateful to Donka Minkova and Thomas
   Cable for careful readings of this paper in a preliminary version. The specific help of Geoffrey Russom and Wolfgang Obst is acknowledged in particulars spelled out below. Most especially I wish to thank Christopher
   McCully and Richard Hogg for including me in the conference of which
   this volume is the fruit, and through them the estate of the late
   G. L. Brook, whose generosity made the conference possible.
2 Subsequently, this high level of interest and achievement has continued,
   perhaps even accelerated, with the publication of Fulk (1992), Whitman
   (1993), and Hutcheson (1995). Here, in fairness to the date of the conference from which this work was derived, I deal only with 1991 and earlier.
   Kendall (1991) appeared in this earlier time frame, but his is not a purely
   metrical theory; it involves so much syntax that it is not directly comparable. I therefore confine myself to the other four.

3 For detailed explication of the Five Types, see e.g. Cassidy and Ringler (1971), Cable (1974 or 1991), C.J.Pope (1942), or Lehmann (1956). Hieatt (1989) provides a compact and useful summary.

4 That is, a rest at the beginning of a bar, where the latter part of the bar is the up-beat to the initial pulse of the next bar.

5 It can be shown that this simplification does not change the rhythmic interpretation, though tertiary stress has some phonological implications that are irrelevant here.

6 A mora is a measurement of syllabic weight equivalent to the weight of a single short vowel (abstracting away from tautosyllabic consonants that precede it; they don't count) in an open syllable. Its usefulness is that it allows certain generalisations to be made neatly which can otherwise be made only cumbersomely. A heavy syllable is one with bimoraic weight. A light syllable is monomoric.

7 Some scholars think resolution was carried into the metrics from the general phonological rules of the language. Dresher and Lahiri (1991: 256) point to contrasts such as *werudes* (where the second syllable of the root is retained to give the necessary weight to the left branch) v. *hēafdes* (from *hēafudes*), with the second syllable deleted by a well-known rule which differentiates between light and heavy stems, seen transparently in pairs such as *lofu* v. *word* (< *wordu*). In effect, whenever S is assigned to a light syllable, the lightness is compensated for by stealing the next syllable. It does not matter whether the next syllable is itself light or heavy: it is still functionally absorbed into the left branch.

Dresher and Lahiri (p. 257) point to the example *færeld* from *færeldu* to demonstrate that the heavy sylable *-rel-* does not block deletion of the final high vowel: the syllable *-rel-* must therefore be part of the left branch.

8 This distinction effectively doubles the number of different verse types he recognises. Comparison of his raw numbers with those of Bliss or Sievers or Pope would be meaningless, for this reason and several others.

9 I say 'metrical constituents' because the statement is true only for metre. In the *language*, the constituents of feet are syllables, with the provision that in Germanic the left branch of a foot may contain two syllables because it must be (minimally) bimoric.

10 I am grateful to Professor Cable for very many kindnesses, not least of which was his willingness to send me a pre-publication version of the relevant chapters in this book. Any errors in this account of his theory are entirely due to my slow learning curve; he has made every imaginable effort to see to it that I am properly informed.

11 Hieatt (1989: 33) and others conflate 'resolution' with 'extrametricality'. The former is used by linguists only as described above, to refer to weight compensation for a light stressed syllable. The latter is indeed used by

metrists to refer to syllables which don't count at all – either to compen-
sate for an underweight stressed syllable or for anything else. Her asser-
tion that 'a drop of two or more syllables is always resolved' makes no
sense linguistically except under the interpretation that two or more syllables in a dip count as occupying only one 'position': i.e. all but one of them
are extrametrical. But this sweeping generalisation will not do: one wants
to be able to say *which* syllables count as extrametrical and why, not
simply that the whole bunch are squished into a single position.

12 Cable has pointed out to me in correspondence, and has mentioned in his
1974 book (p. 35), that 'sometimes they have to count, as in *Fyrst forð
gewāt* (210a)', in order to provide the minimal four positions of the verse.

13 There is a terminological difference between Cable's usage and mine: in his
characterisation of OE metre he refers to 'one optional expansion of
unstressed syllables in either of the first two positions of the verse', and when
he refers to these expansions he prefers to call them 'strong dips'. I have
replaced both 'strong dip' and his earlier usage 'extended dip' with 'expanded
dip' in order to maintain consistency with the basic characterisation.

14 I am not concerned here with whether similar constraints, though not
identical, exist in ME alliterative verse, though Cable believes they do.

15 Anyone in doubt should compare the phrase 'hickory dickory dock' with
'lost white cats'. The latter has zero syllables (empty weak beats) to fill out
the feet, of which three occur in each phrase. Arguments that the timing is
not equal in respect to exact measurements are quite irrelevant; these are
perceptually equal in timing.

16 I would prefer to say 'resolution of clashing stress'. Unfortunately, the
term 'resolution' has been specialised to a very different usage, as already
discussed above, having to do with syllable-weight compensation. That
should have been called 'moraic compensation', and then 'resolution'
could be used here where it would have the sense of 'resolving a clash or
conflict'.

17 Like Cable, Professor Obst has been extremely generous in supplying me
with an advance version of his chapter in this book and a copy of his 1987
book. I am most grateful to him. I have tried hard not to misrepresent his
views, and I can only apologise for errors that may remain despite my
efforts. Quite apart from bilingual inadequacies from which I suffer, Obst's
theory is new and very complex on the surface, even though I believe it to
be conceptually elegant and simple.

18 'Bedingt regelmässige Verse', e.g. *gūð-rinc / gold-wlanc* (1881a), scanned
Ss / Ss by Russom (converting foothills to valleys). The second syllable is
grudgingly (it would appear) demoted into the first foot by Obst: Ss / S / s.
Though the answer is probably buried somewhere in his book, I have not
discovered why Obst is willing to demote the first secondary but not the
second secondary.

19 536b, 1276b, 1739b, 1746b, 2141b, 2277b, 2442b, 2687b, 2975b.

20 But Obst's arguments in favour of verse-final resolution, outlined above, are very strong. My convictions on this point are easily swayed in either direction. I lean toward the linguistic logic of Obst, but the good metrical consequences of the standard unresolved scansion are seductive.

21 485 and 1722.

22 The notation S^{ww} is in accord with Creed's claim that more than one syllable can be resolved into the stressed syllable. This use of the term has no foundation in phonological theory.

23 I double all his values, and I use an exclamation point to indicate a rest of whatever time is implicated by the remainder of the bar. This doubling is only notational, as was pointed out to Pope in 1949. I can't imagine why it took seven years to correct Pope's misapprehension of the nature of time signatures in the notation system of western tonal music. In his 1966 preface he eats humble pie: 'This muddled passage has been duly castigated by Raymond E. Past, to whose article I refer the curious' (p. xvii).

24 Not shared by Le Page (1957) or by Obst, but by almost everyone else.

25 It is impossible to make a really valid generalisation on this point, because Creed reports his scansion of only 386 lines (more or less; I haven't counted occasional readings he gives for lines not included in his 'matched corpus'). On the other hand, Pope scans 663 lines (he of course provides a justly famous and complete catalogue of half-line types, but from this it is not possible consistently to recover what might be called the 'joining function' between the two half-lines). Of those 663, only 141 are the same as those in Creed's corpus to give a basis for comparison. Of the 663, 37 have the up-beat of the third foot assigned to the end of the second foot by Pope. Of the 141, 6 do, namely, lines 28, 35, 39, 220, 225, and 298. Of these 6, *none* are scanned in Pope's way ('straddling') by Creed. In effect, then, he compounds the error Pope made in certain lines by introducing that error at every opportunity.

26 Professor Russom also sent me a copy of his conference paper well in advance, and he has offered me every courtesy in my efforts to understand his work. I am very grateful to him.

27 Recall that the *ge-* of *geweald* is extrametrical.

28 Expanded dip in first position.

29 Five positions, allowed by Cable precisely for this type.

30 Cable would allow an extra beat to minimise the stress clash in this type; perhaps it should be written S!Ssw.

7   Nonprimary stress in early Middle English accentual-syllabic verse

Donka Minkova

1. Background

This chapter addresses some problems of ME stress placement seen in the context of early Middle English (eME) accentual-syllabic poetry. In the absence of any first-hand accounts of accentual prominence relations in earlier stages of the language, we need the evidence from metrics to inform us about the stress rules of the language. The material on which metre and stress will be formulated here is drawn from the *Ormulum*, *c.* 1170. I hope to make this study the first step in a much more ambitious project covering the properties of accentual-syllabic verse composed between 1200 and 1400.

Two assumptions underlie the discussion: first, the metrical intuitions of the people who composed eME accentual-syllabic verse did not differ from the intuitions of poets of later times; then as now, metrical ability was 'an overlaid function, tapping into both linguistic competence and "rhythmic competence"' (Hayes 1988: 246). The early metrical compositions were subject to the general principles of rhythmic activity valid for English today: the English versifier of 1200 followed a pattern of binary stress alternation the violations of which can be captured and projected against either the metric or the prosodic system. Second, poets (versifiers, versecraftsmen/versepersons) would not normally mutilate the prosodic rules of the spoken language; i.e. the language of poetry reflects adequately the phonology and prosody of the spoken language. For years, and through volumes of scholarly production, the combination of these two assumptions has been our only source of information about the prosodic characteristics of earlier language states. More specifically, these assumptions have generated and fostered the familiar basic postulate that strong positions in the verse line are filled by stressed syllables, and its obverse: weak positions are filled by

unstressed syllables. This supposition provides a measure of 'correctness' of the 'fit', the matching, the correspondence, between metrical
and prosodic slots. Similarly to the importance attached to occasional
spellings in phonology, imperfect matching, putative or real, has been a
goldmine for philologists, the corollary being that one can derive valuable information from precisely those forms and occurrences which run
against the expected matching; noncorrespondences between the way
we understand the poetic template and the presumed properties of the
language material fitted into the template provide an exciting line of
enquiry. This study focusses on mismatches involving disyllabic and trisyllabic words; in general I will not be addressing the possibility of
clashes or reversals of phrasal stress attributable to exigencies of the
metrical frame.

Metrical studies of pre-Chaucerian accentual-syllabic verse are virtually lacking in the literature. Early verse is discarded as either too
'monotonous' or as 'irregular', sorely in need of discipline (Partridge
1982: 288). The sections on metre in text introductions customarily list
line patterns and deviations but do not specify the patterns which are disallowed, if any, nor do we in general find comments on the relationship
between these patterns and the prosodic structure of ME. Most detail on
versification and language in some pre-Chaucerian compositions can be
found in Tarlinskaja (1974a, 1976, 1976a), but her findings and conclusions are marred by a questionable system of counting final -e's, as well
as by a failure to distinguish between systematic and nonsystematic noncorrespondences between presumed stress and metric prominence.

One should admit from the start, also, that since the formulation of
metrical rules relies on prosodic stress rules, circularity is the bane of
much of the argumentation in this paper and in other studies of the
topic: I am aware of the problem of making judgements about speech
prosody on the basis of versification rules which we have formulated on
the basis of assumptions about speech prosody. Nor can one be certain
about the time and the way in which versification rules crystallised and
acquired the form we attribute to them with the power and conviction of
hindsight. The alternative to facing the potential circularity is to allow
the unknown to remain unknowable. Rather than being defeatist, I
approach the topic with the conviction that modern metrical theory will
allow us to say something useful about both stress and metre and still
avoid the spectre of circularity.

A terminological note is in order too: I use 'stress' as a term describing the binary prosodic property of syllables in language, alternating (and synonymous) with 'accent', in line with some common practice. The metrically prominent position in verse is referred to as ictus, arsis, strong beat. Another useful distinction is that between 'metrical' and 'prosodic'; see also Minkova (1992: 159). Following Kiparsky (1977: 238), I use 'metrical' to refer to properties specific to poetic compositions. Metrical rules provide the abstract template of any form of verse. They can be defined and modified in reference to one type of verse, to one poet, or even to one poem. 'Prosodic' refers to the properties of any form of language. The abstract metrical template interacts with the prosodic rules of the language. The prosodic rules are a subset of the general range of available linguistic rules and, like them, are subject to synchronic variation and diachronic change.

2. The evidence for mismatches

> All things counter, original, spare, strange;
>   whatever is fickle, freckled (who knows how?)
>   Gerard Manley Hopkins, *Pied Beauty*

The composition of accentual-syllabic and rhymed poetry during what Kaluza (1911: 184) calls the 'Central Middle English Period' (1250–1370) is characterised by progressive generalisation of rhyme and regularisation of the stress alternation within the line. The number of ictuses per line varies from composition to composition; the general perception is that uniformity is not achieved until Chaucer (Tarlinskaja 1974a: 74), when, either through a 'quantitative leap' or as the natural outcome of an earlier steady tendency, the number of ictic positions per line becomes constant. The difference between a fully constant number of ictuses per line, reaching 100 per cent in Chaucer, and some of the earlier compositions is negligible: *The Owl and the Nightingale* reaches 95.5 per cent, *Havelock the Dane*, 97 per cent, and *Speculum Gy de Warewyke*, 94.3 per cent. Putting aside the uneasy question of how many syllables were used to fill the lines with the constant number of ictuses, we still have a solid foundation for investigating the match between the type of metrical position (ictic or nonictic), and the linguistic stress (strong or weak) of the syllable occupying that position. Instances of matching are relatively uninformative: we approach the problem with the a priori conviction that such matching is axiomatic and unexceptional. Mismatches have attracted much more attention; the following section surveys the scholarly reaction to this phenomenon.

2.1. Scholarly reaction to the mismatches

The king was cumand thro Cadden ford
And fiftene thousand men was he;
They saw the forest them before
They thought it awsom for to see
                    The Outlaw Murray, Popular Ballad

The scholarly reactions to apparent mismatches between metrical ictus and presumed linguistic stress in eME accentual-syllabic verse can be sorted out into several strands; the summary of the various reactions and interpretations presented below is based on Tarlinskaja (1974b: 108–9; also 1976b: 43–5).

(1) Mismatches are perceived and construed only by philologists and metrists. In reality, pre-Chaucerian poets could not handle the newly evolved alternating prominence pattern in verse and resorted to counting syllables only without heeding the matching. This practice was based on imitation of the syllabic system of Romance poetry.

(2) Line-initially and after the midline caesura, 'trochaic substitutions' of the predominantly iambic pattern introduced an acceptable variation of the all-iambic lines. For Chaucer the substitution theory is developed fully in Ian Robinson (1971: 118–28), who allows inversions in every position in the line, and for whom Anglo-Saxon words, even the notorious derivatives in *-ing(e)*, *-hed(e)*, and *-ness(e)* in rhyme position, were accented on the first syllable.

(3) Mismatches were a mere poetic convention and as such would require no linguistic explanation.[1]

(4) Noncorrespondences reflect a linguistic reality: they are attributable to the massive influx of French loan words in Middle English. Native English noncorrespondences are due to analogy with the variably stressed words of Romance origin.

(5) Noncorrespondences in native words are due to the reversal in the direction of the application of the Germanic stress rule; Halle and Keyser (1971: 97–109) account for the stressability of the second syllable of *-ing(e)* and *-ness(e)* by the operation of the Romance stress rule which

assigns stress to the paroxytone when the final syllable is a weak *-e*. Tarlinskaja's objection to this analysis (1976b: 44) is based on the observation that there are some disyllabic mismatches, as in:

> I am, thou woost, yet of the companye
> A mayde, and love *hunting* and venerye.
>
> *The Knight's Tale*, 1449–50

The objection is overruled by the argument presented by Halle and Keyser, and developed in Nakao (1977: 134, 142–3), that words with suffixes have an underlying final lax vowel, which is subsequently deleted by the stress cycle. The example cited by Tarlinskaja is in fact an ideal candidate for that procedure because of the elision environment. Alternatively, without engaging in abstract derivations, we might speculate that there are other possible scansions which would not necessitate mismatching: a disyllabic *mayde* and a syncopated *venerye*, i.e. *ven'rye*, or a disyllabic *love* and again a syncopated *ven'rye*.[2]

Tarlinskaja dismisses the interpretation (2) offered by Ian Robinson (1971: 118–19) that the iambic prosodic pattern of native words cannot be violated, i.e. suffixes of the type *-ing*, *-ness* cannot be in a strong metrical position, even in rhyme. She does not offer any comment as to why the theory is implausible. As mentioned above, she also rejects the Halle–Keyser analysis on the basis of the frequency of stress on the second syllable of native words which have no final *-e*. She accepts (somewhat ambivalently) as more plausible the variants summarised as (1) and (4), stating that mismatches are due to lack of understanding of stress alternation, and that polysyllabic words had variant accentual forms stressed on the second syllable.[3]

3. Ormulum

> þiss boc iss nemmnedd Orrmulum
> Forrþi þatt Orrm itt wrohhte
>
> *Preface*, 1.1–2

The decision to look at the *Ormulum* again is dictated by several considerations: the relative precision of the dating and the provenance of the text, the systematic adherence to one metrical form, the absence of detailed discussion of the metrical rules in the text and their implication for the study of the evolution of English stress rules. Very importantly, too, unlike Chaucer's metre, which is claimed to exhibit 'a Romance presence so strong as to constitute a motive rhythmic force in the poetry' (Guthrie 1988b: 30), the almost uniformly Germanic vocabulary of the *Ormulum* would preclude any speculations about prosodic influence from French or Anglo-Norman.

3.1. The metre of the Ormulum: agreements and disagreements

Standard metrical accounts of the *Ormulum* have always assumed an extremely rigid verse pattern.[4] Hall (1920: 486) pronounces Orm's verse 'monotonously regular; every line has its fifteen syllables exactly counted out and ends in x́ x; the caesura comes after the eighth syllable; the rhythm is iambic *without substitution*'. For the sake of this uniformity Orm does violence to the natural accent in *Nipprédd* 35, *Bisscópess* 51, *Enngléss* 69, *sahhtnésse* 140, *drihhtíness* 171.[5] Hall reports Schipper as regarding such cases 'as examples of "hovering accent", wherein the stress is distributed equally over the two syllables having the word-accent and the verse-accent, – a spondee rather than an iamb'.[6] Kaluza states that 'anacrusis and thesis are never omitted' (1911: 156); Mossé (1952: 357) allows a trochee at the beginning of the second half-line and adds that 'it is useless in such cases to suppose any displacement of the word stress'. In a recent study of the development of rhyme in English medieval verse Eric Stanley argues (1988: 33–4), mostly on aesthetic grounds, that in the *Ormulum* the accentuation of the middle syllable in trisyllabic words is regular in the sense that it is 'in line with Middle English practice and with some Late Old English practice', though, to our surprise, he adds that in such words 'it may be that their metre does violence to *natural* accentuation . . .'[7] On the other hand, in disyllabic words the accent should be placed on the stem syllable, i.e. Stanley allows:

(1) *7* tærfore hafe icc turrnedd itt   D 129–30[8]
      inntill Ennglísshe spæche:

compared to:

(2) Hemm hafe itt inntill Ennglissh wennd: D 147–8
      forr þeȝȝre sawle nede

but in (3) he places the accent on the first syllable:

(3a) To frofrenn swillke senndeþþ godd;   D 3798-9
       Enngless 7 hallȝe sawless
(3b) Niþþredd and wannsedd wunnderrliȝ;   3730-1
       7 laȝhedd inn himm sellfenn[9]

Summarising: Kaluza and Hall assume mismatches and attribute them to the exigencies of the verse pattern. In addition, Mossé refers to the caesura, and Stanley to 'linguistic and literary good sense' (1988: 35) as factors which should be included in the metrical account.

4. The basic pattern

> I think that I shall never see
> A poem lovely as a tree
>   Joyce Kilmer, *Poems, Essays and Letters* (1917)

An account covering the vast majority of the lines in the poem is not a problem. The *Ormulum* contains invariably seven strong beats distributed 4:3 across the line. Each strong metrical position is flanked by weaks. The basic template for the septenarius is shown in Fig. 1.

Figure 1

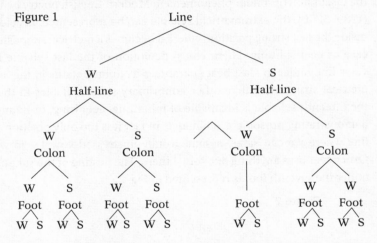

The pattern is not completely symmetrical: the first W in the line is shown to be dominated by weak nodes all the way up; the last S, the fourteenth syllable, conversely, is dominated by S's again all the way up. The binary branching-tree representation (see Hayes 1988: 222) adumbrates a difference between the positions in the line which is crucial in determining the validity of conclusions based on 'mismatches' between prosody and metre.

5. The metrical freedom of line edges

Lines may be varied with a rare
Misplaced syllable here and there
John Hollander, *Rhyme's Reason*

It is a commonplace observation that line edges in accentual-syllabic verse are somehow different from positions inside the line. The next three sections of this study will deal with occurrences of polysyllabic items at line edges.

5.1. The right edge

In addition to the fourteen syllables, the septenarius line in the *Ormulum* always ends with a fifteenth and prosodically weak syllable after the last strong position. Since it falls outside the domain of the last metrical foot (see Fig. 1), this last syllable can be treated as 'extrametrical'. Following the discussion of similar phenomena in Modern English poetry by Prince (1989: 52–6), the extrametrical syllable can be represented as belonging inside the last strong position, where it occupies a metrical subposition; a case of beat-splitting. Hierarchical demotion of the last syllable in the verse line under the last beat guarantees its unique status in the layered metrical structure: unlike other nonprimary stress syllables in the line, the fifteenth syllable is incapable of inheriting, acquiring, or in any way demonstrating prosodic prominence; in fact it is the only position in the line where we can safely assume a fully unstressed vowel – in writing Orm never uses anything but <-e-> there. The nesting of the subposition under the seventh foot is represented in Fig. 2.

Figure 2

(Ultlesedd fra) þe deofell   800

Figure 2 (*cont.*)

Foot

W   S

S   W

(To ben Johann) ჳehatenn   776

This split-position representation reflects two properties of the last S in the string which have been noticed, but not articulated, in terms of the formal metrical characteristics of the line. One is the unparalleled strength of the fourteenth position – the only ictic position capped by four S's. The other is the special prosodic rigidity of the syllable occupying the weak subposition. The combination of the two matches the frequent observation in the literature that this is the most inviolable position in a line of accentual-syllabic verse. It is the rhyme position in rhymed verse. This rigidity of the right edge is manifested in the *Ormulum* through a very concrete constraint: the weak metrical subposition cannot be filled by a lexical monosyllable, nor can the last S be filled by a disyllabic compound. Thus, certain sequences distributed freely over other positions are disallowed in the last foot. While *te king, mann hemm, I kann, off crisst, o boc, himm sellf, shall ben, off uss, to daჳჳ, wiþþ shep*, as well as *onჳæn, Goddspell, œdmod, wifmann*, etc. appear line-initially, in the fourth foot, and elsewhere, they *never* occur in the right edge without the addition of a final weak syllable, most frequently *-e*.

Consequently, this beat-splitting analysis of the right edge enriches our understanding of eME in two ways: first it confirms Lehnert's (1953: 137 and passim) opinion that Orm's language allows free variation of forms with and without final *-e*.[10] Unlike the vexed issue of whether final *-e* should be sounded or not at the end of the line in Chaucer,[11] the *Ormulum* absolutely requires a line-final weak syllable, which can even be inserted unetymologically; witness forms such as *offe* 463, 4097, 15522, *onne* 3753, *þæ rinne* 4127, *tæ ronne* 15475, *þæ roffe* 15305; none of which are recorded in the *Anglo-Saxon Dictionary*. Second, proceeding again from the assumption that the structure of the last position is inviolable, we can draw inferences concerning phrasal and compound stress in the language of the author. The range of syllables appearing in the subposition is clearly limited to inflectional morphemes and parasitic final -e. While the second syllables of disyllabic compounds fill weak metrical positions elsewhere in the line, they are banned from the subposition, which suggests that the pattern / \ is alive in words of the *goddspell* type. Metrical demotion of the secondary stress can occur when the syllable is flanked by two strongs as in the sequence *þiss Goddspell seȝȝþ þatt* ... (255), but it is not an option for the subposition; i.e. no level of stress other than absolute zero can be buried that deep down in the metrical hierarchy.

5.2 The left edge

The line-initial position in the *Ormulum* is predominantly filled by a clearly defined set of prosodically weak items: conjunctions, prepositions, auxiliaries, adverbs of degree, clitic pronouns and cliticized negatives – commonly, but not always, also serving linearly as syntactic phrase openers. Most of them are monosyllabic: *swa, annd, iff, acc, hu, nu, þe, to, onn, forr, att, wiþþ, all, aȝȝ, whan, ær (þan), he, itt, hemm, wass, iss, ne*. In a typical line the matching of the prosodic to the metrical peaks is straightforward as in:

(4) þiss boc iss nemmnedd Orrmulum forrþi þatt Orrm itt wrohhte
    W S W S   W   S   WS   W S W S   W   S (W)

Some questions arise with the so-called transgressions against the 'natural stress' at the left edge, as in (3b). A closer look at the constituency of the first foot may allow us to avoid the postulation of 'unnatural' word stress in accounting for some of these apparent mismatches. In that position one pattern emerges with considerable regularity: in the unproblematic case the anacrusis to the first foot is filled by a word prosodically subordinate to the following constituent. Anacrusis can thus be characterised as a position which *must* be occupied by a prosodic unit which is maximally a member of a clitic group (and by anything below it in the prosodic hierarchy, which would include prefixes), but not by the host of a clitic group. The clitic group is defined as 'a single content word together with all contiguous grammatical words in the same syntactic constituent' (Hayes 1989: 207).[12] Since the only indispensable participant in a clitic group is its host, restricting the anacrusis to a nonhost has the effect of reversing the foot internal prominence relations from iambic to trochaic in the case of line-initial disyllabic words. The correspondence required in this early form of verse becomes a matter of matching the first metrical peak to a prosodically prominent syllable, a nonclitic. The structure of the left edge of the line is represented in Fig. 3.

Figure 3

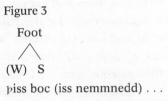

Foot

(W)   S

þiss boc (iss nemmnedd) . . .

The leftmost metrical position is filled by a unit whose prosodic value is that of a clitic word or a unit below a clitic, i.e. a light prefix like the ȝe- in ȝehaten (607) or the a- in amang (D 63) or the on- in onȝœn (99). The correspondence rule which defines the constituency of the left foot with reference to the clitic group is formalised in Figure 4.

Figure 4

Clitic Correspondence Rule

[C . . . Host]
|
W

The nonobligatoriness of the clitic word within the linguistic prosodic hierarchy may be the reason for the special flexibility of the prominence relations within the first foot. The leftmost weak position cannot be labelled extrametrical, yet, like the rightmost one, it is subject to a clearly defined prosodic constraint. The difference in the level on which the constraints operate at the right and the left edges correlates with a well-known observation about the different behaviour of these verse domains, namely, that the left edge is 'freer' than the right. Right-edge extrametricality weighs down the foot, enriches it, and stipulates inflexible prominence relations, sometimes at the cost of violating linguistic expectations such as the addition of unetymological -e. Left-edge clitic matching allows freedom and conformity with the stress patterns.

The proposed structure for line edges in verse composed c. 1170[13] is known to be a possible, though not frequent, feature of later verse. Similar problems have been addressed by Halle and Keyser (1971), Kiparsky (1975, 1977), Hayes (1983, 1989). The optionality of the weak syllable before the first ictus has been attributed to the presence of a syntactic boundary immediately preceding it; see Kiparsky (1977: 231). The evidence in the *Ormulum* suggests that syntactic grouping is only indirectly relevant to the mapping of the prosodic to the metrical constituents, to the extent that syntactic boundaries form only one aspect of the process of clitic group formation.[14] The distribution of various prosodic units at the left edge suggests a strong preference for the clitic group rather than for any other prosodic or syntactic constituent. Why not treat units such as *þatt boc*, *he chœs*, *all þiss*, *þreo kingess* as phrases, phonological or syntactic, rather than as clitic groups? Indeed, in the majority of cases the clitic group is co-extensive with the phonological phrase, or the beginning of a syntactic constituent,[15] but this is not always true in the text. Though Orm is a notoriously unimaginative poet, he allows occasional run-on lines, as in example (5):

> (5) þatt ure Drihhtin *wollde*   3495
>   *Ben borenn* i þiss middellærd

The line begins with a clitic, but syntactically the clitic group straddles the two lines, and therefore reference to a syntactic boundary immediately preceding the weak syllable would be inappropriate.

Finally, it must be admitted that the clitic status of the first word is not always clear or defensible. A possible counterexample to the clitic correspondence rule is provided by example (6):

> (6) Her endenn twa Goddspelless þuss   3490

In this line *her* can be treated as an adverb and might or might not be cliticised to the next word.[16] We can probably scan the line *hér éndenn*, and not *her éndenn*, a headless line with a trochee for the second foot. In a string of weak monosyllables, each one of which could potentially be a clitic, as in: *Icc hafe itt don*, 115; ⁊ *tatt hiss shep*, 14728; ⁊ *icc itt wille*, 14772, etc., the relative prosodic prominence of the second syllable in the string is guaranteed by alternating stress and the fact that these second syllables are flanked by non-major-class words. The additional effect of the metric form will promote the weak monosyllables to ictus. Monosyllabic content words are virtually lacking from the leftmost position. Sometimes, extremely rarely, a monosyllabic verb can appear in the first slot, as in: *Drannc dœþess drinnc* . . . 1374, *Bar ure sinnes* . . . 1372, *Droh ut off* . . . 3064. It is difficult to say whether this is Orm being noncanonical, whether it is a case of verbs being prosodically weak clause-initially, or whether the correspondence rule should be redefined or scrapped altogether.

5.2.1. Trochaic disyllables at the left edge

One aspect of the proposed clitic correspondence rule remains to be clarified: the treatment of disyllabic items line-initially. Quite rarely, about once in a hundred lines, Orm allows disyllabic words in the first foot. Both disyllabic compounds and disyllabic noncompounds can be found in that position: *shammfasst* (2175), *goddspell* (D 157, D 177), *summwhatt* (958), *weppmenn* (3060), *þærþurrh* (2357, 6678), *wærenn* (369), *shæwenn* (393), *wisste* (521), *affterr* (477, 611), *haffdenn* (587), *effnedd* (1206), *turrnedd* (3236). As mentioned in section 3.1, there is disagreement about the scansion of lines beginning with such words. The disagreement ranges from scansions involving full subordination of the linguistic stress to the iambic metrical framework (Hall, Kaluza), through suggestions of a possible initial spondee (Schipper 1910), to trochaic inversion after the caesura (Mossé) and line-initial or half-line trochaic inversion (Stanley). What criteria would render any one of these positions acceptable and defensible?

Our first concern should be to separate the compounds from the non-compounds. Two arguments can be adduced in favour of the suggestion that disyllabic compounds preserved the / \ (primary–secondary) stress pattern in Orm's language. First, such a stress pattern in compounds is assumed to have been part of the phonology of OE. In the absence of evidence to the contrary, we are probably looking at a straight-line continuation of the OESR (McCully and Hogg 1990: 330) with all attendant morphological provisions. Second, the fact that such compounds are consistently banned from the fourteenth position suggests that a secondary stress adjacent to main stress cannot be treated as fully unstressed and cannot occupy a weak metrical subposition.[17] There is nothing surprising about the elevation of a salient secondary stress to a metrical ictus. I believe, therefore, that lines in the *Ormulum* beginning with disyllabic compounds – *eʒʒwhær, goddspell, forrwhi, forrþrihht, forrþi, innto, summwhatt, upponn, whannse* – should present no problem for the iambic structure of the right foot.

For the noncompounds, we have no comparable arguments. One can note that inflexional syllables line-internally are allowed very occasionally to fill strong metrical positions, and this happens invariably in cases where at least one of the flanking syllables is unambiguously unstressed. This is not very helpful, however, because left-edge disyllabic words may be followed by a content word, as in lines P 37, P 75, 481, 593, and 617, but this does not have to be the case; see examples (10) and (11) below. Two alternatives present themselves: Orm ignored the prosodic rules of his language and followed the metrical form slavishly, or Orm 'discovered' the flexibility of the left edge and took advantage of it in a manner very similar to the famous trochaic inversions of later poetry. My own inclination would be to give Orm credit for intuitive knowledge of a phenomenon amply recorded, though unexplained, in the metrical literature. Without being closer to understanding why the left edge is different, I am content to extend this familiar observation back in time to the earliest forms of accentual-syllabic versification in English.

The suggestion is then that lines such as example (7)

    (7) Wærenn rihhtwise ⁊ gode menn   369–70
        Biforenn Godess eȝne

should be scanned with a trochaic opening, in accordance with Stanley's aesthetic preferences.

5.2.2. The fifth foot

It is a commonplace observation that the metrical properties of the line beginning in accentual-syllabic verse and the properties of the foot immediately following the caesura are similar. The first and the fifth metrical positions in Orm's line share the characteristic matching of a prosodic clitic to the weak metrical slot. Lexical items most likely to open the fifth foot are prepositions: *off, i, þurrh, to, att, till*; conjunctions: *⁊, tohh, þatt*; weak adverbs: *þa, aȝȝ, swa, þuss, þær, well, rihht*; pronouns: *icc, þe*; auxiliaries: *iss, wass*. Occurrences such as *rædi* in (8) or *hælennde* in (9) are quite rare but still there.

    (8) ⁊ heore leȝhe birrþ hemm beon   6234–5
        Rædiȝ, þann itt iss addledd

    (9) Jesusess name nemmnedd iss   3054–5
        Hælennde onn Ennglissh spæche

I believe that trochaic substitution should be allowed here too, in nonviolation of the strongest linguistic stress of the syntactic phrases *beon*

rædiȝ and *nemmnedd iss hælennde.* (The matching of *beon* and *iss* to a
metrical ictus is licensed by the preceding syllables.) In (10) both the first
and the fifth foot will be trochaic.

(10) Herrdenn þatt word 7 ȝedenn forþ   12728–9
       Affterrwarrd ur Laferrd.

I have not discussed here the question of possible acephaly (headlessness) in the *Ormulum*. Acephaly is licensed by the extrametricality of
the weak branch in the leftmost first metrical position. It is a verse template phenomenon, while trochaicness is used both in reference to
metre and in reference to the prosodic property of a word. Headlessness
implies the extrametricality of the leftmost edge. That entailment is not
present in trochaic stress-patterning.[18] In (11) we have the option of
scanning the line as headless, since, as we know independently, Orm's
final *-e*'s are not selected on grammatical grounds. Compared with the
widespread assumption about Orm's scansion which would impose
ictus on a final *-e* – an undesirable solution – the headless reading is
preferable in view of the later (and earlier) history of loss of final *-e* in
ME, the fact that the noun is a subject in the clause, and the coexistence
of the forms *strengðu* and *strengð* in OE.

(11) Strenncþe þatt ȝifeþþ lufe 7 lusst   5522
       þe bodi for to pinen.

Rich is the tree of life, though. The solution of reading the line as headless is only one alternative which suggested itself from the other constituency of the second syllable at the left edge. Another and much less
controversial solution would be to treat *strenncþe* like any other disyllabic noncompound and allow it a trochaic scansion. This second
option avoids the problem of elision before a consonant, which, though
clearly attested in other pre-Chaucerian accentual-syllabic verse
(Minkova 1992: 161–2), seems not to occur in the *Ormulum*.

6. Other mismatches

> All natural shapes blazing unnatural light
> Theodore Roethke, *In a Dark Time*

Apparent mismatches in the *Ormulum* occur in positions other than the
first and the fifth foot, of the type cited in (1) above, or as in (12):

(12) ⁊ illc meocnesse is ellenlæs   10908–9
Wiþþutenn herrsummnesse.

Whether we call such usage 'mismatching' or not depends on the definition of our correspondence rules, i.e. on whether we allow secondary
stress to be matched to an ictic position. It was suggested in 5.2.1 that we
have some good arguments to allow secondary stresses to be matched to
ictic positions in the poem. Using the same arguments, we can see
instances such as (12) as unproblematic matching. Yet such usage has
been labelled 'mismatching' or 'noncorrespondence' in the literature;
see the charts in Tarlinskaja (1976a).

Two more points should be made in connection with non-edge-
matching or mismatching. One is that in verse we do run into 'fuzzy'
situations, when the best approach is to establish, if possible, a scale, a
gradience of acceptability, as argued by Youmans (1983) and empirically
supported by the analyses proposed in Hayes (1989) and Youmans
(1989). The second point is related: the non-edge possible noncorrespondence data in the *Ormulum* suggest that we may be indeed dealing
with a range of coexisting innovative and archaic stress patterns, which
defy the terminological separation of clear cases of matching from cases
of mismatching. On the rare occasions when any doubt could arise
about the categorical matching, Orm covers a range of possibilities:
from exploiting inherited secondary stress ('matching') to some genuine
mismatches, the first type exemplified in (13), the second in (14):

(13) þe belle*dræm* bitacnedd ȝuw   922
þatt dræm þatt ȝuw birrþ herenn

(14) To ben un*der* deo*fless* þeowwdom   I 35
to farenn all till helle.

Can we say anything useful about this gradience? First by reference to
the OESR and then by empirical testing of the distribution of doubtful
disyllabic items over various metrical positions, we may be in a position
to draw some inferences about the status of secondary stress in ME.

7.1 The fourth foot

Reliable and unambiguous matching between metric and prosodic
prominence occurs regularly in the fourth foot of the first half-line. (The
seventh foot is also stable, but because of the subposition involving

extrametricality the same tests cannot be supplied there.) In the appendix I list the nonmonosyllabic words found in the fourth foot in one sample of the *Ormulum*. In approximately 90 per cent of the lines the fourth-foot ictus is filled by a monosyllable.[19] Orm uses second roots of compounds as well as derivational morphemes in the eighth position. The largest group of compounds and derivatives clearly accented on the final syllable are trisyllabic and nonproblematic: *oferrhannd, crisstenndom, weorelldþing, unnderrfon*, etc. A small number of disyllabic items appear in the fourth foot, underlined in the appendix – *onnȝæn, twifald, mannkinn, bihet, drihhtin* – to which we can add *gessthus, inssihht*, and *summwhatt* from another sampling of the text. Accounting for these cannot be problematic either.[20] The search produced no instances of syllables which raise the slightest doubt, following the standard accounts of stress placement in OE, that they are legitimate occupants of that metrical position.[21] Thus the fourth position becomes a safe test of matching and mismatching, very much like the special status of the rhyme position in rhymed verse for phonological identification. Without incurring the danger of circularity, we can conclude that the prosodic rules of Orm's language not only allowed but probably required preservation of the OESR in transparent compounds.

What remains to be seen is whether there are sequences or items which might elsewhere suggest noncorrespondence but are excluded from the fourth ictus. Without claiming absolute exhaustiveness, I can say that one separate group of disyllabic items in the *Ormulum* which should be placed on a lower level in the scale of plausible matching seems to be that of words with the derivational suffixes *-ish, -ess, -unng*. Interestingly, none of these appear in the fourth foot of the verse. What does that mean, an accident spread over 20,000 lines? What is the significance, if any, of avoidance of such words in the fourth foot? Let us look at some of the more famous Dedication lines:

(15) Whi icc till *Ennglissh* hafe wennd   D 113–14
      Godspelles hallȝhe lare

and

(16) 7 tærfore hafe icc turrnedd itt   D 129–33
      Inntill *Ennglisshe* spæche,
      Forr þatt I wollde bliþeliȝ
      þatt all *Ennglisshe* lede
      wiþþ ære shollde lisstenn itt

Traditional scansion (including Eric Stanley's, which allows 'natural' stress only line-initially, in Holt's sense of 'line') would have the second syllable of *Ennglisshe* in (16) fill the ictus. I believe that this is correct; one acceptable account of the grammatically perhaps unnecessary -*e* in *Ennglisshe* in (16) – and note the singular verb in line D 133 – would be that it supplied the only available (and linguistically innocuous) metrical filler for a half-line which could not be headless, since only leftmost edges can be allowed that freedom. Alternatively, one can argue that the scansion of the lines is fuzzy: there are two ways to allow perfect stress-alternating scansion. The first would match the derivational morpheme in the ictic position; the other would involve elision of -*e* in consonantal-environment line-initial trochaic inversion and possibly acephaly in the second half-line. The second option is admittedly much more complex, yet until we know more about the embryonic stages of English versification and the stress patterns of eME, the possibility of an alternative treatment of such lines should at least be kept in mind.[22]

The next step down in the scale of secondary stress acceptability (i.e. the group of better candidates for traditional 'mismatching') includes items, again very rare, in which a nonderivational syllable is elevated to S.

(17) Goddspell onn Ennglissh nemmnedd iss   D 157–8
      God word, 7 god tiᵽennde

Kaluza notes that what he describes as 'shift of the accent' is rarer within the verse (1911: 157–8) but still cites two instances involving presumed stress on the inflectional syllable (the accentuation marks in (18) and (19) are Kaluza's):

(18) all ᵽuss iss tatt hallȝhé goddspell

and

(19) rihht alls iff itt wæré ᵽatt waȝȝn . . .

I suggest that even within this group we should distinguish between the types of nonderivational morphemes matched to S. I have no quarrel with (17); the word is trisyllabic historically, and -*end(e)* in this noun could be analogised to the present participle, which alters the prosodic relations. It is also in conformity with the OESR. All of the examples I have gleaned of disyllabic inflected words in which the inflection carries the ictus – (18) and (19) above and also I 35, 1756, 1772, 1766, 1418, 1390 (random list) – place the offender in the third foot.[23] Since I have not identified an inflection in the fourth-foot ictus, I believe that an inflection in an ictus is a genuine violation of the prosodic rules.[24]

8. Towards a conclusion

> For there is good news yet to hear and fine things to be seen
> Before we go to Paradise by way of Kensal Green
>
> G. K. Chesterton, *The Rolling English Road*

This exercise in more rigorous formalisation of the metrical rules in the *Ormulum* offers some advantages over the vague earlier references to rigidity of the verse structure and the ensuing violations of 'natural' stress. First, within generative metrics we can argue that the metrical typology of accentual-syllabic verse which now starts with Chaucer can be enriched chronologically with earlier material. Even in the earliest instantiations of this type of verse we find support for the layered, rather than serial, representation of metrical structure in the differential treatment of line edges. Also, analysed in this way the *Ormulum* lends credibility to the relevance and the universality of the Prosodic Hierarchy and the necessity of including the clitic group in it.[25]

Second, this type of account may be of crucial relevance for the study of the development of English stress. Ideally, armed with a set of metrical norms and statistics, we can set up a scale of archaicness in the application and the direction of the OESR. Such a scale based on the evidence from the *Ormulum* would look like this. Transparent compounds vacillate between compound and phrasal stress, possibly depending on the rhythmic environment: *innsihht, mannkinn, twifald, summwhatt, rodetreo, bodesang*. Historical compounds the second elements of which have lost their independent word status have compound stress – *sikerrli, sinnelæs* – but both primary and secondary stresses can be freely utilised in an ictus. Another group of suffixes which already in OE had been dissociated from whatever ancient historical word status they may have had are less likely to be promoted to the ictic position – *meocnesse, Ennglisshe* – and the potential for promotion is related to the optional insertion of schwa as a third syllable. Any prominence that they may display in the reading of the composition is attributable to the exigencies of the metre. Naturally, inflectional suffixes are excluded from the set of potentially stressable final syllables, especially when they are composed of nothing but a schwa.

Third, on a segmental phonological basis, recall that the *Ormulum* has been used as a test case for the dating of Middle English Open Syllable Lengthening. The special metrical tightness of the last foot in the line, established typologically and in terms of prosodic matching, supports the hypothesis that the text is indeed a good source of information about the weight of the fourteenth syllable.

More questions remain to be asked than have been answered. Are there any more compelling reasons for selecting the domain of the clitic group over syntactic grouping as a factor sanctioning the metrical rules? Has the proposed bounding domain for left line edges in iambic verse changed, and if so, when and why? Can it be suggested that in pre-Chaucerian verse there is any correlation between the preservation of final *-e* and the realisation of anacrusis and, inversely, the acceptability of acephaly? Can we assume that disyllabic and trisyllabic words in the language provided an indigenous source for the Romance stress rule? Are there any really forbidden trees?

Appendix

Nonmonosyllabic words in the fourth foot in the *Ormulum* (lines 5150–775)

Note: Italic type is employed to call attention to disyllables.

Adjectives/Adverbs
bliþeli: 5326, 5330
forr rihht
heþenwarrd: 5490
imæn: 5506
innwarrdliʒ: 5530, 5698
modiliʒ: 5670
oferrhannd: 5460
onnʒæn: 5304, 5444, 5448, 5700
opennliʒ: 5312, 5314, 5764
sikerrliʒ: 5322, 5754
sinnelæs: 5742

Nouns
ædiʒleʒʒc: 5706, 5724
bodesang: 5526
bodeword: 5244
crisstenndom: 5300, 5302, 5306, 5320
endedaʒʒ: 5674, 5690, 5702
fictre: 12816
godspell
goddspellbok: 5634
innsihht: 12674
laʒebok: 13170
larspell: 12686

stallwurrli: 5520

þeþennforrþ: 12930

twifald: 5232

unnderrfot: 5686

witerliȝ: 5168

mannkinn: 5294

rodetreo: 5602

þewdom

weorelldþing: 4644, 4654, 5542,

  5558, 5654

Verbs

bihet: 5574

bisett: 12954

unnderrfon: 5470, 5626

Numerals

seofenniti: 5346

Other

Drihhtin: 5462, 5582, 5722

Notes

1 Borroff (1962: 151) argues that the final stressing of Romance words composed of stem + suffix in the *Cursor Mundi* 'represents an artificial mode of accentuation used solely for purposes of rhyme'. Her conclusion is based on the logic that 'since the pattern xC (noninitial stress) would be as useful within the line as Cx (initial stress) the latter's avoidance in this position' is evidence for its artificiality. The logic is vitiated by the following consideration: in a tetrameter line, for example, the first foot is freely allowed to be either headless or to undergo trochaic substitution, so that position tells us nothing about the stressability of the word in it. Borroff (p. 150) admits that in lines of the type

> *Musik* þat es þe sune o sang (1520)

the scansion of the line allows stress on either syllable of *musik.* The treatment of Romance stem-suffix derivatives in the wheels of *Sir Gawain* also leads to the conclusion that 'the suffix accent they receive in rhyme was not used in the spoken language' – with native parallels provided by *talkying* (927) and *laȝande* (1207) (p. 163).

2 The 'matching' scansion would be in line with the philological tradition according to which loss of final schwa and destressing of the second syllable were simultaneous. The following types of final schwa loss can be observed in words of more than two syllables:

> Words with the stress pattern / \ x (where / = primary stress, \ = secondary stress, and x = unstressed syllable) such as *lafdi,* OE *hlæfdige*; *almes(s),* OE *ælmesse*; *orres,* AN *orresta*; *drinking,* OE *drincinge.* According to Luick (1914–40: §459), this development belongs to the twelfth century and was simultaneous with the suppression of the secondary stress in such words. Crook (1974:

§138) confines this loss to words in which the first syllable was long. Early schwa loss also occurs in the third syllable of adjectives in *-i* of the type *wurrþiȝ*, OE *wurrþiȝe*.

Words of the type / x \ x: *kinriche(e)*, OE *cynerice*; *webster(e)*, OE *webbestere*; *minter(e)*, OE *mynetere*; *herber* (later *herbor*, *harbor*), OE *hereberȝe*; *daisi(e)*, OE *daiesye* underwent syncopation of the medial syllable first. This is followed by loss of the secondary stress and simultaneous loss of final *-e* (Luick 1914–40: §459).

Originally trisyllabic words (e.g. *kindom*, OE *cynedom*; *balful*, OE *bealuful*; *hergong* OE *heregang*; etc.) can be seen as subject to a rhythmic principle of stress-clash avoidance, i.e. in this case too, schwa syncopation in the medial syllable and suppression of secondary stress are causally related.

3 See however the somewhat contradictory statement (Tarlinskaja 1974b: 125–6) to the effect that native English words did not have commonly used forms stressed on the second syllable. Throughout that study, and in the corresponding chapter in Tarlinskaja (1976b), secondary stress is discussed against the background of French influence on stress placement and not as an independent issue having to do with the continuation of the OE stress patterns.

4 Orm has earned the reputation of being the least interesting versifier (and poet, if he can be called that) of the period. Kaluza describes him as standing alone, 'not only in his own time, but in the whole of English literature' for the strict regularity of the verse structure, especially the syllable-counting principle (1911: 158).

5 This passage is also quoted in Stanley (1988: 34).

6 The idea of avoiding the problem of mismatches by treating disyllabic native words (of the type *tackling*, *body*) as spondees rather than iambs is not new; Simpson (1943: 127) attributes it to Samuel Daniel, in *A Defence of Rhyme* (1603).

7 The use of the word 'natural' in this context has irked many scholars; see most recently Duggan (1990b: 332). See also Kaluza (1911: 157) on the *Ormulum*, who writes: 'In general the verse stress agrees with the natural word stress; only those syllables can be used in the arsis, which are stressed in ordinary speech. But he [Orm] was occasionally compelled to shift the accent in order to get a regular interchange of arsis and thesis.' How did Kaluza acquire the magic knowledge of what ordinary ME speech sounded like? This is of course the circularity mentioned earlier, plaguing historical metrics and happily avoided in studies of modern verse based on actual phonetic data; see Kelly and Rubin (1988: 719).

8 All citations from the *Ormulum* are from Holt (1878). D = Dedication (342 lines), P = Preface (106 lines), I = Introduction (108 lines). Citations from the Homilies (approximately 20,000 lines) are given as just numbers. For statistical purposes all figures should be divided in two, since Holt assigns separate consecutive numbers to each half-line. The difference is of no consequence for the discussion.

9 Cited in Stanley (1988: 34–5). It is surprising that Stanley does not refer to the line-initial and post-caesural position of the items he prefers to stress 'naturally' but rather talks of bringing 'grace' to their use.

10 Lehnert's conclusions do not cover the behaviour of weak monosyllabic adjectives, and he notes the special status of the prepositional dative *-e*, but at least the adjectival patterns can be accounted for by the more general principles of eurhythmy; see the proposal in Minkova (1990).

11 Generations of scholars have held opposite views on the last syllable in Chaucer, and no account has been accepted as definitive. It is possible that the only solution to the issue of masculine v. feminine rhymes lies in the differential treatment of lexical items in that position.

12 The Clitic Group:

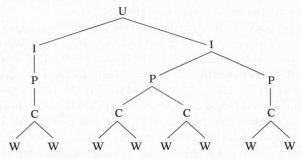

þis gære macod he his gadering æt Oxeneford

U: Utterance
I: Intonational Phrase
P: Phonological Phrase
C: Clitic Group
W: Word

13 For this dating of the manuscript, see the study by Parkes (1983).

14 'CLITIC GROUP FORMATION (modified). Adjunction of clitics to hosts in English is optional. The propensity to cliticize is inversely related to the number of syntactic boundaries separating clitic from host' (Hayes 1989: 239). The metrical relevance of prosodic over syntactic structure in *Hiawatha* is discussed in Hayes (p. 238).

15 The traditional logic that special line-edge phenomena follow a syntactic break entails that line openings would also be syntactic openings.

16 The status of *her* is ambivalent in OE too, where it can be an empty clause opener and as such does not count as syntactic constituent. Like the line-initial finite verbs, the weak adverb *her* may be a member of an intermediate category, a 'particle' in Hans Kuhn's terminology (see also Russom, this volume).

17 A secondary stress can, however, occupy metrical ictus when it is adjacent to unstressed and unstressable syllables in trisyllabic words: *goddspelless*, *rodetreo*.

18 Acephaly was allowed only in the early stages of the development of iambic verse (Prince 1989: 49). Kiparsky also remarks on the rarity of headless lines in Shakespeare and later English poetry (1977: 231).

19 The count is based on 625 lines from the Homilies – lines 5150 to 5775. Out of 315 possible fourth-foot positions, only 47 are filled by nonmonosyllables. My estimate of less than 10% is based on the fact that only 28 items appear there – the remaining 19 are items which are used more than once and should not be included in the statistics. The appendix includes also items noticed and collected outside the 625 lines.

20 The easiest ones are the transparent compounds: *twifald*, *mannkinn*, *innsihht*, and *summwhatt*. They are legitimate by the OE Word Stress rule. *Onȝæn* would be the same as OE *onsacan* (left-edged morphologically defined extrametricality), and *bihet* contains a Marginally Destressed light syllable; see McCully and Hogg (1990: 323–5). *Drihhtin* is a problem, acknowledged but not solved, in Dickins and Wilson (1952: 202), who mention that the second syllable was probably long on the analogy of the semantically close *almihtīn*; notice also Orm's spelling. They admit, however, that 'the explanation remains unconvincing'.

21 It should also be noted that none of the trisyllabic words spanning the ... S / W S sequence of the third/fourth foot can be matched to an odd metrical position which might suggest promotion of the middle syllable; i.e. we get *hóredóm* but not **horédom*, *ópennlíȝ* but not **opénnliȝ*, *wéorelldþing* but not *weorélldþing*.

22 The conference version of this paper made the point about the alternative 'natural' scansion of *Ennglisshe* in these examples with much more conviction. I am grateful to Hoyt Duggan (personal communication) for forcing me to rethink the argument and rephrase my suggestion more cautiously.

23 If we allow acephaly in (18) and a disyllabic pronunciation of 'wagon' in (19), we will have removed the need for classifying these lines as 'original, spare, and strange'. Unfortunately, however, both lines are cited from the Preface of Orm's immortal piece. Compared with the rest of the composition, it seems somewhat rough: it is probably the practice piece which brought him to such heights of craftsmanship in the Homilies.

24 Barring the oddity of *whilumm* in 4868 but not the later history of this
   word, about the only remnant of the dative inflection which remained
   untouched by the ME loss of inflections. It is possible that that word was
   already 'special' and therefore that the -*um* could be treated as noninflec-
   tional.

25 'In the trochaic pentameter of Serbo-Croatian folk epic . . . the fourth syllable in a line must be followed by a Clitic Group boundary, and Clitic
   Group boundaries in general tend to fall after even positions' (Hayes
   1989: 210).

8 Systematic sound symbolism in the long alliterative line in 'Beowulf' and 'Sir Gawain'

Marie Borroff

In the second stanza of *Sir Gawain and the Green Knight*, a well-known allusion to narration in alliterative verse echoes in tantalising fashion a similar passage in *Beowulf*. The *Gawain* poet announces that he intends to recount an adventure, one of 'Arthurez wonderez' (29), and that he will tell it as he himself has heard it told,

> As hit is stad and stoken
> In stori stif and stronge,
> With lel letteres loken,
> In londe so hatz ben longe   (33–6)[1]

In *Beowulf*, after the hero has torn off Grendel's arm and sent him forth to die in his lair, we are told that the celebrations on the following morning included the narration of this exploit in verse by a thane who knew many traditional stories ('. . . ealdgesegena / worn gemunde' *Beo*. 869–70). On this occasion, he 'found other words [that is, new words], truly linked' ('word oþer fand / sōðe gebunden' *Beo*. 870–1). (Translations, unless otherwise specified, are my own.)

Both *lel* (a ME form of the word *loyal* which descends into modern Northern and Scottish English as *leal*) in *Sir Gawain* and *sōðe* ('truly') in *Beowulf* can, of course, be narrowly interpreted as referring to the technique of verse composition: the alliterative links among metrical units in successive lines (the 'letteres' of the *Gawain* passage) are formally correct. But surely this is only part of their meaning – surely we may infer that such linkages, in addition to serving their metrical purposes, somehow enhance the 'truth' (*sōðe*), or 'faithfulness' (*lel*), of the unfolding story.

This effect of enhancement depends on an important aspect of the expressive values we instinctively attach to the sounds of words, especially in poetry. I call it 'systematic sound symbolism'. Operating through chance similarities or identities on the level of sound, the magical incantatory powers of language lend a validity to connections among words which is quite other than the kind of validity having to do with connections among meanings and aspects of subject matter. The influence of systematic sound symbolism is apparent in the everyday uses of language in the numerous proverbial expressions, set phrases, nursery rhymes, and the like, in which alliterating or rhyming words enhance the 'truth' of a generalisation or a story. (In what follows, I shall limit my examples to alliterative combinations.) We feel, without stopping to think about it, that 'fit as a fiddle' defines fitness more fittingly than 'fit as a violin'; that the logical companion for a boy named Jack who goes to fetch a pail of water is a girl named Jill; that more than mere coincidence is at work in the alliteration of *pea* with *pod*; that the proverb 'Early ripe, early rotten' carries more conviction than 'Early ripe, early spoiled.' (In this last example, systematic sound symbolism works ironically to sharpen a contrast between meanings, as it also does, to give but one additional example, in the expression 'as different as chalk from cheese'.)

The alliterating formulas of the verse tradition to which *Beowulf* and *Sir Gawain*, despite the wide chronological gap that separates them, both belong (although see here Cable 1991 and McCully and Hogg 1994) derive a part of their expressive power from the reinforcement of connections among meanings by connections among sounds. 'Systematic' reinforcement of this sort is apparent in such combinations in Old and Middle English as 'wigum on wæpnum' (*Beowulf* 2395; cf. 1559 and *Gawain* 384, 1586); 'heard under helme' (*Beowulf* 342, 404, 2539); 'burne on blonk' (*Gawain* 785, 2024); and 'lorde and . . . ledez' (*Gawain* 1231, 1413). The particular subject matter and cast of characters of a new narrative tend to generate new combinations on the old models. In *Sir Gawain*, for instance, 'burne on blonk' underlies 'þe gome vpon Gryngolet' (748), and formulas combining *kyng* and *court* (cf. 100, 1048) underlie 'þis kyng lay at Camylot' (37). Our sense of the natural affinities of warriors with weapons, helmets, and warhorses is confirmed by the existence of alliterative links among words having these meanings; the first letter of the name of Sir Gawain's horse makes it all the more suitable that he should belong to that particular knight; a castle whose name begins with the *k* sound is a fit residence for a famous *king*.

When two or more words are linked both formally by alliteration and referentially on the level of subject matter, and when they appear a number of times in each other's vicinity as designators of important elements of a narrative, the resultant sound system may take on thematic importance. Such systems can be identified in both *Beowulf* and *Sir Gawain*. Though they are founded on the same expressive principle, they take different forms, and produce different kinds of effect, in their respective contexts. I am especially interested in the relationship between these differences and the differences in metrical structure between the two poems.

In the first part of the narrative of *Beowulf* (I shall arbitrarily define this as comprising Beowulf's journey to Denmark and his reception at Heorot), three important words alliterating on *g* signal key aspects of the identity of the hero: his Geatish nationality, his prowess in battle (*gūð*), and, most important, his intrinsic worth, his goodness. When he enters the poem, having decided to seek out Hrothgar and put an end to the persecution of the Danes by the monster Grendel, he is called first Hygelac's thane, then 'good among the Geats' ('gōd mid Gēatum' *Beo.* 195). He commands that a 'good ship' be made ready ('Hēt him ȳðlidan / gōdne gegyrwan' *Beo.* 198–9), on which he will travel to Denmark to offer his services to that country's 'battle-king' ('gūðcyning' *Beo.* 199). He is 'the good one' ('se gōda' *Beo.* 205) who chooses 'warriors from among the Geatish nation' ('Gēata lēoda / cempan' *Beo.* 205–6) to accompany him. During the banquet in Heorot on the evening of his arrival, he assures the Danish king that the strength and courage of the Geats shall before long offer battle to Grendel: '. . . him Gēata sceal / eafoð ond ellen ungeāra nu / gūðe gebēodan' (*Beo.* 601–3). The words *gōd* and *gūð* are associated with Hrothgar as well. One of the first appellations bestowed on him is 'nobleman good from of old' ('æðeling ǣrgōd' *Beo.* 130). Beowulf, announcing himself at Heorot to the courtier Wulfgar, says that he and his men would like to greet Hrothgar, if he, 'swā gōdne' (*Beo.* 347), will grant them permission. (Talbot Donaldson translates this phrase 'good as he is' (p. 7).) Wulfgar replies that he will enquire and will report back the answer that 'the good one' (355) gives him. *Gūð* appears in association with Hrothgar in the above-cited *gūðcyning* (199), and in his characterisation, on hearing Beowulf's pledge to do battle with Grendel, as 'grey-haired and renowned in battle' ('gamolfeax ond gūðrōf' *Beo.* 608). And Beowulf speaks of Heorot, Hrothgar's royal seat, as a 'battle-hall' ('gūðsele' *Beo.* 443). To the *g* system represented by *gōd* and *gūð*, as it relates to Hrothgar, we should add a third word, one which expresses an important aspect of the Germanic concept of kingly magnanimity, namely, *gold*. Hrothgar is, among other things, a magnanimous ruler. He bestows on those who serve him the lavish rewards that are spoken of in the opening lines of the poem in the narrator's comment on the generosity of his ancestor King Scyld: a young man ought to bring it about by 'goodness' (*gōde*), that is, by 'splendid gifts' ('fromum feohgiftum'), that he will have loyal companions in his mature age (*Beo.* 20–4). At the feast following Beowulf's victorious encounter with Grendel, the Danish queen Wealhtheow, urging her husband to be gracious and generous towards the Geats, addresses him as 'goldwine gumena', literally 'gold-friend of warriors' (*Beo.* 1171). *Goldwine* alliterates with *Gēatum* two lines later, in the sentence that follows; a link on the level of sound thus symbolises the hoped-for link of friendship between the king of the Danes and Beowulf's people.[2]

In Part I of *Sir Gawain and the Green Knight* (henceforth *G.*) the 'goodness' of the hero is underscored by systematic sound symbolism as the poet takes advantage of the alliterative link between his name and the adjective *god*. He is called 'gode Gawan' when he is first mentioned in the poem, at the head of a list of those seated at the high table at Arthur's New Year's feast: 'There gode Gawan watz grayþed Gwenore bisyde' (*G.* 109). He is referred to when he tells the Green Knight his name and when he takes his place at table with King Arthur after the Green Knight's departure as 'þe goode knyȝt' (*G.* 381, 482). In Part II, the narrator's explanation of the five times fivefold symbolic values of the pentangle painted on his shield is prefaced by the statement that

> For ay faythful in fyue and sere fyue syþez
> Gawan watz for gode knawen, and as golde pured   (*G.* 632–3)

(The second of these lines links the two elements of the still-familiar alliterating simile 'good as gold'.)

We must not overlook the emphasis on reputation in this last statement: Sir Gawain was *'known for* his goodness' – specifically, for the mutually reinforcing set of virtues publicly proclaimed as his by the emblem displayed on his shield. From the outset, in fact, the adjective *god*, in appellations for Sir Gawain, is used as an epithet, that is, as signifying an attribute for which the person possessing it is widely known.

('Good Gawain' is paralleled in the line that immediately follows by another combination of proper name and well-known attribute: 'Agrauayn a la dure mayn' *G.* 110). The phrase 'the good knight' is used exclusively with reference to Gawain – it is a 'title that he has', just as 'the Green Knight' is the title of the personage we will later come to know as Lord Bertilak. The adjective *god* is thus part of the hero's unchanging identity in the imagined world of the poem. As Odysseus, in the *Odyssey*, is always *polytropos*, a 'man of many shifts', and Aeneas, in the *Aeneid*, is always *pius*, so Sir Gawain in *Sir Gawain and the Green Knight* is always 'good'. Or so we are assured as the story begins to unfold.

Though, as I have said, the adjective *gōd* functions in *Beowulf* as one element of a system of words alliterating on *g* which help define various aspects of the hero's identity, we do not construe it as an epithet as we do the same adjective in *Sir Gawain*. In the first place, it cannot be linked by alliteration with the name 'Beowulf' (indeed, that name remains unexpressed until the hero identifies himself to the Danish coastguard; see *Beo.* 343). Nor, though Beowulf is indeed referred to immediately after his entry on the scene as 'se gōda', does that appellation serve as his particular title. For one thing, it appears side by side with a number of other equally salient appellations and descriptive statements. Immediately after Beowulf is introduced as 'Hygelac's thane, / good among the Geats,' he is described as 'the greatest in physical strength among the human race at that time, noble and well-grown' ('sē wæs moncynnes   mægenes strengest / on þǣm dæge   þysses līfes, / æþele ond ēacen' *Beo.* 196–8). And the wise men of the kingdom urge him to undertake the journey to Denmark because they see him as one 'valiant of spirit' ('hige[r]ōfne' *Beo.* 204). In addition, the adjective *gōd* is associated with persons other than Beowulf. It sums up the virtues of Hrothgar's ancestor Scyld in the formulaic half-line 'þæt wæs gōd cyning' (*Beo.* 11), and it appears several times, as I have said, with reference to Hrothgar himself (see above).

When we compare the lines in which Beowulf and Sir Gawain are first called 'good', we sense, in little, a crucial difference in tone between the two poems which depends in part on differences in metre. In 'gōd mid Geatum', *gōd* takes up almost one-fourth of the line in which it appears. According to the system of musical scansion applied to the poem by John C. Pope (1942, 1966; and see the contributions by Obst and Stockwell, this volume), it has the temporal value of a dotted crochet (quarter note), or three-quarters of a measure, and it receives the highest grade of stress the metre allows – 'strong primary', in Pope's terminology (1966: 246). For the classification of 'gōd mid Geatum' as Type A.2, see Pope's 'Line Index to the Catalogue' (1966: 390); for the temporal and stress patterns exhibited by half-lines of this type, see Pope (1966: 248). As a self-contained appositive, the phrase is separated by pauses both from the line that precedes it and the half-line that follows. The poet thus speaks deliberately and with emphasis when he tells us that Beowulf is good among his people. But in *Sir Gawain* the *gode* of 'gode Gawan' is rapid and comparatively unemphatic. Because we understand the main thrust of the statement to be the introduction and identification of the hero, we subordinate the descriptive adjective metrically to the first syllable of the proper name that follows it, giving it less than primary stress. (In 'classical' terminology, 'There gode Ga-' would be described as an anapaestic foot.)[3] The adjective can thus be thought of as extending the half-line, supplying it with a third 'lexical' or content-signifying word which also contributes a third alliterating syllable. Metrical structure requires no such additional weight or alliteration; the 'simple' or 'basic' half-line 'There Gawan watz grayþed' would have been fully acceptable. Considered in relation to the noun and verb phrases which make up the 'basic' version, the adjective *gode* is superfluous in terms of grammatical structure as well. This supererogatory character inevitably carries over into the realm of meaning. Gawain's goodness, it seems, 'goes without saying', can be 'taken for granted'. By that same token, the adjective has an attenuated force or generality, comparable, in the realm of moral terminology, to that of a dead metaphor in the realm of figuration.

The two appearances, later in Part I, of the phrase 'þe god kny3t' as an appellation for Sir Gawain are best discussed comparatively. When Sir Gawain tells the Green Knight his name, the poet writes,

'In god fayth,' quoþ þe goode kny3t, 'Gawan I hatte'   (*G*. 381)

When Sir Gawain and King Arthur take their places at table at the end of Part I, he writes,

þenne þay bo3ed to a borde þise burnes togeder,
þe kyng and þe gode kny3t, and kene men hem serued
Of alle dayntyez double, as derrest my3t falle   (481–3)

In both of these lines, the phrase 'þe god knyȝt' occupies the same metrical position, immediately preceding the caesura at the end of an extended first half-line. However, it can and should be scanned in two different ways on the basis of 'rhetorical stress', that is, on the basis of the comparative importance of the meanings of adjective and noun in each line. The correctness of these differing scansions is borne out by the fact that each of them accords with the relation of the adjective to the alliterative pattern. In 381, we feel that the 'goodness' of the good faith with which Gawain speaks and his own intrinsic 'goodness' complement and reinforce each other; both are reinforced in turn by the alliterative link between the adjective and the proper name which appears in the second half-line. We thus read both instances of *god* as what I call 'major chief' syllables, subordinating *fayth* and *knyȝt* to 'minor chief' rank.[4] In 482, we understand the main point of the half-line to be the pairing of Sir Gawain with King Arthur. Accordingly, we subordinate the descriptive adjective to the noun it modifies, as in 'There gode Gawan watz grayþed' in line 109; metrical subordination again corresponds to lack of emphasis in the realm of meaning.

The adjective thus plays three different metrical parts in the three lines in which it refers to Sir Gawain in Part I: in 109, it is an alliterating minor chief syllable; in 381, it is an alliterating major chief syllable; in 482, it is a nonalliterating minor chief syllable. In 381, goodness is imputed to Sir Gawain as he performs an important and courageous action; rhetorical and metrical stress go hand in hand. In lines 109 and 482, in which he is said simply to occupy or take his place at the banquet table, he is called good in passing and without emphasis; the adjective is more an honorific than an accolade.

In *Beowulf*, by contrast, the adjective *gōd* always receives a high degree of stress (in Pope's terminology, either strong primary or strong secondary). With only one exception, it, or, in inflected forms, its first syllable, has the musical value of a crotchet or dotted crotchet, half or more of one of the two measures making up the half-line.[5] Nuances in the poet's use of it with reference to persons derive in part from relationships between the half-lines in which it appears and the sentences, typically drawn out over two or more lines by appositive phrases and other elaborative materials, in which these half-lines are in turn embedded. On a still larger scale, we may respond, as readers familiar with the poem, to connections among sentences in different parts of the story.

Thus, when Beowulf makes his entrance on the scene as 'Higelāces þegn, / gōd mid Gēatum', he is linked first to his king and then, with the aid of systematic sound symbolism, to the other warriors of his nation. The descriptive statement that follows places him, more generally, in the context of all the other male warriors of the human race whom he excels in size and strength. As 'gōd mid Gēatum' and 'se gōda,' he is linked, across the scope of the poem as a whole, to the bygone time of the reign of King Scyld, to the present time of his youth in the reign of King Hrothgar, and to the future time of his old age as king of the Geats, through the thrice-repeated summary statement 'þæt wæs gōd cyning', which refers to the three kings in the order of their reigns (Beo. 11, 863, 2390).

Whether or not we are aware of these verbal linkages as such, we cannot fail, as we read the poem, to sense its all-important theme of continuity: the transmission through historical time, against all odds, of the values embodied by the 'good' Germanic kings and the 'good' thanes who serve them. In affirming these, the voice of the narrator is at all times solemn, emphatic, and unequivocal. The imagined world of the poem is one in which intrinsic goodness and evil manifest themselves clearly in good and evil actions. These in turn are made known through the dissemination of stories, including the story of Beowulf itself, in the course of which praise is bestowed on the former, and blame on the latter, by the poet-narrator.

In Sir Gawain, the bearing out of reputation by performance is by no means a foregone conclusion. The relation between the two is explicitly called into question (with relation not so much to virtue, it would seem, as to virility) by the lady in the first bedroom scene, when she complains that 'So god as Gawayn gaynly is halden . . . / . . . Couth not lyꝣtly haf lenged so long wyth a lady, Bot he had craued a cosse' (G. 1297–1300). The narrator's account of the significance of the pent-angle, which comes immediately before Sir Gawain leaves King Arthur's court in search of the Green Chapel, presents him as a paragon. We are told that he displays the emblem on his shield and coat armour by right, 'as tulk of tale most trwe' (G. 638), and that his perfec-tion consists in part of a set of five virtues which includes 'fraunchyse', or generosity (G. 652). When, at the end of the story, he bitterly reproaches himself for his 'falssyng' (G. 2378) and 'couetyse' (G. 2380), he is acknowledging, as we also must, that the reality of his behaviour under severely trying conditions has fallen short of the ideal 'goodness' imputed to him before the events at Castle Hautdesert and the Green Chapel have taken place.

In underscoring this theme of an uneasy relation between reputation and actuality, the poet avails himself of the numerous metrical options provided him by the late-ME long alliterative line, including the possibility of extending the basic form of the line by the 'gratuitous' addition of descriptive adjectives, among others the adjective *god*. He also makes use of a second adjective belonging to the 'g system', namely, *gay*. This makes its first appearance with reference to Sir Gawain immediately after the poet's account of the meaning of the pentangle:

> Now grayþed is Gawan gay,
> And laȝt his launce ryȝt þore,
> And gef hem alle goud day,
> He wende for euermore   (*G.* 666–9)

The meanings and uses of the adjective *god* in ME, for all their variety and scope, include nothing disparaging. *Gay*, however, had not only its most common modern sense, 'joyous, light-hearted, carefree', but a number of other senses which have not survived in modern English, some of them bordering on or actually encroaching on morally dubious territory. These include 'wanton, . . . lascivious', 'glittering', 'showy', and 'superficially pleasing, specious' (MED s.v. *gai* adj.). *God* and *gay*, as monosyllabic lexical adjectives, are interchangeable for metrical purposes,[6] and the poet's deployment in the long alliterating lines now of one, now of both, is of great interest.

God in *Sir Gawain* is associated almost exclusively with men, especially the hero, and *gay* with women, especially the lady of the castle.[7] As *god* becomes, in effect, an epithet for Sir Gawain, so *gay* becomes an epithet for the lady. At the moment when Gawain first sees her, the narrator refers to her as 'þat gay' (*G.* 970); when she opens the dialogue in the first bedroom scene, and later in that same conversation, she is called 'þat . . . gay lady' (*G.* 1208, 1248); Gawain addresses her as 'gay' (*G.* 1213) in the first bedroom scene and as 'my gay' in the third (*G.* 1822). But Gawain himself is also referred to as 'gay' at moments when he is splendidly attired. I have already quoted the line 'Now grayþed is Gawan gay' (*G.* 666). Attending the Christmas Eve service at Hautdesert in his fine new mantle, having feasted on fish and warmed himself with wine, he 'glydez ful gay' toward his host and hostess (G. 935). An ominous distinction between inner qualities of 'goodness' and outer ones of 'gaiety' or splendour would seem to be suggested when we are told, on the morning of the first hunt, that 'Gawain þe god mon in gay bed lygez' (G. 1179). The two adjectives are grammatically superfluous, and they elaborate on, rather than figuring in, the gist of the statement. Nonetheless, they are thrust on our attention by the chief metrical rank given them in a properly expressive reading.

The g system I identified in the first five hundred lines of *Beowulf* as consisting of *Gēat*, *gūð*, and *gold* remains operative in Part II of the poem, when the aged Beowulf, having reigned fifty years as king of the Geats, undertakes his final and fatal adventure. The all-important theme of the historical continuity of kingly and 'thanely' virtues thus continues to be reinforced, in part, by systematic sound symbolism. In particular, expressions containing the words *gūð*, *gōd*, and *gold* which in Part I were used with reference to Hrothgar reappear in references to Beowulf as king of the Geats (see F. C. Robinson 1985: 24). The hero is referred to four times (*Beo.* 2335, 2563, 2677, 3036) as a 'gūðcyning', a title he himself, in Part I, had bestowed on Hrothgar (*Beo.* 199); the narrator had also used it of Hygelac, who was king of the Geats in Beowulf's youth (*Beo.* 1969). Beowulf, like Hrothgar before him, is a 'nobleman good of old', an 'æþeling ǣrgōd' (*Beo.* 130, 2342). Whereas Hrothgar had been described as 'gold-friend of warriors' ('goldwine gumena' *Beo.* 1171, 1602), Beowulf is called 'gold-friend of the Geats' ('goldwine Gēata' *Beo.* 2419, 2584). Among the endlessly varied appellations devised by the poet for his aged hero, there are of course a number in which the adjective *gōd* appears. Thus Beowulf is described, as he gazes on the fiery stream flowing from the dragon's cave, as 'the one, good in accordance with manly virtues, who had survived many battles':

> sē ðe worna fela
> gumcystum gōd   gūðe gedīgde   (*Beo.* 2542–3)

In Part I, the young Beowulf had used the phrase 'gumcystum gōd' in praising King Hrothgar for his generosity towards him (*Beo.* 1486).

The narrator's concept of the qualities that make kings and warriors worth celebrating remains unaltered to the end, and his belief in them remains unshaken. Nonetheless, a sea change has occurred. In the fatal venture against the marauding fire dragon, the goodness of the hero is manifest still. But it now no longer prevails. In view of the poem's fore-gone conclusion, late references to Beowulf and his war gear as 'good', though they remain unequivocal and emphatic, take on an ironic ring, especially when the adjective is linked with other words that have par-ticipated in the g system: 'The gold-friend of the Geats did not boast of victories in combat; the battle-sword failed, bared in hostility, as it should not have done, the iron good from of old.'

> Hrēðsigora ne gealp
> goldwine Gēata; gūðbill geswāc,
> nacod at nīðe, swā hyt nō sceolde,
> īren ǣrgōd.   (2583–6)[8]

When the word gōd makes its final appearance in the poem, the alliter-ative link in which it participates has tragic significance. Wiglaf orders that wood for the funeral pyre should be carried to the body of the 'good one' ('gōdum tōgēnes' Beo. 3114); the alliterating word in the second half of the line is glēd 'fire'.

As the plot of Sir Gawain approaches its denouement, the complexity of the relationship between 'goodness' and 'gaiety' (in the latter word's two ME senses of 'visible splendour' and 'showiness or speciousness') continues to be underscored by the appearance of the two relevant adjectives, singly or juxtaposed, in varying metrical positions and with varying degrees of metrical and rhetorical emphasis. After he has accepted the green girdle and promised to conceal the fact, Sir Gawain, awaiting his host's arrival, is blandly referred to as 'Sir Gawayn þe gode' (G. 1926); the adjective receives full metrical emphasis in an unex-tended first half-line. Telling us how Gawain dressed himself for his visit to the chapel the following morning, the poet assures us that he did not leave that magic talisman behind:

> Ʒet laft he not þe lace, þe ladiez gifte,
> þat forgat not Gawayn for gode of hymseluen . . .
> Swyþe sweþled vmbe his swange swetely þat knyʒt
> þe gordel of þe grene silke, þat gay wel bisemed.[9]
>   (G. 2030–1, 2034–5)

Here gode has strategic rather than ethical significance, and 'þat gay' is unusual in that it refers to a man rather than a woman. The implications are obvious.

The adjective *good* figures several times in the scene at the Green Chapel. When Sir Gawain calls out to whoever is making an unconscionable racket up on the hill, he bestows the appellation 'gode Gawayn' on himself, perhaps with feigned self-confidence: 'now is gode Gawayn goande ryȝt here' (*G.* 2214). A few moments afterward, when he has flinched from the first blow of the axe, his tormentor accuses him of being, not 'good Gawain', but someone else:

> 'þou art not Gawayn,' quoþ þe gome, 'þat is so goud halden,
> þat neuer arȝed for no here by hylle ne be vale'   (*G.* 2270–1)

After all has been revealed, of course, the Green Knight speaks more kindly, saying, among other things, that

> 'As perle bi þe quite pese is of prys more,
> So is Gawayn, in god fayth, bi oþer gay knyȝtez'   (*G.* 2364–5)

In the second of these lines, *oþer* is a major chief syllable, *gay* being subordinated to minor chief rank.[10] We are to understand that Gawain is intrinsically good, whereas other knights are outwardly gay, or perhaps that Gawain, unlike other knights, is one in whom praiseworthy outward and inward qualities coincide.

When the hero reappears at Camelot at last, he is joyfully received:

> þer wakened wele in þat wone when wyst þe grete
> þat gode Gawayn watz commen; gayn hit hym þoȝt
> (*G.* 2490–1)

What are we to make of this ascription of goodness to the hero, now that he has shown his true colours? I have no space here to address the endlessly debated questions of moral judgement raised by the poem, but I shall make one further observation founded in part on metrical analysis: the matter of Gawain's goodness, as alluded to on his return to the court, is of no great moment. We can see this if we return to line 109, 'There gode Gawan watz grayþed Gwenore bisyde', where the hero is first mentioned and at the same time the adjective is first used with reference to him. The phrase 'gode Gawan' in that line and the same phrase in line 2491 stand in identical positions and have identical metrical values. And the adjective in the two lines is equally lightweight, both metrically and in meaning (see the discussion of line 109 above). It is almost as if the aristocratic members of King Arthur's court ('þe grete') had learned that Gawain, 'that good fellow', or even 'good old Gawain', was once again among them.

Fred Robinson has well said that 'in reading *Beowulf*, as in reading all great poetry, we have the sense that the author's genius has been happily merged with the one style and language which alone could convey his poetic apprehension of his subject' (1985: 80). To this I would add 'and the one metrical form'. The rapid, voluble long lines of *Sir Gawain* and the slow-paced, stately measures of *Beowulf* seem alike suited to the stories these poems have to tell, and to the meanings of those stories, locked by two superbly skilled poets in letters tried and true.

Notes

1 The word *loken*, in the line 'With lel letteres loken' is worth pausing over for a moment. It means, not 'secured with a key' but simply 'fastened together'. Later in the poem, other forms of this same verb (*louken* in ME) refer to the intertwining of the five lines of the pentangle, or 'endless knot', and to the tying of the green girdle, first around the lady's sides (*G*. 1830), then under Sir Gawain's left arm (*G*. 2487). Its use to signify the linkages among 'letters' that form the long alliterative line thus introduces a theme of knottings or attachment – the invulnerable perfection of the pentangle knot and the ambiguousness or duplicity of human 'ties' – that runs through the narrative and enhances its meaning.

2 Reinhard presents comprehensive lists of 'Basic Collocations' in which lexically congruent words are joined, including, among others, collocations whose members begin with the letter <g> (see Reinhard 1976: 39). Space forbids my discussing a 'countersystem' in which the name *Grendel* alliterates not only with adjectives denoting monstrous attributes, such as *grimm* and *grædig* (*Beo*. 121), but with *guðcræft* (*Beo*. 127), a word signifying the human arts of war that are wholly unknown to such a creature. See Reinhard (p. 58) for the link between *Grendel* and *guð*; also p. 195, where *gōd*, *Gēatum*, and *Grendles* are listed among 'Contrastive' word groups; and p. 152, where a 'Grendel–gold motif' is discussed (Grendel is the 'opponent of all the values represented by gold').

3 The fact that the second syllable is heavy does not rule out this description. So-called anapaestic verses in English may contain feet whose first or second syllables, or both, receive considerable stress, as in 'Not a word to each other; we kept *the great pace*' and 'Till over by Dalhem a dome-spire *sprang white*', in Browning's 'How They Brought the Good News from Ghent to Aix'.

4 See Borroff (1962: esp. 173–5 and 192–8). The poetry of Chaucer provides evidence for alternative scansions, in the iambic pentameter line, of similar phrases, such that either the adjective or the noun is assigned chief rank; I confine myself to a single example of each. In *Troilus* 2.162 '"In good feith, em," quod she, "that liketh me"', *good* is a chief syllable; in *The Parliament of Fowls* 24 'And out of old bokes, in good feyth', it is an intermediate syllable. The scansion of Chaucerian lines in which *good* modifies words referring to persons is complicated by the fact that the adjective is usually disyllabic when declined weak or used in apostrophes. But cf. *Troilus* 2.309 'Now, good em, for Goddes love I preye' (a 'headless' line) and 2.499 'Til at the laste, "O goode em," quod she tho'. Here a disyllabic pronunciation (as in *Clerk's Tale* 852 'O goodë God, how gentil and how kynde') is ruled out by elision. The two instances of *goode* in *Troilus* 2.309 and 2.499 have intermediate and chief rank, respectively. See also Duffell (1991) and this volume.

5 *Gōd* appears in the first 400 lines of the poem in lines 11, 195, 199, 205, 269, 279, 347, 355, and 384; for scansions of these, see the 'Line Index to the Catalogue' in Pope (1966: 389–409). The first syllable of *godan* is scanned by Pope as a quaver (eighth note) in *Beo.* 384 'Ic þæm gōdan sceal' (Pope 334, type B1.2).

6 I am scanning *Sir Gawain* in accordance with my own theory that the final -*e* of these adjectives is not sounded in the long alliterating line in positions in which it would be sounded in Chaucer's decasyllabic verse (see Borroff 1962: 154–60, 182–9). Syllabication, in this line or that of the poem, may or may not be reflected in spelling (compare e.g. the plural forms in 'goude ladyez' 1625 and 'goud chepez' 1939).

7 *Gay* is used only once of persons in Part I of the poem, with reference to Guenevere. Thereafter it refers to Gawain and the lady of the castle (but not to Lord Bertilak). *God* refers to masculine persons seventeen times, to feminine persons only once ('þe goude ladyez were geten, and gedered þe meyny' (1625)). I suspect that the 'gode halʒez' of line 2122 are exclusively masculine.

8 In his pathbreaking 1963 essay, Randolph Quirk showed that the appellation 'goldwine' takes on a poignant rather than an exalted resonance when, late in the poem, it is linked with 'geōmor' ('sad'). I would add that such effects are not produced exclusively by the juxtaposition of terms of contrasting emotional value; the tried-and-true combinations themselves may take on tragic force.

9 Davis construes the last half-line as a relative clause with the pronominal head unexpressed, and translates 'which well suited that handsome man'. 'Splendidly dressed' would translate *gay* equally well.

10 If we read the line with natural expressive emphasis, *oþer* rather than *gay* will receive chief metrical rank, even though the latter alliterates and the former does not. For further examples in the poem, see Borroff (1962: 171 and 202).

9 Non-aa/ax patterns in Middle English alliterative long-line verse

A. T. E. Matonis

1

Not very long ago, Angus McIntosh called attention to something so basic that we often overlook it, namely, that the phrase *alliterative verse* 'tends, misleadingly, to accord to the term *alliterative* the status of somehow seeming to define rhythmical characteristics that are in many respects quite independent of alliteration' (1982: 20). The extent to which our thinking about this verse has been conditioned by this traditional but misleading label may be argued, but a bias in favour of alliteration can be detected both in textual emendation and often in the way verses are scanned.[1] This bias can no doubt be accounted for by the dominance of the *aa/ax* pattern and the traditionally accepted principle that alliteration is structural in ME long-line verse – hence we speak of metrical alliteration v. nonmetrical alliteration. Yet on the formal structural level, a line of alliterative verse, strictly speaking, needs only two alliterating staves, one in the first half-line and, more critically, one to the immediate right of the caesura, i.e. on the first strong stress of the second half-line. OE verse, which is often invoked in discussions of the ME long line, demonstrates the structural function of such alliteration in its high representation of *ax/ax* verses. However, even in OE the preference for *aa/ax* and *ax/ax* as against the slight use of *xa/ax* reflects the presence of a nonstructural factor operating over and beyond the metrical line.

Few would question the structural function of alliteration in OE.[2] Although it is largely assumed that alliteration also has a structural role in ME long-line poetry, the issue is by no means closed.[3] In fact, the topic of alliterative function in ME awaits detailed study. The reasons that it has not received this study are several. First, it has long been accepted that the structural constraints of this verse allowed the ME poet few options. Add to this that whatever theoretical potential alliteration has as a topic is tied up in the larger and more formally beguiling issue of metre, to which distinctions between metrical and nonmetrical alliteration and of structural v. ornamental alliteration have to be attached. Thus, alliteration has been subsumed under metrics. Indeed, the difficulty of detaching alliterative features from metrical ones becomes apparent as soon as one attempts to describe alliteration as an independent element. For instance, when representing the alliterative pattern in a line of verse as *aa/ax* or *ax/ax* or *xa/ax* we do not confine our description to alliterative variables. By including *x* in the notation and by excluding all alliterating words or syllables with an alliterative register but which do not bear metrical stress, our account of the alliterative texture of the line is made subordinate to metrical value. Thus at a basic descriptive level, alliteration is neither perceived nor represented as independent of metrical considerations.

In addition, questions concerning alliterative function have had to wait until the metrical system of this verse was more adequately charted. Recent work on metrical theory in general and in OE in particular, as well as the work of Cable on ME metre (1988, 1991) and of Duggan on rhythm (1986a, b, 1987, 1990a, b, c), has greatly advanced our understanding of the metrical and linguistic factors, structural norms, and constraints embedded in early English verse, so that it now becomes possible to begin to talk about alliteration on a more informed and informal level than in the past. One question that might be reexamined is that of the structural (as v. ornamental) role of alliteration; another has to do with the determinant power of the normative *aa/ax* pattern and the degree to which it allows or checks deviations from the norm, and the conditions, if any, under which the norm may be violated (see also McCully, this volume, and McCully and Hogg 1994). This chapter is but a preliminary enquiry into the authority of the normative pattern and into some of the narrative and rhetorical contexts where we might expect to find departures from it. In a large number of lines, however, the use of a nonnormative pattern is not governed by linguistic, narrative, or rhetorical exigencies but appears to have been adopted simply as an optional alternative available to the alliterative poet.

2

While alliteration corresponds with metrical stress most of the time, there are occasions when it unmistakably does not and others when it may not. Despite the compelling force of alliterative convention, the authority of the *aa/ax* pattern could be gainsaid not only as an exercise in creative manipulation but in quite ordinary lines as well. The *ax/ax* and *xa/ax* patterns in the examples below do not represent imaginative crafting but are quite ordinary lines. In rhythm, metre, syntax, and diction, they conform to the conventional norms of alliterative composition. In some of these verses, such as *Morte Arthure* 637, we find formulaic staples of alliterative diction; in others, the line has to accommodate a borrowed polysyllabic proper noun (e.g. *Cleanness* 958); and in yet another group, a nonalliterating word or syllable which ordinarily goes unstressed receives metrical prominence for narrative, argumentative, or rhetorical emphasis, such as in *Wars of Alexander* 257, *Mum & the Sothsegger* II 42, and *Patience* 78.

ax/ax:
>   Sir Perceualle de Galeys þat preued had bene ofte
>   (PTA 478)[4]
>   At the cetee of Rome assemblede at ones   (MA 609)
>   With alle the perez of the rewme, prelates and other
>   (MA 637)
>   And the south-westrene wynd on Saterday at even
>   (PP1 B V 14)[5]
>   Be it hee, be [it scho], haly þere werdes   (WarsA 257)
>   Is erdand in Jude, as Isoder sais   (DestTr 923)
>   If he hem stowned vpon fyrst, stiller were þanne
>   (GGK 301)

xa/ax:
>   Here ene as a trendull turned full rounde   (DestTr 453)
>   Thane he takes hys leve at ladys in chambyre   (MA 713)
>   For on þat ȝe merkyd ȝe myssed ten schore   (M&S II.42)
>   'þaghe I be vnworthi', al wepand he sayde   (StErk 122)
>   Abdama and Syboym, þise ceteis alle faure   (Clean 958)
>   I com wyth þose typþynges, þay ta me bylyue   (Pat 78)
>   Durst nowhere for roȝ arest at þe bothem   (Pat 144)

Since any style, including the alliterative style, allows for paradigmatic deviation, verses written in *ax/ax* and *xa/ax* patterns can be accepted as permitted alternatives to the norm.

2.1

Less certain as paradigmatic alternatives but worth looking at nonetheless are a number of verses in which the absence of an alliterating stress in one of the three expected positions may be compensated for by the presence of nonmetrical alliteration in the environment of expected metrical alliteration. Such an alliterative adjustment might at least have satisfied the alliterative aesthetic by providing an implicative rhyme in verses which would otherwise lack three alliterating stresses. On the formal level, it is as close as we can come to witnessing as structurally separate the operations of alliteration and metre. The question of whether nonmetrical compensatory alliteration was intentional – indeed, of whether the strategy exists at all – is bound to be controversial. Schmidt has claimed that some such phenomenon is operating in Langland's verse,[6] and a similar process was recognised by Schumacher in his identification of the liasonal stave.[7] In Langland verses lacking three alliterating lexical words, Kane and Donaldson assign stress to alliterating grammatical words, or 'little words', entirely on the basis of alliterative presence (Kane and Donaldson 1975: 134–5). More recently, Kane has postulated a theory of modulation which accounts for those lines in Langland in which metrical stress and alliteration fall on different syllables. Indeed, here Kane sees alliteration and metrical stress as constituting two quite separate patterns (1981: 53), and this amounts to accepting that the two exist on different systemic levels in the verse line.

The examples of compensatory alliteration below are gathered in four groups. The first three contain a nonmetrical alliterating stave in first half-lines which would otherwise alliterate *ax/ax* and therefore be deficient by the conventional normative standard. The compensatory alliteration, which is italicised in these three groups, typically falls on a word which is normally excluded from stress and which if awarded stress would convert the verse from a normal to an expanded one. In the fourth group, compensatory alliteration compensates for the absence of metrical alliteration in the critical position of third stress across the caesura. It is notable that in the second half-lines the compensatory alliterating staves fall either on grammatical words or on syllables that under few conceivable circumstances would be elevated to metrical stress.

Non-aa/ax verses with compensatory alliteration

1. (a)ax/ax:

þat *m*ade his moder þe queene þat moste was adouted
    (AlexA 33)
*S*ithen it is sonde of a god, soothelich iprooved   (AlexA 973)
*M*ay no man but God maken us tine   (AlexB 36)
He *d*othe hym doun one þe bonke & dwellys a while
    (W&W 109)
*S*one sendeþ hym to & þe soþe tolde   (SJ 206)
*L*o, lordlynges, her, þe lyknesse of Crist   (SJ 245)

2. a(a)x/ax:

What kid *K*ing Philip þat keene is of hert   (AlexA 801)
His grete *g*od Amon grates too ȝelde   (AlexA 661)
And als I waytted *w*ithinn, I was warre sone   (W&W 85)
And buskyd þiderwarde *b*y tyme on his blonke after
    (StErk 112)
Furst tomurte *m*ony rop and þe mast after   (Pat 150)
For soþely, as *s*ays þe wryt, he wern of sadde elde
    (Clean 657)
Elanes *a*une doghter, abill of chere   (DestTr 7940)
Bot mon *m*ost I algate mynn hym to bene   (GGK 141)

3. (a)xa/ax:

In *G*lamorgane with glee, there gladchipe was euere   (MA
    59)
A*m*onge enmyes so mony and mansed fendes   (Clean 82)
Now þat London is neuenyd hatte þe New Troie   (StErk 25)
*B*ot of alle þat here bult of Bretaygne kynges (GGK 25)
*W*atz– not þis ilk my worde þat worþen is nouþe
    (Pat 414)

4. aa/(a)xx:

Bisshopes and bachelers, *b*othe maistres and doctours
    (PP1 Pr 87)
For fere of othere foweles and *f*or wilde beestes
    (PP1 X1 354)

Corseth he no creature, ne he *k*an bere no wrathe
   (PP1 XV 171)
Whitte als the whalles bone, *w*ho-so the sothe tellys
   (W&W 181)
Er me wont þe wede, *w*ith help of my frendez   (GGK 987)
þat was þe athill Alexsandire, *a*s þe buke tellis   (WarsA 17)
þat alder hight Alisaunder *a*s I right tell   (AlexA 22)
Sir Ectore was euerous *a*ls the storye telles   (PTA 306)
Bot Arthure oure athell kynge *a*noþer he thynkes
   (PTA 484)
But alisaundrine þer-after *a*non be a wile   (WmPal 834)
Als wemles were his wedes *w*ytouten any teche   (StErk 85)

2.2

In contrast to OE, *ax/ax* lines in ME are remarkably limited in number. On the other hand, ME poets used the expanded variant *aax/ax* to a considerable degree, especially in highly stylised passages in which expanded verses are dominant or appear in successive strings. It is also the *aax/ax* pattern which seems to have been preferred as the verse type to accommodate loans over three syllables. As we would expect, and corresponding to the slight numbers of lines patterning *xa/ax* across the corpus, there are fewer *xaa/ax* expansions than *aax/ax*; however, the expanded *xaa/ax* variant is more highly represented than the normal *xa/ax*. Of course, expanded verses, including the *axa/ax* type, which appears to have its own syntactic and prosodic patterns, bring up a corollary set of metrical and linguistic problems. Most immediate for the purpose of this chapter is that the difference between the degree of stress on those syllables which remain metrically weak (in a metrical reading as opposed to ordinary speech) and those which bear minor chief emphasis (to use Borroff's term) is often extremely slight. Accordingly, there will be lines among the following examples that some readers will read as normal, some as expanded.

1. *aax/ax*

A. First half-lines ending in a prepositional phrase with a non-alliterating headword.

The trewe toure of Londone in his tyme he makede
   (PTA 408)

A grete gartare of ynde girde in the myddes   (W&W 94)
Kiddes clouen by þe rigge, quarterd swannes   (W&W 340)
As lauce leuez of þe boke þat lepes in twynne   (Clean 966)
þe verray vengaunce of God schal voyde þis place   (Pat 370)

B. First half-lines ending in a nonalliterating adverb
And the see satillede agayne and sanke thaym thereinn
   (PTA 437)
þe rauen raykez hym forth, þat reches ful lyttel   (Clean 465)
þe segge sesed not ȝet, bot sayde euer ilyche   (Pat 369)

C. First half-lines ending in a nonalliterating polysyllabic noun
The gentill Judas Machabee was a Jewe kene   (PTA 454)
And sett the Sege Perilous so semely one highte   (PTA 470)
The gates towardes Glasschenbery full graythely he rydes
   (PTA 494)
He come to Comonthonham, full cumlich a place
   (AlexA 255)
þe lordship of Lacedemonie loþed hem than   (AlexA 335)
þe gentil Genosophistiens þat goode were of witte
   (AlexB 23)
Addrus and ypotamus and oþure ille wormus   (AlexB 157)
And careful cocodrillus þat þe king hette   (AlexB 158)
And kenely be conjurisons callis to him spiritis   (WarsA 58)

D. First half-lines ending in a phrasal unit of alliterating adjective
   + nonalliterating noun
Bet on þe broun stele, while þe bladde laste   (SJ 542)
Tytus at þe toun ȝate with ten þousand helmes   (SJ 1185)
And drifes thurȝe his depe hert as he ware dart-wondid
   (WarsA 225)
With grete glesenand eȝen grymly he lokis   (WarsA 603)
Fyndes he a fayr schyp to þe fare redy   (Pat 98)

2. *axa/ax*

A. First half-lines which divide *axa/-* into *ax:a/-*
Bolde sqwyeres of blode, bowmen many   (W&W 194)
A kynde herueste to cache and cornes to wynn   (W&W 274)
Hir shire face all for shame shot into rede   (DestTr 451)
Grim arowes and graie with grounden toles   (AlexA 270)
Harde stones for to hewe wyt eggit toles   (StErk 40)
In rouh erþe to be reke, to roten hure bonus   (AlexB 594)

B. First half-lines which divide *axa/*- into *a:xa/*-

   Kyng of Galile ycalled, whan þat Crist deyed   (SJ 6)

   Trynes one a grete trotte and takes his waye   (W&W 122)

   Wyth scheldeȝ of wylde swyn, swaneȝ and croneȝ
      (Clean 58)

   þroly into þe deueleȝ þrote man þryngeȝ bylyue   (Clean 180)

   Rwly wyth a loud rurd rored for drede   (Clean 390)

   þy long abydyng wyth lur, þy late vengaunce   (Pat 419)

   Her bagges and her feþer-beddes and her bryȝt wedes
      (Pat 158)

   So blyþe of his wod-byne he balteres þer-vnder   (Pat 459)

   Leches by torche-liȝt loken her hurtes   (SJ 846)

   3. *xaa/ax*

   His purse weghethe full wele that wanne thaym all hedire
      (W&W 162)

   þe blod schot for scham into his schyre face   (GGK 317)

   The firste was gentil Josue þat was a Jewe noble   (PTA 426)

   Cam with a fair ferde þe fals men to mete   (SJ 551)

   þ[at] kne-depe in þe dale dascheden stedes   (SK 572)

   Tricerberus þe helle hound þat holden is kene   (AlexB 536)

3

Few would claim that every alliterating syllable should be read with strong stress or that nonalliterating syllables are to be rejected as bearers of stress solely for alliterative reasons. If the context or occasion calls for it, there are few words in the language that are categorically ineligible for stress elevation.[8] Even prefixes, which exert semantic modification, will sometimes be promoted to stress in verse as in ordinary speech. Thus, although the degree of stress operating in verse is usually insufficient to raise bound morphemes and minor category words to ictus, they may occasionally be metrically promoted for reasons of rhetorical or dramatic emphasis or when the context urges it. In the following verses, the prefixes *vn-*, *vt-*, *in-* and *mis-* are both stressed and alliterating:

   In owttrage, in vnthrifte, in angarte [of] pryde   (W&W 267)

   As be honest vtwyth and inwyth all fylþez   (Clean 14)

> Al watȝ þe mynde of þat man on misschapen þinges
> (Clean 1355)
> The mysscheff & þe mysserule þat men þo in endurid
> (M&S Pr 22)

Similarly, the morphemes -fore, -hynde:

> Two with flowres of Fraunce before and behynde   (W&W 78)
> Harm of eny man, byhynde or bifore   (PP1 V1 117)

In the following lines, alliteration on the same or similar morphemes does not coincide with metrical stress. Whereas the contrasting morphemes *vt-* and *in-* have been forwarded in *Cleanness* 14 above, in *Cleanness* 20 they appear in their normal position as the second element in the compound, where they nonetheless retain their contrasting semantic force and should therefore retain stress even though nonalliterating. Moreover, like all the preceding lines (except *Cleanness* 1355), *Cleanness* 20 is structured around an anaphoric parallelism, in which the rhetorical balance additionally recommends that the contrasting *-inne* and *-outen* receive stress rather than the alliterating *wyth-*.

> Boþ wythinne & wythouten, in wedeȝ ful bryȝt   (Clean 20)

Similarly, a reading which recognises the sense expressed in the following verses will give stress to the italicised nonalliterating negatives, pronouns, and bound morphemes. In doing so, the normative *aa/ax* pattern will have been violated but adjusted for if we allow compensatory alliteration. The rhetorical balance of these lines and the emphasis demanded by the contrasting morphemes suggest, in their different ways, that ME alliterative poets were responsive to semantic principles no less than to alliterative ones.

1. Bound morphemes
> For cristene and *u*ncristene claymeth it ech-one   (PP1 I 89)
> Hir brest bare bi*f*ore, and bi*h*inde eke   (GGK 1741)
> That wroute any wrake with*i*n or with*o*ute   (M&S I 44)

2. Negatives
> a. I salle *n*euer no saynt bee, by my fadyre sawle!   (MA 1169)
> b. Was *n*euer syche noblay, in no manys tyme   (MA 76)
> a. þat is markid to me and to *n*o mo kingus   (AlexB 90)
> b. 'Nay, sertus', saide þe noble, 'þat may *n*ot be graunted'
> (AlexB 73)

3. Pronouns
   a. For hitt they *the* or thy horse, it harmes for euer
      (MA 2437)
   b. For to hurte *h*yme or his horse with that hard wepne
      (MA 2427)
   c. & layte as lelly til þou *me*, lude, fynde   (Clean 146)

While alliterative poets were constrained by alliterative demands, they were equally responsive to meaning. The examples given here suggest that they knew full well that the 'little words' of ordinary speech, and units smaller than a word, have potential semantic and dramatic force. And while it is true that when invoking interpretive criteria we face opening to debate a sizeable number of lines, we cannot ignore the non-formal elements of the narrative altogether. Although I have not made a point of it in the preceding discussion, I would add that it is often in lines of dialogue (and many of the preceding examples are drawn from such lines) that the professional poets show themselves receptive to manipulation of the normative alliterative pattern in order to fore-ground a pronoun, negative, or other minor-category word on which hinges an expressive reading. As a final example of this group, we might look at *Cleanness* 517, which is spoken by God to Noah. Here the non-alliterating auxiliaries are elevated to stress within the framework of an anaphoric parallelism which uses the verb *to be* in a remarkable rhetori-cal *traductio* adapted to English. The result is a line which has the untidy alliterative pattern $x(a)x(a)x/ax$, but which displays an altogether ortho-dox metrical and rhythmical pattern:

    & ay *h*atȝ ben & *w*yl be ȝet fro her barnage

4

The importance of context has been part of the argument for justifying non-*aa/ax* readings in the verses thus far reviewed.

Traditionally, scholars have both acknowledged the importance of reading lines within their context and accepted that a poet's practice throughout an entire poem must be part of the consideration when analysing ambiguous, difficult, or nonstandard patterns. Using *Saint Erkenwald* and *Sir Gawain and the Green Knight*, I should like now to look at nonnormative lines in particular poems and passages. While numerically such verses constitute deviations from the norm in both poems, they are not rare. Moreover, they are sufficiently finished in execution to suggest that they are intentional authorial creations. Just as *Piers Plowman* opens with a nonnormative pattern, so does *Saint Erkenwald*, albeit one of a decidedly different cast:

> At London in Englond noȝt full long sythen

In fact, of the first fifty lines in the poem, seventeen use a nonnormative pattern.

ax/(a)/ax	At London in Englond noȝt full long sythen	(1)
aba/ab	Sythen Crist suffrid on crosse & Cristendome stablyd	(2)
aa/aa	Saynt Erkenwolde, as I hope, þat holy mon hatte	(4)
(a)ax/ax	ffor hit hethen had bene in Hengyst dawes	(7)
(a)xa/ax	Til saynt Austyn into Sandewiche was send from þe pope	(12)
aax/ax	þen prechyd he her þe pure faythe & plantyd þe trouthe	(13)
aax/ax	And chaungit cheuely hor nomes & chargit hom better	(18)
aa/(a)xx	þat ere was of Appolyn is now of Saynt Petre	(19)
aa/aa	Iubiter and Iono to Iesu oþir Iames	(22)
(a)xa/ax	Now þat London is neuenyd hatte þe New Troie	(25)
aax/ax	þe metropol & þe mayster toun hit euermore has bene	(26)
aax/ax	þe mecul mynster þerinne a maghty deuel aght	(27)
aa/aa	þe thrid temple hit wos tolde of Triapolitanes	(31)
aab/ab	At loue London toun and the laghe teches	(34)
aaa/(a)xx	Syttes semely in þe sege of Saynt Paule mynster	(35)
aax/ax	Hit was a throghe of thykke ston thryuandly hewen	(47)
aax/ax	Wyt gargeles garnysht about alle of gray marbre	(48)

The nonmetrical alliteration (indicated by (a) in the pattern notation) may be a compensatory adjustment to bring the lines closer to the alliterative norm. In lines 12 and 35, for example, the epithet *saynt* has sufficient relative significance lexically and phrasally to allow its alliterative register to be recognised on a stylistic level even though in this metrical system the appellative functions much as a proclitic (as do *Sir* and *King*). In order to make these lines conform to the normative alliterative pattern, we would have to give strong stress to *saynt*, which would contradict its treatment elsewhere in the poem and the corpus.[9] Neither of these lines, then, belongs to the normative pattern; rather they alliterate *(a)xa/ax* and *aaa/(a)xx* respectively.[10]

Line 19 provides quite a different example of how nonnormative patterns could be accommodated to the alliterative line. Here the temporal adverb *ere* at once recommends itself as the first strong stress of the line. Since *Appolyn* carries vocalic alliteration and since foreign proper nouns are variously accommodated to ME alliterative and metrical schemes, the initial *A* was no doubt intended to carry metrical alliteration. However, in the second half-line the copula *is* cannot compete for metrical prominence with the temporal adverb *now*, which must have been intended to form a rhetorical antithesis with the earlier *ere*, the two adverbs marking out the temporal distance between the two creedally distant figures. Here, too, alliterative compensation may be present on the copula and in the form of supplementary-alliteration on the syllable initiating *p* in *Appolyn* and *Petre*. Given the rhetorical structure of the line, we are probably correct in reading it *aa/(a)xx*, or, if accepting the supplementary alliteration on *p*, as *aa(b)/(a)xb*.

4.1

When we look at non-*aa/ax* lines in *Sir Gawain and the Green Knight*, we find exceptional alliterative and rhythmical variety, the two often combining to impressive effect and not infrequently supplemented by internal assonance or consonance. In lines 151–61 from the description of the Green Knight, half or more of the lines contain nonnormative patterns. Throughout the example for *SGGK*, I have marked only those alliterative patterns which depart from the norm.

	Ande al grayþed in grene þis gome and his wedes:
axa/ax	A strayt cote ful streȝt þat stek on his sides,
aax/ax	A mere mantile abof, mensked withinne
	With pelure pured apert, þe pane ful clene
aaa/xa	With blyþe blaunner ful bryȝt, and his hod boþe,

þat watz laȝt from his lokkez and layde on his
    schulderes;

aaa/?(a)xx   Heme wel-haled hose of þat same grene,

aa/?xax   þat spenet on his sparlyr, and clene spures vnder

?axa/ax   Of bryȝt golde, vpon silk bordes barred ful ryche,

And scholes vnder schankes þere þe schalk rides.

aa/xa   And alle his vesture uerayly watz clene verdure.

The *Gawain* poet's ear and technical versatility prove especially valuable in passages conveying direct speech, which he intersperses with vocatives of address, mild oaths, enjambed lines, variously heavy junctures at the caesura, the use of prolonged anacrusis, and the kind of syntactically independent parenthetical assertions common in speech but not in formal or written language (see, for example, lines 1218, 1251–2). It is not surprising, therefore, to find that he manipulates the alliteration as well, but discreetly. Throughout both scenes, a dramatically expressive reading urges promotion of a certain number of non-alliterating syllables, as in lines 1218, 1222, 1487, 1493.

Gawain's first words to the lady in the first Temptation Scene:

'Goud moroun, gay', quoþ Gawayn þe blyþe,

'Me schal worþe at your wille, and þat me wel lykeȝ,

For I ȝelde me ȝederly, and ȝeȝe after grace,

a(a)x/ax   And þat is þe best, be my dome, for me byhoueȝ nede.'

ax/ax   And þus he bourded aȝayn with mony a blyþe laȝter.

xaa/ax   'Bot wolde ȝe, lady louely, þen, leue me grante

And deprece your prysoun and pray hym to ryse,

aa/aa   I wolde boȝe of þis bed and busk me better;

I schulde keuer þe more comfort to karp yow wyth.'

(1213–21)

The lady's reply:

?xaa/aa   'Nay for soþe, beau sir', sayd þat swete,

ab/ab   'ȝe schal not rise of your bedde, I rych yow better,

aa/(a)aa   I schal happe yow here þat oþer half als,

And syþen karp wyth my knyȝt þat I kaȝt haue.'

(1222–5)

and:

ax/ax   Bot hit ar ladyes innoȝe þat leuer wer nowþe

(a)aa/aa   Haf þe, hende, in hor holde, as I þe habbe here,

To daly with derely your daynte wordez

aa/aa	Keuer hem comfort and colen her carez,
xa/ax	þen much of þe garysoun other golde that they hauen.

(1251–5)

From Gawain's reply at the close of the first Temptation:

	'Madame', quoþ þe myry mon, 'Mary yow ȝelde …
	Bot þe daynte þat þay delen for my disert nys euer –
ax/ax	Hit is þe worchyp of yourself, þat noȝt bot wel connez.'

(1263–7)

The same distinctive hand is at work in the second Temptation Scene. As before, metrical and rhythmical variation alternately move and halt the narrative. Instead of the formula of address, and with it the normative alliterative pattern, it opens with direct words from the lady in a nonnormative pattern:

xa/ax	'Sir, ȝif ȝe be Wawen, wonder me þynkkez,
a(a)a/x(a)x	Wyȝe þat is so wel wrast always to god
	And connez not of compaynye þe costez vndertake,
	And if mon kennes yow hom to knowe, þe kest
	hom of your mynde:
	þou hatz forȝeten ȝederly þat ȝisterday I taȝt te
xaa/ax	Bi alder-truest token of talk þat I cowþe.'
xa/(a)ax	'What is þat?' quoþ þe wyghe. 'Iwysse I wot neuer.
xa/ax	If hit be sothe þat ȝe breue, þe blame is myn awen.'
	'ȝet I kende yow of kyssyng', quoþ þe clere þenne,
aa/aa	'Quereso countenaunce is couþe, quikly to clayme;
	þat bicumes vche a knyȝt þat cortaysy vses.'
(a)xa/ax	'Do way', quoþ þat derf mon, 'my dere, þat speche,
?xaa/ax	For þat durst I not do, lest I deuayed were.
	If I were werned, I were wrange, iwysse, ȝif I
	profered.'
(a)xa/ax	'May fey', quoþ þe mere wyf, 'ȝe may not be
	werned;
	ȝe ar stif innoghe to constrayne wyth strenkþe, if
	yow lykez …'

(1481–96)

xa/ax	And ȝe, þat ar so cortays and coynt of your hetes,
xa/ax	Oghe to a ȝonge þynk ȝern to schewe
	And teche sum tokeneȝ of trweluf craftes.

xa/ax   Why! ar ȝe lewed, þat alle þe los weldeȝ?

(1525–8)

The second exchange ends with Gawain's apology, and although the alliterative line is more orthodox than variant, the rhythms expressed in the linguistic segmentals and enjambed lines deflect the attention of both listener and reader from the alliterative style.

'In goud fayþe', quoþ Gawayn, 'God yow forȝelde'. . .

aax/ax   Bot to take þe toruayle to myself to trwluf expoun
           And towche þe temez of tyxt and talez of armez

xa(a)/ax   To yow, þat (I wot wel) weldez more slyȝt

?xaa/ax   Of þat art, bi þe half, or a hundreth of seche
           As I am, oþer euer schal in erde þer I leue,
           Hit were a fole felefolde, my fre, by my trawþe.'

(1535–45)

If all these many verses, or any proportion of them, are scribal corruptions, it was a most crafty and creative scribe, and one who deserves equal credit for much of the imaginative energy behind this exceptional poem.

To paraphrase Abraham's negotiation with God over the numbers to be saved (*Cleanness* 715–65), if fifty, or ten, or even five lines composed in a nonnormative pattern (including the eccentric and anomalous ones) can be shown to be *reȝtful*, should we not then reconsider the possibility that such patterns might equally have served the poet's needs, and even upon occasion served them better?

Notes

1 The textual emendations of Gollancz (1921) will be well known; the scansions supplied by Sapora (1977) are equally governed by alliterative considerations.
2 Russom (1987) has mapped out the metrical and linguistic factors regulating alliteration. McCully, however (this volume), suggests that even in OE, alliteration may be merely a stylistic ornament rather than a structural linguistic feature of the underlying verse line. On some rule-governed features of ME alliteration, see also McCully and Hogg (1994).
3 Compare the views of Derek Pearsall: 'In Old English, alliteration served the structural function of linking the freely-running half-lines in couples; in Middle English, the half-lines are bound together by natural rhythm in a

strongly end-stopped line and alliteration is no longer structurally indispensable' (1977: 160), and Norman Davis: 'There is no fixed rhythmical relation between the first and second half-lines, but they are knit together into a single whole by means of alliterating sounds, of which at least one must obviously fall in each half. These alliterating sounds nearly always begin stressed syllables' (1968: 149).

4 Abbreviations

AlexA	*Alexander* (A/B texts)
Clean	*Cleanness*
DestTr	*Destruction of Troy*
GGK	*Gawain and the Green Knight*
MA	*Morte Arthure*
Pat	*Patience*
PTA	*Parlement of the Thre Ages*
PP	*Piers Plowman*
StErk	*St Erkenwald*
SJ	*Siege of Jerusalem*
WarsA	*Wars of Alexander*
W&W	*Wynner and Wastoure*

5 A. V. C. Schmidt (1987) uses this line as an example of a 'minimally-staved' verse (i.e. *ax/ax*) which, despite the judgement of Kane–Donaldson (1975), we should accept as genuine, particularly since it is 'uniformly attested in all versions (A V 14 / C V 116 / Z V 32)'. Schmidt answers the Kane–Donaldson objection that the line was allowed to stand in C because it was so well known. He argues that this 'logically tells *for* rather than *against* the authenticity of *ax/ax*' (p. 33 n. 46).

6 Schmidt (1987: 36) refers to nonmetrical alliterating syllables as 'mute' staves, the term of course borrowed from Schumacher, and defines a mute stave as one which carries alliteration but not stress and which may be understood as a 'correlative' to the 'blank' stave (i.e. nonalliterating stress).

7 See Schumacher (1914: 57–62).

8 Thus, function words may in certain contexts receive the strongest stress of the utterance, as, for example, in hyperbolic speech: 'My dear, it was simply THE event of the year!'

9 For example: *St Erkenwald* 4, 20; *Siege of Jerusalem* 232, 894; *Morte Arthure* 899, 940, 1069; *Piers Plowman* C II 87.

10 While Modern British English gives reduced or weak stress to the titular *saint*, other dialects of English (North American, for instance) accord the honorific a degree of stress which could make it metrically salient in verse, and it may be that ME (or some dialects of ME) granted *saint* a similar degree of stress. If so, *Saint Erkenwald* 35 is the only example I can find of such treatment in long-line alliterative poetry.

10   The prosody of Middle English 'Pearl' and the alliterative lyric tradition

Richard Osberg

Appreciations of the ME poem *Pearl* are unanimous in their admiration of its technical mastery, its brilliant and demanding stanza, its complex concatenation, and its numerological virtuosity. The history of editorial and critical opinion regarding *Pearl*'s metrics is therefore doubly remarkable for the uncompromising polarity of its conflicting postulates, epitomised in Cawley's (1962: 150) and Tolkien's (1975: 146) respective descriptions of the line:

In order to recapture the rhythms of *Pearl* the line should be read as a development of the native four-stress alliterative line, and not as a clumsy attempt to put together four iambs or anapaests.[1]

The line in *Pearl* is a French line, modified primarily (a) by the difference of English from French generally, and (b) by the influence of inherited metrical practices and taste, especially in the areas where the alliterative tradition was still strong. The essential features of the ancient English alliterative practice are wholly unlike, in effect and aim, what is found in *Pearl*.[2]

There is oddly little middle ground.[3] Although the alliterative lyrics of MS Harley 2253 exhibit similar prosodic features, the relationship of *Pearl*'s metrics to those of rhymed alliterative verse has been infrequently observed.[4] Like the verse of the earlier Harley lyrics, *Pearl*'s verse is essentially heteromorphic,[5] composed in the tumbling rhythms of alliterative half-lines, the chief metrical features of which are sketched by John Thompson (1966: 38):

The structure of *Pearl* is identified as four-beat by the pattern of junctures and the pattern of the stresses . . . The essential feature of the pattern of junctures is that the line is formed of two half-lines, indicated by the phrasing of the language. The essential metrical elements within the half-line are 'lifts' and 'dips', the lift being the metrical equivalent of a relatively strong stressed syllable, the dip the metrical equivalent of a relatively weak-stressed syllable.

My chapter amplifies Thompson's notion of half-line composition in *Pearl*, establishing lexical stress rules for the scansion of 408 lines in which final *-e* and plural and preterite suffixes are not present. Noting that rhyme provides a designated terminal element independent of lexical or syntactic boundaries (Hogg and McCully 1987: 209), I will suggest that rhyme exerts in the second half-line a strong tendency towards alternating stress (footing), even against lexical prominence or alliterative patterns. The tendency towards footing can also be discerned in first half-lines containing only one lexical prominence, where nonmetrical features (alliteration, rhyme, syntactic parallelism) support an alternating-stress interpretation. With the exception of a limited number of lines in which clashing stress can be shown to fall into four syntactic frames, application of rules governing lexical stress and secondary footing to the lines of *Pearl* suggests that suffixes and etymological and historical final *-e* are metrically significant syllables in *Pearl*'s prosody. A comparison of the half-line types in *Pearl* with those of the alliterative Harley lyrics points to the underlying similarity of their metrics.

I. Rules of scansion

Following Thompson's intuitions about the line, I suggest the following rules for scansion.[6]

1. The rhythmical unit is the two-stress phrase, corresponding usually to a half-line.
2. In the phrase, the root syllable of lexical words (verbs, substantives, adjectives, and adverbs) exhibits prominence.[7]
3. Final *-e* occurring before a vowel or *h* is elided.[8]
4. When two lexical stresses are present in the half-line, trisyllabic forms are usually syncopated.

Leaving aside for the moment lines in which final *-e* or a plural or preterite suffix complicates matters, *Pearl* contains 178 lines whose first and second half-lines provide a range of recurrence for basic half-line types (see Table 1, col. 1). In so far as it is reasonable to expect groups of lines to exhibit roughly similar distributions of half-line types, this primary sample constitutes a baseline of distributions against which to compare the scansion of groups of lines complicated by stress elevation, by suffixes, and by final -e. First-half-line N types (see note 5) range between 47 and 52 per cent recurrence; A types between 38 and 43 per cent; B types between 4 and 7 per cent; and C types 2 per cent. Second half-lines exhibit 71.3 per cent N types, 27.4 per cent A types, 1.6 per cent B types, and 2 per cent C types.

Since the so-called clashing stress constitutes a characteristic feature of alliterative verse, excluded from accentual-syllabic verse, an examination of C types and the role of final -e in their occurrence is warranted. Northup (1897) identified 13 first half-lines and 17 second half-lines as potentially exhibiting clashing stress, although most of these are scribal.[9] There remain, however, a small but significant number of lines, conforming to four grammatical-metrical (grammetrical) frames,[10] in which prominence produces a clashing, or at least an ambiguous, stress. I find that 22 first half-lines and 29 second half-lines exhibit clashing stress.

In the absence of two lexical stresses, some half-lines are composed of a disyllabic substantive containing two long vowels. (Gordon 1953: 108 notes that the poet likes the combination $/ \setminus$ x, as in 'wodshawe, godnesse'). This combination may occasionally substitute for a first half-line (39, 81, and 1014, for instance); more frequently for a second:

> Bot my Lorde þe Lombe   þur3 hys godhede (413) wwssw
> Arayed to þe weddyng   in þat hyl-coppe (791) wwssw
> þat is to say   as her byrþ-whate3 (1041) wwssw

A second formula has the syntactic frame (adv $<>$ v $\pm$ pron) or ($\pm$ pron + adv $<>$ v):

> Now tech me   to þat myry mote (936) ssw   wwSwSw
> þer hit doun drof   in molde3 dunne (30) wwSS   wswSw
> þat þou so styke3   in garlande gay (1186) wwSSw   wSwwS

In second half-lines especially, minor modification of word order would give rise to alternate-stress constructions (i.e. 980 'as forth I dreued'):

> þe sunne wat3 doun   and hit wex late (538) wsws   wwss
> And blusched on þe burghe   as I forth dreued (980) wSwwwS
> wwssw
> To swymme þe remnaunt,   þa3 I þer swalte (1160) wSwsw
> wwsSw

A third formula in both first and second half-lines entails an uninflected modifier and a substantive:

> Suche odour   to my herne3 schot (58) Ssw   wwswS
> Nis no wy3 worþe   þat tonge bere3 (100) wwSSw   wswsw
> þre worde3   hat3 þou spoken at ene (291) ssw   wwswws
> Al blysnande whyt   wat3 hir beau biys (197) wSws   wwSSw
> Vch pane of þat place   had þre 3ate3 (1034) wSwwS   wssw

A fourth formula involves a nominative or accusative substantive and a verb in final (and usually rhyme) position. It is worth noting that in a number of these cases, a minor syntactical change would have precluded the question of clashing stress (i.e. 69 'þe ly3t of hem no mon my3t leuen'):

> Hys lef is.   I am holy hysse (418) wsS   wwSwS
> þe ly3t of hem   my3t no mon leuen (69) wSws   wwsSw
> So gracios gle   couþe no mon gete (95) wSwS   wwsSw
> þen I cowþe telle   þa3 I tom hade (134) wSwS   wwSsw

as well as 637, 667, and 815.

These C types account for roughly 2 per cent of first and second half-lines, a percentage that tallies almost exactly with that in the Harley lyrics. Not as salient as in the alliterative long line, clashing stress persists nonetheless as a feature of rhymed alliterative verse.

In addition to the 178 lines without final -e or a suffix, there remain 230 lines requiring stress elevation. In such lines, it seems desirable to invoke an alternate-stress rule for two reasons: footing is frequently exhibited in second half-lines employing French loan words,[11] and both second and first half-lines employing polysyllabic words often result in alternate stress.[12] However promoted by rhyme, the tendency towards alternate stress (to be found also in the rhyme use of prepositions – 'þat alle þys worlde hat3 wro3t vpon', 824 – or forms of to be – 'If þou wyl knaw what kyn he be', 794) is not simply a result of it but may be found in first half-lines as well.[13] Evidence of footing in the stress elevation of pronouns, prepositions, and forms of to be may be discovered in the deployment of certain nonmetrical features: alliteration, internal rhyme, and parallel syntactic structures.

II. Semantic and lexical markers of prominence

Aside from a natural tendency towards footing in the language itself or a hierarchy of nonlexical items, i.e. modals before pronouns, pronouns before auxiliaries, auxiliaries before prepositions, and so on (Hogg and McCully 1987: 259), heteromorphic verse offers little justification for invoking a secondary alternate-stress rule. However, among a number of nonmetrical features seconding prominence to nonlexical syllables, alliteration, internal rhyme, and rhetorical parallelism are conspicuous in reinforcing rhythms of alternating syllables.[14] Line 199 exhibits all three of these nonmetrical features:

> Al blysnande whyt watȝ hir beau biys,
> Vpon at sydeȝ, and bounden bene
> Wyth þe myryeste margarys, at my deuyse,
> þat euer I seȝ ȝet with myn ene   (197–200)

The question of whether 'at' or 'my' in this line is elevated to prominence resists an easy answer. Does Gollancz's 'trisyllabic rhythm' govern the expectation for prominence on 'at'? That is:

> x   x   /   x x   /   x x   /   x   x /   x
> Wyth þe myryeste margarys at my deuyse

Alternatively, does half-line composition, with rhythmically dissimilar half-lines joined by alliteration, govern the expectation of prominence on 'my'? That is:

> x   x   /   x x   /   x x   x   /   x /   x
> wyth þe myryeste margarys / at my deuyse

I will argue for the second reading, an A-type first half-line joined to an N-type second half-line, with prominence seconded to 'my' by alliteration, rhyme, and a syntactic strategy of contrasting first-person and third-person pronouns ('*hir* beau biys' / '*my* devyse').

A frequent companion of lexical syllables in *Pearl*, alliteration might well underline the stress of elevation of function words, as in line 748, 'þat wroȝt þy wede he *watȝ* ful wys', or in line 843, in which the auxiliary alliterates, 'þat mot ne masklle *moȝt* on streche'. Syntactic inversion may also provide the occasion for elevating alliterating prepositions to prominence, as in line 46, 'A fayr reflayr ȝet *fro* hit flot', in which the rhyme of the first half-line (underscoring the juncture of the half-line) is mirrored in the consonance of the second half-line. Matonis (1988) has shown how the Harley lyrics reveal complex patterns of consonance, and in many of *Pearl*'s lines consonants are likewise intricately inter-woven; here, for instance, the line plays on fr/rflr/ /tfr/tflt.

The alliteration of function words may serve not only to provide prominence in the half-line but to link half-lines as well. In line 710, 'He loke on bok and be awayed', internal rhyme marks the juncture of the half-lines, and the alliteration of 'bok' and 'be' links the two half-lines. Alliteration of atonic words serves as one nonmetrical marker by which the *Pearl* poet signals prominence for a nonlexical syllable and (as many of these examples suggest) underscores a rhythm of alternating strong and weak stressed syllables.

In addition to marking the juncture of the half-line, internal rhyme also seconds the prominence of function words, as in line 979: 'Tyl on a hyl þat I asspyed', (swws / wswsw). Notice that, as in the previous exam-ples, rhyme defines the juncture of the half-lines: 'tyl/hil', 'I/spye' in this line. However, it also marks prominence even against the syntactic sense of the line: prose rhythm suggests that prominence might fall on the demonstrative pronoun 'þat' – the 'mote', or 'burgh' – but the narra-tive 'I', elsewhere thematically salient, is here marked by internal rhyme as well.

In some cases, internal rhyme, like alliteration, not only defines the junctures of the half-lines but links rhythmically dissimilar half-lines as well: 'If ȝe con *se* hyt *be* todone' (914) or 'Schal *sve*, tyl *þou* to a hil be *veu*ed' (976). In line 976, rhyme helps promote the pronoun 'þou', but 'hil' picks up the unstressed 'tyl' in much the way secondary alliteration (the r's and t's of line 46, for example) decorates the line. Some poignancy resides in the secondary rhyme of 'tyl' and 'hill', since these are the Pearl maiden's last words; she will follow the jeweller along the opposite shore until (imagine the jeweller's reaction if he had under-stood that as 'only until') he comes to the hill with its view of the celes-tial city. She then rejoins the virginal procession, breaking off the dialectic of personal pronouns so neatly balanced in her final speech:

> If I þis m͡ote þe schal vnhyde
> Bow vp towarde þys borneȝ heued
> And I anendeȝ þe on þis syde
> Schal sve, tyl þou to a hil be veued   (973–6)

The chiastic 'I' and 'þou' of this passage (I/þe, I/þe, þou/. . .) ironically finds its concluding term in the jeweller's 'þen wolde I no lenger byde'; 'þou' does not reappear until line 1183, following the jeweller's wakening affirmation 'Now al be to þat Prynceȝ paye'.

Third in the poet's repertoire of nonmetrical markers of stress elevation is a series of parallel syntactic constructions which direct the placement of emphasis, particularly antimonies of personal pronouns and prepositions. For example, the contrasting structure of the narrative 'I' and the 'þou' of direct address may be read as an index of the jeweller's wilfulness in mistaking the good, as in the opposition of 'I' and 'your' in line 393: 'For *I* am ful fayn þat *your* astate'. So controlling is this dialectic that, in some lines, lexical prominence is subordinated. The jeweller's indignation at what he takes to be Pearl's claim that she, in her innocence, has been rewarded above one who has endured temptation is given expression in the stress reduction of 'com' and elevation of 'hym' (the one who has endured) in contrast to 'þou': 'And *þou* to payment com *hym* before' (598). In the parable of the vineyard section, such advancement of one pronoun at the expense of another is given thematic resonance in the labourer's complaint that the Lord considers of equal merit those who worked two hours and those who worked all day: 'And þou dotȝ hem vus to counterfete' (556). Here it is impossible to assign prominence to one or another of the pronouns; in contrast to 'þou', 'hem' and 'vus' are unresolved. This play with pronouns (the labourer is insisting that 'vus' should take precedence over 'hem') picks up a major theme of the poem, the dichotomous key on which hierarchy (at least from the jeweller's perspective) is based.

That perspective, however, the jeweller finally relinquishes, signalled by the unambiguous subordination of the 'I' and concomitant elevation of 'hit', his last reference to Pearl: 'And syþen to God I hit bytaȝte' (1207). When we recall the pronominal ambiguity of the opening stanza, the stress elevation of the pronoun here (aided perhaps by the consonance of d and t's) signals that the jeweller has subordinated his will to God's.

Like the binary opposition of pronouns, pairs of prepositions are elevated to prominence by structures of contrast as in line 13: 'Syþen in þat spote hit fro me sprange'. In the juxtaposition of 'in þat spote', with its connotations of domain, dominion, and control, and 'fro me sprange', with its connotations of mishap, distress, and loss, resides one of the jeweller's most ineradicable misapprehensions, the prepositional security of place and possession maintained against the Pearl maiden's insistence on transformation and transcendence.

The Pearl maiden's attempt to distinguish her present state from that of the earthly rose occurs in a speech in which the shifting prominence of atonic words serves a singularly playful, if nonetheless didactic end:

> To say your perle *is* al awaye
> þat *is in* cofer so comly clente
> As *in* þis gardyn gracios gaye
> *Hereinne* to lenge for euer and play
> þer mys nee mornyng com neuer nere.
> *Her* were a forser for þe, in faye.   (258–63)

In these lines the contrast between what is lost ('is al awaye') and found ('Her were a forser') plays itself out in the repetitions of the phrase 'is in here': unstressed 'is' in line 258 becomes elevated to prominence in 259; unstressed 'in' of 259 is elevated to prominence in 260; 'here' and 'inne', ambiguously stressed in 261, are finally resolved as 'Her' in 263, a resolution reinforced by the quadruple rhyme of 'þer', 'nere', 'Her', and 'were'. In the absence of two lexical stresses in the half-line, nonmetrical features reinforce a pattern of alternate stress and support the invocation of a secondary alternate stress rule.

III. Scansion with an alternate stress rule

The application of an alternate-stress rule in 230 half-lines without final -*e* or plural or past suffixes and containing a single lexical prominence gives rise to a significantly different distribution of types from the half-line distribution of the 178 lines with four lexical stresses.[15] Half-lines requiring a nonlexical element to be raised to prominence (Table 10.1, col. 2) are notably more regular rhythmically than are those half-lines with two lexically stressed elements (Table 10.1, col. 1). Among N-type first half-lines, for instance, the type wSwS rises from 27 per cent of the 178 lines with four lexical prominences to 33.6 per cent of the total 408 lines. If nontetrameter lines were the result of scribal error or of scribally unrecorded apocope, syncope, elision, and so forth, rhythmic variation should be evenly distributed between first and second

Table 10.1. *Frequency of half-line types in 'Pearl' percentages*

	1st half-lines	1	2	2nd half-lines	1	2
N types	**(1: 46%; 2: 55%)**			**(1: 68.5%; 2: 73.3%)**		
SwS	More and more (145)	3.9	4.6	ryche arayed (719)	–	1.7
SwSw	Weþer welnygh (581)	0.5	1.4	for þe layned (244)	3.3	5.6
wSwS	þe blod vus boȝt (651)	27	33.6	hit syȝ wyth syȝt (985)	22.4	23.3
wSwSw	Ne neuer nawþer (485)	12.9	12.3	me comfort kenned (55)	42.6	41.6
wwSwwS	Bot þe water watȝ depe (143)	1	2.3			0.9
A types	**(1: 44.3%; 2: 35.5%)**			**(1: 24.7%; 2: 20.7%)**		
SwSww	Oute of oryent (3)	1	0.7			
SwwS	Delyt me drof (1153)	5	5.5	out of þat flet (1058)	5	3.1
SwwSw	Wrypen and worchen (511)	5	3.8	ȝet with myn yȝen (200)	2.8	5
wSwwS	Vch pane of þat place (1034)	14.6	13.8	by stock oþer ston (380)	4.4	0.9
wSwwSw	Is worpen to worschyp (394)	7.3	4.7	wyth lyttel atslykeȝ (575)	5.6	4.3
wSwwSww	þer wonys þat worþyly (47)	0.5	0.1	I sette hyr sengeley (8)	1	3.9
wwSwS	As þat foysoun flode (1058)	6	4.6	of þys gracious gote (934)	6.7	3.4
wwSwSw	On þe mount of Syon (868)	1.6	1.1			
wwSwwSw	Fro þat maskeleȝ mayster (900)	1	0.5			
B types	**(1: 4.4%; 2: 4.7%)**			**(1: 1.6%; 2: 1.8%)**		
Swwws	Doun after a strem (125)	2	1.1	hider arn we wonne (517)	1.1	1.2
Swwwsw	Temen to hys body (460)	0.5	–			

Table 10.1. (cont.)

Pattern	Example	1	2	Example	1	2
wSwwwS	And don me in þys del (250)	0.5	0.5			0.3
wwSwwws	For a pene on a day (510)	0.5	–			
wwwSwSw	Hit is a dom þat neuer (667)	0.5	1.4			
Swww(*)S		–	1.7	neuer for to declyne (333)	0.5	0.2
C types (1: 3.3%; 2: 2.6%)				C types (1: 2.2%; 2: 2.2%)		
*wSS	þer hit doun drof (30)	2.2	0.4	watȝ hir beau biys (197)	1.6	–
SSw*	þre wordeȝ (291)	1.1	1.4	God gaue (197)	0.6	–

1: Scansion of half-lines using lexical word stress in 178 lines without -e, preterit or plural suffixes, or stress elevations; 2: 408 lines when stress elevations are included.

half-lines. However, this is not the case; second half-lines exhibit regular alternation of stressed and unstressed syllables more frequently than do first half-lines; N types in second half-lines account for 73 per cent of the 408 lines studied; in first half-lines, they represent only 54 per cent of that total. Likewise, A types in second half-lines account for only 20 per cent, whereas in first half-lines they account for 35.5 per cent.

Moreover, first half-lines offer a greater variety of A types than do second, with ten varieties of A types in first half-lines, six in second half-lines. The incidence of B types in first half-lines (4.7 percent) is more than that in second half-lines (1.8 percent), again suggesting the greater frequency of rhythmic variation in first half-lines.

Although second half-lines in rhymed alliterative verse do not conform to the rules of composition discovered by Cable (1988a) and Duggan (1986a,b) for the alliterative long line, this distribution conforms to a general principle of the alliterative tradition, that the line tends to a right-edge metrical strictness. The lack of variety of types and greater frequency of N types in second half-lines suggests a right-hand rule in the line and vitiates the argument that *Pearl*'s line is iambic tetrameter disguised by scribal error.

IV. Scansion of lines with suffixes and final -e

Of the 669 first half-lines exhibiting either final -*e* or a suffix, 218 exhibit only a suffix, 68 of which contain suffixes 'required' as metrical syllables by an alternate stress rule.[16] The use of inflection in *Pearl* for metrical purposes is conservative but conforms in the main to what Jordan (Crook 1974: 246) suggests was the standard in the North in the later fourteenth century. When a suffix is required, the recurrence of N types is high (72%), as is the recurrence of N types in the first half-lines when a stress elevation is required – that is, the alternate-stress rule is more in evidence in these two situations, and regular alternation of syllables is more likely than not.

In addition to these lines, 158 lines exhibit a suffix that is not metrically required.[17] Combined with the 68 lines in which a suffix is necessary for metrical purposes, these lines provide the distributions shown in Table 10.1a; they fall within that range suggested by scansion of lines without final -*e* or suffixes.[18]

Table 10.1a. *Distributions from*
Table 10.1

	No stress elevation	Stress elevation
N types (41%)	46%	55%
A types (52%)	44%	35.5%
B types (7%)	4.4%	4.6%

Table 10.1b. *Distributions from*
Table 10.1

	No stress elevation	Stress elevation
N types (40.4%)	46%	55%
A types (53.7%)	44%	35.5%
B types (7.4%)	4.4%	4.7%

Three hundred and sixty-three first half-lines of *Pearl* exhibit at least one final -*e* but are free of suffixes, including 78 half-lines in which final -*e* is a necessary metrical syllable.[19] Including these 78 half-lines in the group of first half-lines that have one or more final -*e* but no suffixes (363 lines), the distribution in Table 10.1b obtains, counting all -*e*'s as metrical syllables.[20] The rhythm wSwwSw, occurring often when final -*e* is read as a metrical syllable, is characteristic of alliterative lyric poetry.

Clearly, however, scribal final -*e* in *Pearl* has functions unrelated to etymological and historical final -*e*.[21] A comparison of the recurrence of first-half-line types in lines without final -*e* or suffixes with the recurrence of first half-line types in lines in which an etymological, scribal -*e* is present reveals the greatest congruence of any of the scansions proposed (Table 10.2).[22] Columns 3, 4 and 5 show reasonably similar distributions of N, A, and B types in first half-lines, suggesting that the scansion of lines with etymological and historical final -*e* as metrical syllables comes closest to replicating the metrical grammar obtaining in lines without final -*e* or suffixes. Column 5, showing the effect of stress elevation, and column 6, showing suffixes as metrical syllables, both reflect an increase in types whose rhythms are regular

Table 10.2. *Comparative scansions for first and second half-lines (percentages)*

	1	2	3	4	5	6	7	8	9	10	11
N types	40.4	70.2	45.4	46	55	69.2	89.5	32.3	81	44.7	71.3
A types	53.7	27.8	48.5	44.3	35.5	29.8	9.5	60	17.9	53.7	24.7
B types	7.4	4.9	4.8	4.4	4.7	1.9	0.9	4.6	1	2.4	1.6

1: First half-lines with final -*e* as metrical syllable.
2: First half-lines with final -*e* suppressed except for alternate stress rule.
3: First half-lines with etymological and historical -*e*.
4: First half-lines without final -*e*, suffixes, or stress elevation.
5: First half-lines without final -*e* or suffixes, with stress elevation.
6: 104 first half-lines with suffixes as metrical syllables.
7: 104 first half-lines with suffixes suppressed except for alternate stress rule.
8: Second half-lines with final -*e*.
9: Second half-lines with -*e* suppressed except for alternate stress rule.
10: 204 second half-lines with etymological -*e*.
11: Second half-lines without final -*e*, suffixes, or stress elevation.

alternations of syllables – that is, the effect of an alternate-stress rule – but even these increases in N types do not begin to approach the high incidence of N types if final -*e* and suffixes are suppressed except where they satisfy an alternate stress rule. The same appears to be true for second half-lines.

V. Lines with no caesura

Although in no line are second and third lifts contained within a single word, in some lines the two 'grammetrical' half-lines are difficult to discern. In a small group of lines, the mediation of two principles of composition – alliterative half-lines dominated by lexical prominence and half-lines dominated by an alternate-stress rule – allows half-lines to be consolidated into larger syntactical units. Half-lines are incorporated into lines that retain the loose rhythmical structure of half-line composition but in which the syntactic boundaries of the half-lines are no longer visible. One example of the ways in which the alternate-stress rule restructures the half-line prosody of *Pearl* involves a syntactic frame composed of a first half-line (sb <> v) joined to a second half-line

(prep ± pron + sb) in which the prepositional phrase functions adverbi-
ally:

> So schon þat shene   anvnder shore (166)
> þat beren þys perle   vpon oure bereste (854)
> His lyf wer loste   anvnder mone (1092)

In the absence of a lexically stressed substantive, this formula may be
modified to (aux <> v) or (v + v) in the first half-line: 'Oþer proferen þe
oȝt agayn þy paye' (1200).

In a number of lines, however, the prepositional phrase intervenes
between the substantive and verb, so that the contours of the half-lines
are obscured: 'þe wal abof þe bantels bent' (1017). In a few lines, this
formula is slightly modified: 'þay wente into þe vyne and wroȝte' (525),
'For pyty of my perle enclyin' (1206). In such lines there is no clear division of 'grammetrical' units into half-lines; instead, the prepositional
phrase occupies the second and third lifts in the line and the initial syntactic frame is broken up and accommodated by the first and fourth lifts.

A third modification of the formula, again one that obscures half-line
contours, occurs when a pronominal subject and verb are followed by a
prepositional phrase (prep + adj + sb): 'I felle vpon þat floury flaȝt' (57),
'I slode vpon a slepyng-slaȝte' (59), 'þay songen wyth a swete asent' (94),
'And brede vpon a bostwys bem' (814). The initial verb establishes the
alliterative pattern; consonance generally occurs on the adjective mod-
ifying the object of the preposition. In every case, an alternate-stress rule
is in effect. Since in a number of these lines syntactical elements can
easily be rearranged while leaving the rhyme word in the terminal position (i.e. 'Into þe vyne þay wente and wroȝte'), it seems likely that the
position of the preposition either in the second lift (sandwiched between
two alliterated lexical prominences) or in the third (generally following
two alliterated lexical prominences) is a response to a stress-elevation
rule for prepositions arising from the alternate-stress rule.

VI. Comparison with alliterative Harley lyrics

As I have shown elsewhere (Osberg 1984), accentual-syllabic verse in
the lyrics preserved in MS Harley 2253 demonstrates a variety of half-
line types quite distinct from those exhibited by that manuscript's
rhymed alliterative verse. Greater congruence obtains between half-line

Table 10.3. *Half-line types in 'Pearl' and the Harley lyrics (percentages)*

	Pearl		Alliterative Harley lyrics		Accentual-syllabic Harley lyrics	
	1st h-l	2nd h-l	1st h-l	2nd h-l	1st h-l	2nd h-l
N type	55	73.3	62.6	60.9	81.5	83.1
A type	35.5	20.7	22.8	31	17.2	14.2
B type	4.7	1.8	11.8	5	0.4	1.3
C type	1.8	2.3[a]	1.4	2	0.0	0.0

[a]These percentages exclude lines that do not fall into half-lines.

types in *Pearl* and in the alliterative Harley lyrics than between *Pearl*'s half-lines and those of the accentual-syllabic Harley verse. While the distribution of half-line types is by no means identical, Table 10.3 reveals greater similarities than differences between the half-line types of *Pearl* and those of the alliterative Harley lyrics. *Pearl* and the alliterative Harley lyrics exhibit clashing stress in roughly the same percentage of their lines, a bit more frequently in second than in first half-lines. Although the alliterative Harley lyrics make more frequent use of B types, especially in first half-lines, in his deployment of both B and N types the *Pearl* poet pays increased attention to the regular alternation of syllables in second half-lines. However, the increased iambic character of second half-lines in *Pearl* does not give rise to lines of regular iambic rhythm. The N type wSwS may well be followed by wwswwsw, swwsw, or sSwwSw:

I do me ay   in hys myserecorde (366) wsws   wwswws
Of erytage   ʒet non wyl ho chace (443) wsws   wwsws
Innoghe þer wax   out of þat welle (649) wSwS   SwwSw

In lines where one half-line is a rhythmically regular N type, the other half-line may not be; in fact, of the 178 lines without stress elevation and uncomplicated by questions of final -*e* and other suffixes, only 37, that is, 20 per cent, combine N-type first and second half-lines to compose iambic tetrameter lines (i.e. 859, acephalous; and 644, 645, 1017, etc.). Furthermore, of the 408 lines without -*e* or suffixes, 124, or 30.3 per cent, combine types of all variety into regular and acephalous iambic tetrameter lines. In the alliterative Harley lyrics, by comparison, 33.6 per cent of the lines are regular iambic tetrameter, while in the nonalliterative Harley lyrics, 54.4 per cent of the lines are iambic tetrameter. Though syllabic regularity is more frequent in *Pearl* (especially in second half-lines) than in the alliterative Harley lyrics, there remains considerable latitude in the rhythmic variety of the whole line. That some scholars see in *Pearl* something like an iambic tetrameter line is not surprising, for two systems are at work – one, the tumbling rhythms of half-line composition, the other, an alternate-stress rule providing stress elevation for strings of nonlexical items.

Critical admiration for *Pearl*'s technical brilliance is seldom extended to the line itself. Seen against the metrics of rhymed alliterative verse, however, *Pearl*'s prosody reveals subtlety, intricacy, power, and grace. In the following lines, for instance, half-line 'grammetrical' structures, alliteration, syntactic parallelism, and associative rhythmical grouping work together to underscore a principal theme:

> þe oȝte better þyseluen blesse
> And loue ay God in wele and wo
> For anger gayneȝ þe not a cresse
> Who nedeȝ schal þole be not so þro
> For þoȝ þou daunce as any do
> Braundysch and bray þy braþeȝ breme
> When þou no fyrre may to ne fro
> þou moste abyde þat he schal deme (341–8)

The first 'for' in this passage functions unambiguously as a coordinating conjunction, meaning something like 'for this reason', linking the two imperative clauses with the third declarative. The ambiguity of the second 'for', however (part of the subordinating conjunction 'though' (as in the construction 'And for because þat he was so wel with god, þerfore þei worschipe him', *Mandev.* 109, 35) or a coordinating conjunction introducing a clause stating the reason for or cause of something), has led at least one editor to punctuate 'Be not so þro' as an independent clause, against the grain of all earlier editions. In Vantuono's edition, 'Be not so þro' follows as syntactically parallel to 'loue ay God', with 'for' as a coordinating conjunction linking the much-postponed second independent clause, 'þou most abyde'.[23] That is, the imperative 'Love God' with its 'for-this-reason' clause 'for anger gains you nothing' is parallel to the imperative 'Don't be stubborn' with its 'for-this-reason' clause 'for you must submit to God's will'. In such a reading, 'for' must be elevated to prominence to signal the suspension of the completed thought.

How the nonlexical string 'For þoȝ þou' is to be scanned, as wswS or as swwS, depends on which reading of the syntax one is prepared to accept. Some support for Vantuono's reading may be found in the prosody. The four first half-lines preceding 345, N types (wsws), establish a rhythmical pattern; the two first half-lines following 345, A types, 346 (SwwS) (the only first half-line in this passage marked by alliteration of both lexical syllables) and 347 (SwwSww), vary the rhythmical pattern; and the final line, an N type (wsws), resolves the variation. Half-lines in the alliterative Harley lyrics often show such associative rhythmical groupings. Possibly the three first half-lines of initial prominence, all associated with subordinate clauses and all hanging, as it were, on the suspended 'For this reason', mirror prosodically the limits of 'to ne fro' which one may traverse before submitting to God's will. The inevitability of that submission is suggested by the return to alternate stress in the final line's emphatic subjugation of 'þou' to 'moste', to the necessity of obeying God's will.

Notes

1 Gollancz took exception to Northup's analysis for 'not giving sufficient recognition to the trisyllabic character of the metre', but he also criticises Osgood's claim of the influence of the alliterative long line on the poem (1921: xxiii–xxiv, n 1). In addition to C. G. Osgood (1906), those who take the influence of the alliterative long line to be paramount include J. P. Oakden (1930, 1935) and particularly E. V. Gordon: 'The essential basis of the line consists of four stresses ("lifts"), around which are arranged unstressed elements ("dips"), varying in number from three to five. The position of the dips and the number of syllables in them is variable, the old rhythmic variety of the alliterative line being inherited and only slightly reduced by the addition of rhyme' (1953: 89–90). See also Sara DeFord (1967: ix), P. M. Kean (1967: 5), Charles Moorman (1986: 50), and most recently William Vantuono (1984: I, 368).

2 Among those editors and commentators arguing for an iambic tetrameter line in *Pearl* are Clark S. Northup (1897), Oliver Farrar Emerson (1921), and Frederick Von Ende (1973), who maintains that the poet was 'more familiar with the accentual-syllabic, end-rhymed, stanzaic verse style . . .

than he was with the older alliterative verse form'(p. 3065). Marie Borroff qualifies this: 'The meter of *Pearl* is more like musical rhythm than that of the traditional iambic line' (1977: 32). Thorlac Turville-Petre (1977: 67) points out that *Pearl*'s line is more regularly syllabic than the long lines of *Gawain*, linking *Pearl* to the regularly iambic poems of the Vernon manuscript, and Malcolm Andrew and Ronald Waldron argue for 'four-stressed accentual verse of an iambic pattern' (1978: 50). Most recently this position has been restated by Hoyt Duggan (1988a). See also Duggan, this volume.

3 Margaret Williams suggests the difficulty of formulating a middle ground: 'The prosody is the French four-beat line assimilated into the Anglo-Saxon alliterative line, or the alliterative cadence modified by the French syllabic beat. The balance eludes definition' (1967: 63).

4 Gollancz, p. xxiii n. l; Oakden, I, 235; and Turville-Petre, p. 67. *Pearl* belongs to a genre of rhymed alliterative verse whose metrics are little understood; see A. T. E. Matonis (1981) and Susanna Greer Fein (1989). The comparisons between *Pearl* and the Harley lyrics made here are based on my analysis of the alliterative Harley lyrics reported in 'Alliterative Technique in the Lyrics of MS Harley 2253' (Osberg 1984).

5 Angus McIntosh distinguishes heteromorphic rhythmical material, 'in which the basic "foot" units have a number of different forms', from homomorphic rhythmical material, which contains 'only one basic foot-unit' (1982: 21–2). Although I believe half-lines to be more useful than feet in describing *Pearl*'s rhythm, the distinction between heteromorphic and homomorphic forms is useful, and I differentiate four varieties of half-line: N types, which are homomorphic (wwSwwS, wSwS), and three varieties of heteromorphic half-lines: A types, (wSwwS, wwSwS); B types, three or more unaccented syllables in a dip (wwwSwS, SwwwS), and C types, the so-called clashing-stress half-lines.

6 I rely on Gordon's edition, noting emendations where they have metrical consequences. As Waldron and Andrew note to 'fayr reflayr', or 'faryre flayr' (1. 45), the scribe is not to be trusted even on matters of word division, although he is fairly consistent in reflecting the assimilation of *d/t* before thorn, and in recording apocope and syncope, especially in nasal environments. Gordon also notes the scribal loss of final -*e*, especially in the dative singular.

7 These two rules correspond to Duggan's Rules III and IV for the alliterative long-line. The major divergence between alliterative long-line prosody and that of alliterative lyrics seems to be in the coincidence of lexical stress and alliteration. Alliteration of the third lift is a condition of metricality in Duggan's (1986a, b, 1988a, b) analysis of the alliterative long line, although even on this point there is little consensus. It seems not to be a requirement in rhymed alliterative verse.

J.P. Oakden found that 63.7% of *Pearl*'s lines alliterate on stressed syllables; my scansion, including vocalic alliteration, finds 72.8% of the lines so alliterating:

4-stress	67 lines	5.5%
3-stress	240 lines	19.8%
2-stress	488 lines	40.2%
abab types	60 lines	4.9%
vocalic	36 lines	2.8%

OE types account for 16% of the alliterative types in both *Pearl* and the Harley lyrics; but in the deployment of late OE types, and in those which fail to bridge the caesura, significant differences emerge:

Types found in late Old English

Pearl 36.2%			Harley lyrics 54.2%	
aa/xa ;	88	7.2%	49	8.4%
xa/aa ;	57	4.7%	54	9.3%
aa/aa ;	67	5.5%	54	9.3%
ax/aa ;	53	4.3%	37	6.4%
aa/bb ;	40	3.3%	22	3.8%
ax/xa ;	55	4.5%	32	5.5%
xa/xa ;	79	6.5%	57	9.8%
Failures		*21.1%*		*12.8%*
aa/xx ;	124	10.3%	26	4.5%
xx/aa ;	131	10.8%	48	8.3%

The significant difference between the use of alliterative types in *Pearl* and in the Harley lyrics rests on the *Pearl* poet's willingness to use alliteration in one half-line exclusively. In the alliterative Harley lyrics, syllables with prominence alliterate in 83% of the lines; in *Pearl*, syllables with prominence alliterate in 72.8%.

8 As in the Harley lyrics, there seem to be occasional exceptions to this rule in *Pearl*: 'þaȝ I hente ofte' (388) (wwSSw or wwSwSw), for example.

9 Northup identified first half-lines in lines 30, 68, 87, 100, 393, 406, 527, 928, 1004, 1046, 1076, 1130, 1152, and second half-lines in lines 69, 105, 134, 197, 286, 381, 466, 486, 564, 586, 635, 667, 678, 995, 1034, 1036, 1041 as potentially clashing stresses. As Northup showed, a number of these may be ascribed to the loss of historical and etymological -*e*:

    a. ask: OE *axian*. Northup gives *ask[e]*, inf.

    b. bliss: Gordon lists the loss of this final -*e* as probably a scribal omission.

c. carp: ON *karpa*. An infinitive whose appearance here without final
   -*e* Gordon lists as scribal.

d. fyrst (twice): OE *fry(e)st*. Likewise noted by Gordon as scribal.

e. hy: OE *heh*. With acc. pl., *heh*[*e*] as weak adjective.

f. ilk: OE *ilca*. Northup compares the use in the acc. with *Gawain*, line
   1385.

g. long: OE *lengra*. Northup gives *long[e]* in the dat.

h. much: OE *mycel*. Northup here gives *much[e]*, a dat. he compares
   with 'muche', *PPl*. A. viii. 70.

i. nw: OE *neowe*. Northup lists both *nwe* and *newe* without noting line
   527. Gordon remarks that plural -*e* is often dropped.

j. rych (3 times): OE *rice*; OFr. *riche*. Northup gives *rych[e]*, nom. pl.,
   168, dat p., line 1036.

k. þryd: OE *þridda*. Northup gives *þryd[de]* with dat.

Other cases are at best problematic.

l. ber: OE *beran*. Here in the subj., which may or may not have -*e*.

m. com: OE *cuman*. Preterit subj. pl. ending -*en* reduced to -*e*.

n. frech: OE *fersc*, OFr *freis*. Gordon observes that the pl. -*e* is dropped
   in this case.

o. luf: OE *lufu*. Northup does not catalogue this word, but again, dat.
   sing. -*e* was often dropped by the scribe.

p. on: OE *an* declined as a strong adj.

q. self (twice): OE. *self*. Wright and Wright suggest that 'self' was
   declined either in a strong or weak declension in the nom. (p. 163),
   and Gordon notes the -*e* of the weak declension 'is one of the more
   stable final -*e*'s in the middle of the line' (p. 109).

Additionally, some words may have alternative forms or alternative pronunciations:

a. hed, also heued, OE *heafod*.

b. daunger (twice), OF *da(u)nger*; in line-terminal positions in
   Chaucer, wS (RR 1049; KT 1849); in medial position, Sw (Pr. 402)

c. doungoun, AF *doungoun*, in line-terminal position in Chaucer, wS
   (KT 1057).

10 See Wexler (1966) for 'grammetrical' and a discussion of the jointure of
   grammar and metre.

11 The strong tendency towards alternate stress (footing) at the expense of
   the alliterative pattern of the line is a tension not to be found in tetrameter
   verse – *The Owl and the Nightingale*, for instance. As has been long noted,
   words of French derivation shift lexical stress readily from one syllable to
   another, depending on rhyme, and in some poems, on ictus. In *Pearl* one

frequently meets such shifts; in line 193, for instance, 'of ryal prys', 'ryal' is stressed on its first syllable, but in line 191 'Ryseȝ vp in hir araye ryalle', it is stressed on the second syllable at the expense of a third alliterative syllable in the line. Such tension between the rhyme syllable and the alliterative syllable, fairly common in the Harley lyrics (i.e. 'heo is lilie of largesse / heo is paruenke of prouesse' (14.48–9)) is nearly invisible in accentual-syllabic poetry like *The Owl and the Nightingale*. The *Pearl* poet, however, makes extensive use of stress-shifting French rhymes:

> I hoped þat gostly watȝ þat porpose (185)
> And bornyste quyte watȝ hyr uesture (220)
> Caȝte of her coroun of grete tresore (237)

Furthermore, the *Pearl* poet often embellishes lexical stress in the lift with alliteration, so that there is a tension created between the expectation of stress occasioned by alliteration and the expectation occasioned by rhyme:

> Blysnande whyt watȝ hyr bleaunt (163)
> And don me in þys del and gret daunger (250)
> Thow demeȝ noȝt bot doel-dystresse (337)
> Quo formed þe þy fayre fygure? (747)
> þou telleȝ me of Jerusalem þe ryche ryalle (919)

Although alternate-stress rhythm is not an inevitable outcome of rhyme's shifting stress to the final syllable of French loan words (e.g. 'For ferly of þat frelich fygure', 1086; 'Watȝ sodanly ful wythouten sommoun', 1098), it does illustrate the tension between a system in which lexically stressed syllables are marked by alliteration and a system in which alliteration is subordinated to footing.

12   Polysyllables in second half-lines also tend to invoke footing, not only in homomorphic lines, but in lines with epic caesura as well:

> In helle in erþe   and Jerusalem (840) wSwS   wsws
> Of half so dere   adubbemente (72) wswS   wSwsw

Even when the rhythms of first half-lines are heteromorphic, or the initial rhythm of the second half-line seems to strain against alternate stress, polysyllables in rhyme position nearly always result in footing. The single exception I have been able to find is 'Gilofre, gyngure and gromylyoun' (43, SwwSw   wSwwS), although 'gromylyoun' may be trisyllabic, producing a line like 'In Jerusalem, Jordan, and Galaye' (817, wSwwSw   wsws).

13   This may be the result of a principle of rhythmical alternation; see Hogg and McCully's discussion of Selkirk (1987: 149, 183, and 208). In first half-lines containing two lexical stresses, trisyllabic forms are treated as syncopated. In a number of first half-lines, however, only one lexical stress is present, requiring the stress elevation of a second syllable:

Of courtaysye   as sayt3 Saynt Poule (457) wswS   wSwsw
By innocens   and not by ry3te (708) wsws   wswsw

See also lines 206, 443, 481, 672, 695, 829 for instances of alternate footing in polysyllables in first half-lines. Because we cannot be sure how radically the *Pearl* poet employs syncopation, a number of lines remain open to interpretation. In line 109, 'The dubbemente of þo derworth depe' (wSws wwSwSw), a scansion based on half-lines (that is, excluding 'of' from an ictus position) requires 'dubbemente' to be trisyllabic (as it is in rhyme; line 120, for instance). Duggan reads 'dubbement' here as disyllabic (compare line 121), throwing 'of' into ictus. A particularly vexed example is line 827, 'Hys generacyoun quo recen con', which might be scanned wwwsws   wsws (on the model of 'In þys veray avysyoun', line 1184) or wswSw   wSws (on the model of 'Jerusalem' as disyllabic). That the poet could employ multiple pronunciations is illustrated by his use of 'apoka-lypse', which ranges from four to two syllables in various lines:

In Appocalyppece   is wryten in wro (866) wwsws   wSwwS
In þe Apokalypce   is þe fasoun preued (983) wwSws   wwswSw

The deployment of polysyllabic forms in both first and second half-lines in *Pearl* suggests that in the absence of lexical stress an alternate stress rule may be invoked.

14 Clearly, such ornamental, rhetorical, and semantic features occur else-where in the poem without specific metrical consequences. It does not seem unreasonable to suppose that in diverse contexts similar features might have quite different effects.

15 Forty-three lines require at least one such promotion in each half-line; in addition, there are 93 lines in which only the second half-line requires a stress elevation. Additionally, there are 94 lines in which the first half-line requires a stress elevation but the second half-line does not.

16 Although even Skelton alternates forms in the plural of trisyllabic sub-stantives, none of these 68 lines occur in hiatus. Only one occurs follow-ing an atonic auxiliary, 'þou wolde3 knaw' (410), while three follow trisyllables, 'Dysplese3 not' (422), 'þe sunnebeme3' (83), and 'In Apokalype3' (834). In at least one case where we would expect syncope, 'And I hyred þe' (560), the scribe provides the suffix. Otherwise, these 68 suffixes conform to the principles outlined in Jordan's *Handbook of Middle English Grammar* (1974): covered *e* in inflectional endings *-es* (more rarely in *-ed*, *-eþ*), is lost, particularly in older (i.e. fourteenth-century) texts in third-syllable, hiatus (i.e. *day-es*), and atonic words. Inflections of adjectives and verbs, *-es*, *-e*, and *-ed*, are required as metrical syllables in, for instance, the following: 'Blome3 blayke' (27), 'Pensyf, payred' (246), 'Wyth lappe3 large' (201), 'My wreched wylle' (56), 'þe fyrre

I stalked' (152) (with enclitic pronoun), and lines 1112, 1144, 1189, etc.

Second half-lines also require a suffix as a metrical syllable to comply with an alternate-stress rule: 'burnist broun' (990), 'harmeʒ hate' (388), 'of ʍo gladneʒ glade' (136), and 'wythouten spotteʒ blake' (945).

17 In reading these suffixes, I have disregarded suffixes in hiatus, in trisyllabics (those required by alternate-stress rule are considered above), and in atonic auxiliaries. That is, 'I watʒ payed anon' (584) is an example of hiatus scanned wwSwS, and 'Hundreth ʍowsandeʒ' (1107) is an example of trisyllabic syncopation, scanned swsw.

18 It might be argued, however, that lines exhibiting suffixes do not use them as metrical syllables. Reading suffixes in these 226 lines only as needed to follow an alternate-stress rule gives rise to the following distributions: N types, 161 (71%); A types, 62 (27.4%). Thus, two very different distributions of types can be found in these lines. When suffixes are read as metrical units, a high percentage of A types occurs; when suffixes are discounted, a high percentage of N types occurs:

With suffix	Without suffix	No stress elevation	With stress elevation	
N types	41%	71%	46%	55%
A types	52%	27.4%	44.3%	35.5%
B types	7%	0.4%	4.4%	4.7%

The relationship between this sample set of lines and those without final -e or suffixes remains much closer when all suffixes are treated as metrical syllables than when suffixes are disregarded except to fulfil an alternate stress rule: a difference from the initial set of lines of 5 percentage points for N types and 8 percentage points for A types, as opposed to a difference from the initial set of lines of 25 percentage points for N- and 16.9 percentage points for A types.

Also, even in the relationship between specific types, a closer correspondence obtains between scansion including suffixes and the scansion of the primary group of 178 lines than otherwise. When suffixes are not considered as metrical syllables except for alternate-stress rules, a much higher incidence of Sws (5.7% v. 3.4%) and wSwS (46% v. 27%) occurs than is found in the primary group. Conversely, however, when suffixes are considered as metrical syllables, a much higher incidence of wSwSw and a much lower incidence of wSwS obtains.

19 In addition to the high percentage of the N-type wSwS (with final -e serving as the second dip) that might be expected, a number of other types occur, notably:

Hiȝe pynakled (207) (3 lines)	SwSww
Gotȝ to my vyne (535) (4 lines)	SwwSw
Gos into my vyne (521) (1 line)	Swwwsw
And when in hys place (405) (5 lines)	wSwwSw
And þe self[e] sunne (1076) (8 lines)	wwSwS(w)

In at least one case, final *-e* seems to sound even before a vowel: 'þaȝ I hente ofte' (388) wwSSw or wwSwSw.

As with suffixes, final *-e* is also required in some lines by an alternate-stress rule. Sixty-nine of the 804 lines require final syllabic *-e*:

N types

sute schene (203) (3 lines)	4.3%	SwSw
hys face flayn (809) (16 lines)	23.1%	wSwS
of rych[e] plateȝ (1036) (30 lines)	43.4%	wSwSw

A types

watȝ her lombe lyȝt (1046) (3 lines)	4.3%	wwSwS
in þe worlde rounde (657) (14 lines)	20.2%	wwSwSw

20 A revised scansion of these 363 lines, in which final *-e*'s that are not necessary for an alternate-stress rule are not sounded, provides the following distributions of types: N types, 255 lines (70.2%); A types, 101 lines (27.8%); and B types, 18 lines (4.9%).

21 Duggan notes, for instance, that scribal *-e* tends to occur after monosyllabic stems ending in a consonant cluster and following a single consonant to indicate the length of the tonic vowel.

22 The table presents the specific percentages of types.

	No final *-e*		Etymological *-e*	
N types				
sws	13	3.4%	8	1.9%
SwSw	5	1.3%	13	3.1%
wsws	106	27.8%	71	17.1%
wSwSw	48	12.6%	84	20.2%
wwSwwS	8	2.1%	10	2.4%
SwwSww	–	–	2	0.4%
Total	180	47.3%	188	45.4%
A types				
swsww	3	0.7%	3	0.7%
SwwS	21	5.5%	17	4.1%
SwwSw	19	5.0%	17	4.1%
wSwSww	3	0.7%	4	0.9%
wSwwS	58	15.2%	63	15.2%

Table (*cont.*)

No final -*e*			Etymological -*e*	
wSwwSw	24	6.3%	55	13.2%
wSwwSww	1	0.2%	1	0.2%
wwSwS	16	4.2%	14	3.3%
wwSwSw	6	1.5%	20	4.8%
wwSwwSw	3	0.7%	6	1.4%
wwSwSww	–	–	1	0.2%
Total	154	40.5%	201	48.5%
B types				
SwwwS	5	1.3%	6	1.4%
wwwSwS	4	1.0%	2	0.4%
wSwwwS	3	0.7%	3	0.7%
Total	21	5.5%	20	4.8%
C types				
SS	23	6.0%	2	0.4%

23 Vantuono (1984: I, 28). Unhappily, Vantuono provides no rationale for this reading.

11 Alliterative patterning and the editing of Middle English poetry

Gerrit H. V. Bunt

Recent work in ME unrhymed alliterative poetry, especially publications by Cable and Matonis (see references and their contributions to this volume) and the long series of articles by Duggan and Turville-Petre preparatory to and following their recent edition of *The Wars of Alexander* (1989), has greatly extended our understanding of alliterative conventions and practices. Duggan and Turville-Petre have argued (although they did not invariably speak with one voice) that poets of the alliterative revival wrote their lines on only one pattern of alliteration, *aa/ax*, and that they applied quite strict criteria to the structure of their b-verses, and Cable (1988, 1991) has independently arrived at very similar conclusions. Duggan has argued that if alliterative patterns and b-verses which fail to meet these rules nevertheless occur in varying numbers in the manuscripts in which these poems have been transmitted to us, such lines must have become corrupted through scribal error or interference. An editor should therefore aim at removing scribal corruption and restoring authorial, and consequently metrically regular, readings, if necessary through conjectural emendation. His argument is based on those few alliterative poems that exist in more than one manuscript, and he and Turville-Petre were able to show that when a deviant line occurred in one manuscript, text-critical methods could be used to establish a properly alliterating line as the archetypal reading.

The views expressed by Turville-Petre and especially by Duggan have called up dissent from various quarters. Duggan has, I think without much justification, been accused of circularity. Matonis (1984, and see the chapters by Matonis and Borroff here) has emphasised the variety of alliterative practice and has questioned the theory of consistent adherence to the *aa/ax* pattern. Stephanie Trigg, in her recent edition of *Wynnere and Wastoure* (1990: xxvii–xxxvi), has also questioned

Duggan's assumption of uniform practice for all alliterative poets. She has argued that under certain conditions *aa/xx* lines could be authorial, and three such lines are therefore left unemended in her edition. She also accepts one line each with the patterns *aaa/bb* and *ab/ba*, which Duggan rejects. In this paper I shall bring forward evidence which suggests that, in one poem at least, non-*aa/ax* patterns have every appearance of being authorial.

In April 1985 I published an edition of the alliterative romance *William of Palerne*. Its text is preserved in a single manuscript now in the library of King's College, Cambridge, where it is bound in a volume together with a version of the *South English Legendary*. I have argued elsewhere that the manuscript was probably produced somewhere in Norfolk, but the dialect of the original poem appears to be that of southern Worcestershire or Warwickshire (Bunt 1990). The language of the sole manuscript of *William of Palerne* is quite mixed, and there may well be further dialectal layers involved. The composition of the poem can be dated, on the basis of two references to the poet's patron, Humphrey IX de Bohun, Duke of Hereford and Essex, between 1335 and 1361; the manuscript, which is all in one hand, cannot be very much later, probably between 1360 and 1375. The romance was translated from the French *Guillaume de Palerne* of *c.* 1200 and follows its source quite closely in narrative outline while treating individual scenes with some freedom. There exists a brief fragment of a later prose redaction, printed by Wynkyn de Worde *c.* 1515,[1] and we also possess an Irish version probably based on this largely lost English prose redaction (ed. O'Rahilly 1949).

William of Palerne tells the story of a young prince of Sicily, the son of King Ebrouns and his queen, who is abducted by a werewolf who thus intends to save him from the murderous plans of his uncle. The werewolf is a Spanish prince, who has been wickedly transformed by his stepmother, who wishes to secure the succession for her own son. William is found by a cowherd in the vicinity of Rome, who fosters him for seven years. He is later brought to the imperial court at Rome, where he and the emperor's daughter Melior fall in love and elope to avoid Melior's marriage to a Greek prince. The werewolf guides the lovers, disguised first as white bears and later as a hart and a hind, to Sicily, where William frees his widowed mother from the war waged on her by the king of Spain, who wants her daughter in marriage for his son, the werewolf's half-brother. The identity of William and the werewolf is revealed, and the werewolf is disenchanted. William and Melior are married and become king and queen of Sicily. Alphouns, the former werewolf, marries William's sister and succeeds his father as king of Spain. When the emperor dies, William succeeds to the imperial throne.

The text of this alliterative poem as it has come down to us is in several places clearly corrupt. Some of these corruptions can be emended with some confidence, but in other cases no suitable emendation suggested itself, and the corrupt passage had to be allowed to stand largely unaltered. An example of such corruption apparently beyond repair is:

> for feire floures schal we finde, of foulen song here,
> and þurth cumfort may cacche swiche happ may falle,
> to have þe better hele at ȝoure hom-kome.   (805–7)

Line 806 is clearly deficient in both sense and alliteration. In my edition I transposed *þurth* and *swiche*, which improves the sense but leaves a very odd syntax as well as a faulty alliterative pattern and, according to the criteria formulated by Duggan (1990a: 159), an unmetrical b-verse.

More numerous, however, are lines which make passable or even excellent sense, but which, as they stand in the only manuscript, show unorthodox alliterative patterns or are otherwise unmetrical. In some cases, the defective alliteration was clearly the result of scribal substitution of one synonym for another. In one instance the scribe has himself corrected such a substitution. In line 5192 he wrote at first

> ȝif it bitide eni time þat þou nede have

which shows the pattern *aa/xx*, but he recognised his error and wrote the correct *tene* in the margin, subpuncting *nede* for deletion. A few other examples of scribal substitution are

> þerfor, lady, go we loke wat sekenes him eyles (842)

where *sekenes*, which also occurs in the preceding line, appears to be substituted for *langour*; and

> þan William was gretliche glad and loveliche hire þonked (975)

where we could read *godliche* for the nonalliterating *loveliche*. The defective *xa/ax* pattern in line 46

> and evere þe dogge at þe hole held it at abaye

can be restored to the standard pattern by substituting the synonymous *hound* for *dogge*, as was suggested by Kaluza (1881: 283) and Simms (1973). It would not be difficult to give numerous similar examples.

There is one line in which the other versions of the poem help us to recover an original reading and restore alliteration. William's vanquished opponent, the king of Spain, tells us of his first wife,

> þe kinges douȝter of Naverne was þat gode burde (4076)

In the French *Guillaume* (line 7287) and in the Irish version (lines 2842, 3822, 3831), however, the lady is the daughter of the king of Gascony. As Charles Dunn (1960: 76–7) points out, 'Gascony' would alliterate properly, and if we accept *k/g* alliteration, the line would exhibit the standard *aa/ax* pattern.[2] Since the Irish version depends on the English prose redaction, which in turn goes back to the alliterative poem, we may conclude that there must once have been another manuscript of the poem which duly read 'Gascony' at this point. Dunn also suggests plausibly that the scribe, or a predecessor, substituted *Naverne* for 'Gascony' because he realised that Gascony was not a kingdom, whereas Navarre was. There was thus an element of scribal pedantry involved here, and there is an interesting parallel with Thornton's interference, also disrupting the alliterative pattern, with the text of *The Parliament of the Three Ages*, lines 546, 548, 558, and 569. As Duggan (1986b: 81–2 and 100–1) plausibly suggests, in MS BL Add. 31042 Thornton substituted correct but non-alliterating names of heroes associated with Charlemagne for the erroneous but properly alliterating names of the original poem, which have been preserved in the Ware MS (BL Add. 33994).

Most editors of ME alliterative poetry would probably feel little hesitation in emending lines where scribal substitution seems to have destroyed an original correct alliteration so as to make them conform to the standard pattern, or would at least make confident suggestions in their commentaries. But matters are not always as straightforward as this. Some lines show defective alliteration where suitable emendation is not so easy to come by. One such line is

> þat quen and hire douȝter and Meliors þe schene (3299)

which contains no alliteration at all. It is difficult to see how alliteration, supposing it was originally present, could be restored. There is some alliteration in and þre þousand þro men in his eschel were (3564)

but it is restricted to the a-verse, and the line contains the defective pattern *aaa/xx*. Again, it is not so easy to emend this line so as to make it alliterate satisfactorily.

In a few lines 'Stab der Liaison' might be assumed to yield correct alliteration, for instance in

þat þe same seg hade slawe his em þertofore (3435)

but Schumacher (1914: 57–8) plausibly argued that such alliteration on the final /s/ (or was it /z/?) of *his* before an initial vowel was probably not intended by our poet. Another line where 'Stab der Liaison' would give some alliteration, although not in this case a proper *aa/ax* pattern, is

but his ost þat tide he left in þe see stille (4952)

So far we have considered lines whose b-verses had a significant information content. However, *William of Palerne* also contains many lines with defective alliteration where the b-verse can be said to have the character of a tag. Examples are

and clipt it and kest oft and many siþes (2470)
and realiche were araiȝed in a litel while (3375)
at þe last þei him left, for miȝth þat þei couþe (3508)
of alle maner armure þat to werre longed (3769)

In many such lines we must also conclude that there is no obvious emendation which would result in correct alliteration. In passing we should note that all nonalliterating b-verses that we have discussed so far conform to the rhythmical requirements defined by Cable and Duggan.

Lines which seem to defy emendation are even more numerous than those in which scribal corruption can be more or less confidently assumed to be responsible for the defective alliteration. It is impossible to draw a clear line of demarcation between the set of emendable lines and the set of lines which seem to resist emendation. No doubt some of the lines which I would place in this latter category would be regarded in another light by critics with more experience and more creativity. It seems fair to say that there is a continuum, with easily emendable lines at one extreme and possibly authorial lines at the other.

Above I discussed a line with defective alliteration where comparison with the French source and with later redactions suggested a suitable emendation. Comparison with the French *Guillaume* may, however, also lead to quite different results. Let us consider lines 364 and 365. The hero of our story, now eleven years old, is about to accompany the emperor of Rome to his imperial court and to leave the cowherd who has been his foster-father for seven years. The young William asks the cowherd to greet his friends, of whom he mentions some by name. The French source (I use Michelant's edition of 1876)[3] reads:

> Salués moi Huet le nain,
> Et Hugenet et Aubelot,
> Et Martinet le fil Heugot,
> Et Akarin et Crestiien,
> Et Thumassin le fil Paien   (594–8)

The English adapter must have mistaken the names of *Crestiien* and *Paien* for common nouns, and he translates the last two lines as follows:

> and þe Cristen Akarin, þat was mi kyn fere,
> and þe trewe kinnesman, þe payenes sone   (364–5)

It is obvious that *kinnesman* is a scribal error for something like *Thumassin*. But even after this error has been removed, the line is still *aa/xx*. However, although it contains an error of translation and fails to alliterate properly, it is so close to the French source that it can hardly be anything but substantially authorial.

There are not many passages where the English poet follows his French source so closely that we can use it for textual purposes. Another such passage is

> ful godli þei him gret gladli, as þei ouȝt,
> ferst in Alphouns half, þat king was of Spayne,
> for þemperour and he hadde be felawes ȝore;
> seþen in worþi Williams, þat king was of Poyle
> and soverayn of Cisile, as schold a king bene;
> and seþen in Meliors name, þat was hise mery douȝter.
>   (4825–30)

This corresponds to the following lines in *Guillaume:*

Salué l'ont et sa compaigne
De par le roi Amphoul d'Espaigne,
Que jadis furent compaignon,
Et puis de par le fil Embron
Cui est Puille et toute Sezille,
Et de par Melior sa fille.   (8425–30)

The English lines 4826, 4628, and 4830 fail to alliterate in the proper way, and the metricality of the b-verse of line 4827 is doubtful unless we place the caesura after *be*, in which case the alliteration is defective in this line too. Yet the English text is so close to its French source that it appears likely that these lines are also in substance authorial.

Other examples of this kind are perhaps less compelling. A few more parallel passages are the following:

He gat him, as God ȝaf grace, on his ferst wyve   (112)

Il estoit fix le roi d'Espaigne
De sa feme la premeraine.   (281–2)

Messangers ful manly þemperour þanne sente
byfore to his dere douȝter to do hire to wite   (1330–1)

L'emperere a messages pris,
A sa fille les a tramis. (2447–8)

The following English line has the pattern *aa/bb*, which Duggan regards as scribal:

þe king bisouȝt þe quene, ȝif it were hire wille (3977)

Yet it also closely follows its French source:

Li rois requiert forment et prie
La roine, se li plaisoit   (7162–3)

and may therefore well be authorial rather than the product of scribal corruption.

In the following passage from the alliterative poem the heroine's confidante, Alisaundrine, pleads William's cause with her:

and seide, 'A mercy, madame, on þis man here,
þat neȝh is drive to þe deþ al for youre sake!'
'How so for my sake?' seide Melior þanne.   (978–80)

Line 979 shows defective alliteration. The English poet has followed his source less closely, but there is nothing in the line that does not correspond to a phrase in the French poem:

'Damoisele, por Jhesu Crist,
Et por pitié et por amor,
Aies pieté de la dolor,
Que cis vallès sueffre por toi.'
Meliors dist: 'Bele, de coi?'
– Dame, por toi languist enfin.
Por toi se muert et fait tel fin.
– En quel maniere, bele suer?   (1672–9)

Moreover, the echo of 979b in 980a makes it unlikely that the former is not authorial.

If it can be made plausible that the author of *William of Palerne* wrote lines which do not conform to the regular *aa/ax* pattern, the assumption that the poets of the alliterative revival shared an unvaried adherence to the *aa/ax* pattern needs qualification. Indeed, in his earlier articles Duggan expressed himself more guardedly on this issue; thus, in his 'Alliterative Patterning as a Basis for Emendation in Middle English Alliterative Poetry', which appeared in *Studies in the Age of Chaucer* in 1986 (1986b: 102), he states his belief that in *The Parliament of the Three Ages*, *The Siege of Jerusalem*, and *The Wars of Alexander* (all three of which are preserved in more than one manuscript) 'irregularity in alliterative patterning is a certain indication of scribal corruption', adding that this is true of '*most* of the other alliterative poems written in the unrhymed alliterative long line' (my emphasis). At the time Duggan wrote this, he still considered *Piers Plowman* an exception; in his later work, however, he succeeded in bringing the recalcitrant Langland to heel (Duggan 1987 and 1990a), and this may well be the reason why the reservation which was still present in 1986 has disappeared in his more recent work. I believe it should be brought back.

What I also find slightly worrying in Duggan's theory is the sharp distinction that he draws between the regularity of the poets and the lawlessness of the scribes. An impression is created of poets and scribes moving in entirely separate worlds, at least as far as their understanding of alliterative poetics was concerned. This picture is contradicted by Thomas Hoccleve, in whom we know of at least one ME scribe who was also a poet, although not one who wrote alliterative verse. Surely our alliterative poets cannot have been working within conventions which were fully known only to themselves?

The evidence which I have presented undoubtedly contains lessons for editors too. It cannot be assumed, I think, that regularities discovered in one group of alliterative poems necessarily apply to the whole corpus without qualification. As Stephanie Trigg (1990: xxix) argues persuasively, the poets must have written each with his own understanding of the metre, and have evolved each his own rules and licences within a basic grammar of alliterative composition; and there must have been degrees of competency within that grammar, which may have varied from place to place and from time to time. Editors should therefore be cautious in assuming authorial regularity of practice unless there is good textual evidence for such a virtue.

It follows that a moderate conservatism is perhaps the best editorial policy, at least in the case of a text for which only one manuscript is available. Conservatism is not, as Duggan suggests in 'Alliterative Patterning' (1986b: 73), only based on a belief that the shape of ME alliterative verse is too indeterminate and its organisation too loose to permit emendation on purely metrical grounds. It also stems from a certain measure of respect for the work of scribes and not only of poets, and from a disinclination to believe that a modern editor is always a better judge of medieval poetry than a medieval scribe. Another consideration is that if we cannot retrieve the author's original text, we are possibly as well off with a near-contemporary witness as with a modern editor's partial reconstruction. Of course we must treat such a witness critically, and correct if his testimony makes no sense.

In my own edition of *William of Palerne* I decided not to introduce any emendations on metrical grounds alone. Some of my reviewers have taken me to task for this, and if our present knowledge had been available earlier I might well have decided differently. As it is, if I erred, it is on the side of caution. I cannot help thinking that is by far the best side to err on.

Notes

1 The text of the prose fragment is given in an appendix in my edition of the alliterative *William of Palerne*. An earlier edition is in Brie (1907).

2 On *k/g* alliteration in *William of Palerne*, see Rosenthal (1878: 446) and Schumacher (1914: 129), and my own discussion in Bunt (1985: 81).
3 The recent edition by Micha (1990) came to my notice too late for me to make use of it for the present chapter.

12 Reconsidering Chaucer's prosody

Gilbert Youmans

And your true rights be term'd a poet's rage
And stretched metre of an antique song
Shakespeare, *Sonnet* 17

My title alludes to Halle and Keyser's 1966 article 'Chaucer and the Study of Prosody', which inaugurated the school of metrical analysis that has come to be known as generative metrics. During the last twenty-five years, generative metrical theories have evolved so rapidly and so completely that all of Halle and Keyser's original principles have been revised or replaced (see e.g. Attridge 1982; Duffell 1991). However, most of the changes in the theory have been introduced to account for the metrical practice of post-Chaucerian poets. Therefore, a reconsideration of Chaucer's prosody from a generative viewpoint might reasonably begin with reexamination of Halle and Keyser's earliest definition (1966) of the iambic pentameter line:

(1) **Principle 1.** The iambic pentameter verse consists of ten positions, to which may be appended one or two extrametrical syllables.

     Principle 2. A position is normally occupied by a single syllable, but under certain conditions it may be occupied by more than one syllable or by none.

     Condition 1. Two vowels may constitute a single position, provided that they adjoin or are separated by a liquid or nasal or by a word boundary, which may be followed by *h-*, and provided that one of them contains a weakly stressed or unstressed vowel.

     Condition 2. An unstressed or weakly stressed monosyllabic word may constitute a single metrical position with a preceding stressed or unstressed syllable.

185

Principle 3. A stress maximum may only occupy even positions
within a verse, but not every even position need be so occupied.

Definition: A stress maximum is constituted by a syllable bearing
linguistically determined stress that is greater than that of the
two syllables adjacent to it in the same verse.

Condition (1) is usually interpreted as an elision rule. It accommodates
lines such as those below:

(2) Ful many͡a deyntee hors hadde he in stable   A.Prol.168
     1   2 3   4   5   6   7   89 10 x
(3) Wyd was his pari͡sshe and houses fer asonder   A.Prol.491
     1   2   3   4   5   6 7 8 9 10 x

The crucial issue raised by these and similar examples is not whether
Chaucer actually intended readers to elide the relevant syllables when
performing his verse. Rather, such lines illustrate that *syllable* is a gradient category rather than a clear-cut one. At opposite extremes, *back-
pack* is obviously disyllabic and *cat* monosyllabic. However, words such
as *hour* and *power* are borderline cases, as their contrasting spellings
suggest. Based on spelling alone, for example, one might conclude that
hour is monosyllabic and *power* disyllabic. Actually, of course, the two
words rhyme, and both are metrically ambiguous. In verse, such words
are treated sometimes as monosyllables and sometimes as disyllables.

Halle and Keyser (1966) predates the theories of syllable structure
that were later developed by generative phonologists (see, for example,
Kahn 1980). Nevertheless, Condition 1 can be interpreted as an early
attempt to specify syllabic boundaries that are phonologically ambiguous. Not surprisingly, this early attempt is flawed in some of its descriptive details, as pointed out by Weismiller (1989) and others (Tarlinskaja
1976a, b, Schlerman 1989, Kiparsky 1989). However, an adequate
theory of iambic pentameter must include some principle comparable
with Condition 1, that is, some acknowledgement that *syllable* is a fuzzy
rather than a well-defined phonological category. Condition 2, by contrast, is in no sense an elision rule. It accommodates extra unstressed
syllables in lines such as the following:

(4) Of͡a solempne and a greet fraternitee   A.Prol.364
     1   23   4   5   6   78 910
(5) As wel of this a͡s of other thynges more   D.WB.584
     1   2   3   4 5 6 7   8   9   10

Traditionally, lines such as (4) and (5) are said to contain anapaestic substitutions (in the first and third feet, respectively). However, this traditional description is inaccurate, since it fails to account for the metrical constraints on extra syllables in these lines. If poets were truly free to substitute anapaests for iambs, then metrical W positions in iambic verse should permit not only sequences of unstressed syllables such as *of a* and *as of*, but also stressed words such as *early* and *light's last*, which occupy W positions in an anapaestic tetrameter poem such as 'The Star-Spangled Banner':

(6) (x) Oh! say, can you see, by the dawn's *early* light,
     (W)W S   W W S   W W S   W WS
     What so proudly we hailed at the twi*light's last* gleaming?
     W W S   W W S   W W SW   W   S   x

Iambic verse occasionally includes 'light' anapaests such as *by the dawn's* and *at the twi-*, but never 'heavy' ones such as *early light* and *light's last gleam-*. Hence, the underlying metrical pattern of iambic verse remains duple rather than triple even if some metrical positions are allowed to include disyllables. Kiparsky (1989) claims that such split positions are governed by the following constraint: two syllables may occupy a single metrical position provided that both syllables are short and the second is unstressed. Kiparsky's (1989: 312) definition of short syllables includes complicated details, but his constraint on split positions is stricter than Halle and Keyser's Condition 2 and therefore is to be preferred. Weismiller (1989) points out that such extra syllables seldom occur in nondramatic iambic verse before the Romantic period, and I have not investigated Chaucer's constraints on split metrical positions. Instead, the remainder of my chapter focuses upon the arrangement of stressed and unstressed syllables in Chaucer's iambic pentameter verse.

Halle and Keyser's Principle 1 defines the iambic pentameter line as a sequence of alternating W and S positions with one or two optional extrametrical syllables:

(7) (W)* S W S W S W S W S (X) (X)

The first W position is normally occupied by an unstressed syllable, but it may remain empty in the case of headless lines such as the following:

(8)   Ø   Alderfirst his purpos for to wynne.   TC 1.1069
(W)S   WS   W   S   WS   WS   (x)

According to Halle and Keyser (1971), unstressed syllables typically occupy W positions and stressed syllables typically occupy S positions in a line of verse. Every deviation from this pattern increases metrical tension. However, the only categorical constraint in Halle and Keyser's theory is Principle 3, the Stress Maximum Principle (SMP): stress maxima are prohibited from all W positions in verse.

In Halle and Keyser (1966), a stress maximum is defined as any syllable bearing stress greater than that of the two syllables adjacent to it in the same line of verse. In 1971 (hereafter referred to as HK), the authors modify this definition because they believe it incorrectly identifies lines such as (9) as unmetrical:

(9) Arsenyk, sal armonyak *and brimstoon*   G.CY.798

HK assume that (9) violates their 1966 version of the SMP because *brimstoon* bears primary stress on its first syllable (like most compound nouns). Actually, this assumption can be questioned. It is possible, perhaps even probable, that Chaucer intended syllables such as *stoon* to receive greater-than-usual stress when occupying rhyming positions. Certainly there are many other disyllabic words in Chaucer's verse that are aligned exclusively with SW positions except when these words occur at the end of a line – that is, when they are used as rhymes. This distribution suggests two alternatives: either Chaucer relaxed the SMP in position 9 (which would be unusual, because verse tends to become more, not less, regular at the end of lines), or he followed a stress-promotion convention for rhyming syllables, changing a line-final word such as *brimstoon* from falling stress to level or rising stress.

Regardless of the intended stress pattern for *brimstoon* in (9), many poets writing in iambic pentameter, even metrically strict ones such as Pope, allow disyllabic compounds to occupy either SW or WS positions. In order to accommodate this permissible variation, HK narrow the definition of the stress maximum to 'a fully stressed syllable . . . between two unstressed syllables in the same syntactic constituent within a line of verse'. Because both syllables are stressed in compounds such as *black-board* and in phrases such as *black board* (= board that is black), these sequences are exempt from the revised version of the stress-maximum constraint: they can occupy either SW or WS positions in iambic verse.

Also exempt are fully stressed syllables at the beginning of a phrase – because of the requirement that a stress maximum must be flanked by unstressed syllables *in the same syntactic constituent*. This revision accommodates metrical inversions after midline caesuras as well as at the beginnings of lines. Unfortunately, it also suspends the SMP at the ends of phrases, where stress patterning is likely to be strictest. Partly for this reason, Kiparsky (1975) substitutes the Monosyllabic Word Constraint (MWC) for the SMP. Briefly, the MWC prohibits stressed syllables in metrical W positions unless (a) the stress is on a monosyllabic word or (b) it is preceded by a phrase boundary (a potential caesura). In effect, this rule constrains polysyllables rather than monosyllables: it requires stressed syllables in polysyllabic major-category words to occupy metrical S positions unless these stresses are immediately preceded by phrase boundaries (where inversions are permitted). Thus, the MWC requires *inspired* to begin in an odd-numbered position in (10a). The rephrasing in (10b) violates the MWC (as well as the SMP):

>   S
>
> (10a) Inspired hath in every holt and heeth   A.Prol.6
>   1   23 4 5 6 7 8 9   10
>
>   S
>
> (10b) *Hath inspired [Violates both the MWC and the SMP]
>   1   2   34

Kiparsky (1977) adds a comparable, though less strict, constraint upon clitic phrases, that is, upon major-category words that are preceded by proclitic words or followed by enclitic ones. Chaucer's line (11) includes four such clitic phrases:

> (11) [The droghte] [of March] [hath perced] [to the roote]   A. Prol.2
>   1 2   3 4   5   6 7   8 9 10

The revised version of the MWC treats clitic phrases such as *the droghte* and *of March* like iambic words. They are normally aligned in WS position, obligatorily so at the end of a phrase. Empirically, then, the chief difference between the MWC and the SMP is that the MWC may be suspended after, but not before, phrase boundaries, whereas the SMP may be suspended both before and after such boundaries.

In a series of articles (Youmans 1982, 1983, 1989), I have argued that the MWC succeeds better than the SMP in accounting for Shakespeare's and Milton's metrical practice. Nevertheless, both poets violate the MWC and the SMP occasionally, especially in positions 3 and 7 of their lines (as Koelb 1979 points out). Consequently, the MWC and the SMP appear to be strongly normative principles rather than categorical ones in Shakespeare's and Milton's verse. Therefore I have proposed that these principles should be incorporated into a tension metric rather than being treated as definitions of an exact boundary between metrical and unmetrical lines. More generally, I have argued that this reclassification of the MWC and the SMP is not an isolated case; it is evidence that the set of iambic pentameter lines is fuzzy rather than well defined, resembling the set of gourmets rather than the set of U.S. Congressmen. If so, then the primary task of metrical theory is to determine degrees of metricality rather than to define a clear-cut dividing line between metrical and unmetrical lines. Treating metricality as a gradient concept rather than a categorical one may seem to deny it a strict meaning. 'But', as Wittgenstein (1958: 27) points out, 'this is not a defect. To think it is would be like saying that the light of my reading lamp is no real light at all because it has no sharp boundary.'

If the primary goal of metrical theory is to determine degrees of metricality, then the first step in describing a given poem's metre is to discover its metrical prototype. Such a prototype should not be confused with a statistical norm. Prototypes are necessarily normative, but they are rarely norms. Achilles and Romeo, for example, became prototypes primarily because they exceed the statistical norms for warriors and lovers respectively. Similarly, metrical prototypes are the yardsticks by which metricality is measured; they need not find any counterparts in actual verse, any more than perfect triangles must exist in nature. Using the notation of Liberman and Prince (1977), I have proposed the following prototype for Milton's iambic pentameter (Youmans 1989):

(12a) Iambic line (4/6)

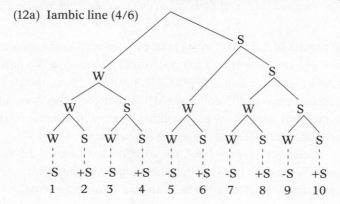

(12b) Abbreviated version
       [W 2S] [W 3S] // [W 2S] / [W 2S] [W 5S]

The prototype in (12a, b) implies a hierarchy of stresses: all odd-numbered positions are [−stress] and all even-numbered positions are [+stress]; in addition, positions 2, 6, and 8 are dominated by one S; position 4 is dominated by two S's, and position 10 by four S's. Hence, the strongest stress in the prototypical line is in position 10; the next strongest is in position 4; the next strongest are in positions 2, 6, and 8; and the least strongest are in odd positions. The prototype in (12) also implies a hierarchy of metrical boundaries, typically (a) a syllable boundary between metrical positions, (b) a word boundary between feet, (c) a subsidiary phrase boundary after the sixth position, (d) a major phrase boundary after the fourth position, and (e) a clause or sentence boundary at the end of the line.

Recent work in metrical phonology (Hogg and McCully 1987, Giegerich 1992) subdivides the syllable into three parts: an optional onset (of one or two consonants), a nucleus (with a vowel plus an optional glide or resonant), and an optional coda (of one or two consonants). Stress is a phonological feature of the nucleus (in terms of Giegerich 1992, the 'core' of the syllable), whereas syllabic boundaries normally coincide with onsets and codas. At one extreme are consonant clusters, which form clear-cut syllabic boundaries. At the opposite extreme are nuclei separated only by a glide, as in the first two syllables of words such as *reëstablish* and *coöperate* and phrases such as *the acceptance*. Disyllabic strings such as these (*e-e, o-o, e-a*) are frequently elided in speech, and poets often treat them like monosyllables for metrical purposes.

Halle and Keyser's Condition 1 can be interpreted as a first attempt to specify the relative weakness of marginal syllabic boundaries. Hogg and McCully's (1987) sonority scale (derived from Selkirk 1984) provides a more recent and more accurate tool for this same purpose (see also Giegerich 1992: ch. 6). Syllabic boundaries are weaker when nuclei are separated by single [+sonorant] segments and stronger when separated by [−sonorant] segments. The weakest boundaries are the glides [w, j] and [h], next weakest are the liquids [r, l], next are the nasals [m, n, ŋ], and next are the voiced fricatives [v, ð, z]. The voiceless fricatives and the stops are the lowest on the sonority scale, and they form clear-cut syllabic boundaries that block elision.

Halle and Keyser's Condition 2 addresses a different sort of deviation from the syllabic prototype. Kiparsky's version of this condition states that two syllables may occupy a single metrical position provided that both syllables are short and the second is unstressed. Kiparsky defines short syllables as ones with monophthongal nuclei and no codas. Additionally, in Hopkins' verse final unstressed syllables that end in a single consonant are metrically ambiguous: they can be treated as either short or long. Metrical constraints such as Kiparsky's suggest that the stressed syllables in an iambic pentameter prototype such as (12) are 'heavy' rather than 'light', that is, the prototypical occupant of an even position in (12) is a stressed syllable with a coda and/or diphthongal nucleus. Lighter syllables may be metrically ambiguous.

Hayes (1989) is an excellent source for a discussion of phonological boundaries above the level of the syllable. Hayes contends that there is a strictly layered prosodic hierarchy that includes five levels: (a) the word, (b) the clitic group, (c) the phonological phrase, (d) the intonational phrase, and (e) the utterance. Phonological words include not only the usual words entered in dictionaries but also contractions such as *wanna* (in *we wanna go*) and *whyncha* (in *whyncha come?*). Clitic groups include one and only one content word (lexical category word), which serves as the host of the group. Attached to this host may be one or more clitic words (function words). A phonological phrase is formed from one or more clitic groups. Phonological phrases coincide with syntactic phrases defined by X-bar notation: N″, V″, and so on.

Intonational phrases, which have a characteristic pattern of high and low pitches, include one or more phonological phrases. According to Hayes (1989: 218), intonational phrase boundaries occur obligatorily at '. . . the edges of parentheticals, nonrestrictive clauses, and constituents displaced by stylistic or root transformations. The boundaries of clauses and the breaks between subject and verb phrases also strongly tend to attract I-phrase breaks.' (Length is a major determining factor: short sentences often contain just one intonational phrase, whereas long sentences contain more than one.) An utterance includes one or more intonational phrases; utterances are bounded by structural pauses that normally coincide with sentence boundaries.

Applying Hayes' prosodic hierarchy to (12) suggests a prototypical arrangement of metrical constitutents: the iambic pentameter line typically ends with an utterance or intonational phrase boundary.

Demoting this boundary results in enjambement – a clear deviation from the central prototype. The line, in turn, is subdivided into two or more phrases, with a phonological phrase or intonational phrase boundary after the fourth syllable. If this boundary is promoted to an utterance boundary, then a strong caesura results. If this boundary is demoted, then the midline caesura is likely to shift to another position in the line – usually after the sixth syllable, less frequently after the fifth. The longer hemistich is also subdivided; typically, there is a phonological phrase boundary after the sixth syllable in (12). If this boundary is promoted, the result is usually a 6/4 line (the most common variation from the 4/6 prototype). If this boundary is demoted, then the subsidiary boundary is likely to shift to another position in the hemistich, usually after the seventh or eighth syllable (see also Duffell 1991 and this volume).

Finally, the iambic foot is typically occupied by an iambic word or clitic phrase. Of course, the boundary between successive feet is often demoted to a syllable boundary; conversely, the boundary between syllables within a foot is often promoted, sometimes even to an utterance boundary. Hence, the foot is defined by statistically normative, rather than by categorical, rules. This variability has led many prosodists to deny that the foot is a metrical constituent at all, but the same argument could be applied to the hemistich. Hemistich boundaries are also variable in English iambic pentameter verse, but they are clearly normative for such poets as Chaucer, Shakespeare, and Milton.

One detail in Hayes' analysis is particularly important for the purposes of this chapter: namely, that phonological phrasing is strongly affected by syntactic transformations. For example, each line in (13) includes two intonation groups:

(13) [₁Full fathom five]   [₁thy father lies].
      [₁Of his bones]   [₁are coral made].   Temp. 1.2.396–7

By contrast, when these lines are rephrased in their normal prose word order, they are more likely to include only one intonational phrase each:

(14) [₁Thy father lies five full fathoms (deep)].
      [₁His bones are made of coral] / [₁Coral are made of his bones]

Of course, other intonational patterns are possible, but internal intonation boundaries are likely to be more clear-cut in (13) than in (14). That is, the syntactic movement transformations underlying (13) tend to make the midline phonological boundaries more emphatic, promoting them from phrase boundaries to intonational boundaries. The consequent increase in pitch contrasts results in more musical lines as well as in an increase in the number of prosodic layers.

Hayes discusses only the relation between stylistic transformations and intonational boundaries, but examples such as (15) suggest that lower-level phonological boundaries can be affected by stylistic transformations, too. (Both versions of the line are divided into clitic phrases.)

(15a) [$_C$That time] [$_C$of year] [$_C$thou mayst]
      [$_C$in me] [$_C$behold]   Son. 73
(15b) [$_C$Thou mayst behold] [$_C$that time] [$_C$of year in me]

Minor-category words such as *thou*, *mayst*, *in*, and *me* normally attach themselves to a clitic host, as in (15b). However, movement transformations prevent this cliticisation in (15a), and they also tend to promote the phonological boundaries of the moved constituents. Consequently, the phrases *thou mayst* and *in me* become separate clitic phrases in (15a). In this case, then, Shakespeare's stylistic transformations tend to reinforce the division of his line into iambic feet. Furthermore, clitic groups must by definition include a host. Hence, in (15a) it is plausible to claim that the auxiliary verb *mayst* and the pronoun *me* are promoted to the status of clitic hosts, which is to say that they receive greater-than-usual stress, like that of semantic content words rather than that of syntactic function words. Consequently, the stylistic transformations in (15a) tilt the line strongly toward the iambic prototype (12a), with respect to both bracketing and stress patterning. Chaucer achieves a similar effect in (16a):

(16a) [$_C$Forthi] [$_C$som grace] [$_C$I hope] [$_C$in hire]
      [$_C$to fynde].   TC 1.980
(16b) [$_C$Forthi] [$_C$I hope] [$_C$to fynde] [$_C$som grace in hire]

Partly because of the joint demands of metre and rhyme, the incidence of movement transformations tends to be much higher in rhymed iambic verse than it is in prose. For example, roughly 34 per cent of the lines in Shakespeare's sonnets include transformations such as those in (15a), whereas this ratio drops below 3 per cent in the prose passages of

Hamlet (Youmans 1983). The percentage of lines including movement transformations is even higher in the General Prologue to *The Canterbury Tales* (roughly 44 per cent), whereas the *Treatise on the Astrolabe* contains few such transformations. A higher density of movement transformations ensures that the frequency and magnitude of stress and intonation contrasts will be significantly greater in verse than in prose, and these contrasts are one source for the greater musicality of verse. Furthermore, movement transformations not only tend to make phonological stresses and phonological boundaries more emphatic but in verse these transformations also tend to align stresses and (to a lesser degree) phonological boundaries with metrical S positions and metrical boundaries in the prototype (12).

Even in rhymed verse, however, most lines do not include stylistic movement transformations. One such hypothetical line, which matches the iambic pentameter prototype very closely, is shown in (17):

(17) Contrite designs // invite / divine delight (a 4//2/4-constructed line)

This sort of sentence, which is composed entirely of iambic words (linked closely by assonance and consonance), comes very close to matching the iambic pentameter prototype, but it goes against the natural grain of English. Disyllabic nouns are usually trochaic rather than iambic, words are more often monosyllabic or polysyllabic than disyllabic, assonance and consonance are the exceptions rather than the rule, and so on. Consequently, it is not surprising that Chaucer's verse includes no lines that match the iambic pentameter prototype as closely as (17) does, but a large number of his lines *are* divided 4//2/4:

(18) And of his craft // he was / a carpenter.   A.MT.3189
(19) Aboute this kyng // ther ran / on every part   A.KT.2185
(20) I am not def. // Now pes / and cry no more,   TC 1.752
(21) I hadde a lord, // to whom / I wedded was,   TC 5.975

Examples such as these are traditionally classified as 4/6 lines, and prosodists have long noted that the most common position for a caesura in iambic pentameter verse is after the fourth syllable. This observation is accurate as far as it goes, but the prototype in (12) implies that there is a tripartite as well as a bipartite division in the typical iambic pentameter line. Such tripartite divisions are often very clear in Chaucer's verse, so much so that 'subsidiary' midline boundaries are sometimes difficult to distinguish from 'major' ones, as in the following 4/2/4 lines:

(22) For of his wo, / God woot, / she knew ful lyte.   TC 1.826

(23) His worthynesse, / his lust, / his dedes wise,   TC 3.1550

Examples such as these could be classified as either 4/6 or 6/4 lines, and they illustrate why the 6/4 line is the most common variant of the 4/6 norm. If 4/6 lines are prototypically subdivided 4//2/4, then reversing the major and minor boundaries will result in a 4/2//4 sequence – that is, a 6/4 line. Such 4/2//4 lines are also commmon in Chaucer:

(24) Til on Criseyde / it smot, // and there it stente.   TC 1.273

(25) Or feynede hire / she nyste, // oon of the tweye   TC 1.494

(26) And gan to sike, / and seyde, // 'O Troie town, . . .'   TC 5.1006

(27) 'My lady bright, / Criseyde, // hath me bytrayed, . . .'   TC 5.1241

Of course, other subdivisions within the line are also possible, as in lines that are divided 4//4/2, highlighting the final iambic foot:

(28) And dredeless, // yf that my lyf / may laste,   TC 1.1048

(29) My lyf, my deth, // hool yn thyn hond / I leye.   TC 1.1053

(30) Wo was that Grek // that with hym mette / that day!   TC 1.1075

Lines divided 4//3/3 are especially common:

(31) Thou shalt nat love // my lady / Emelye.   A.KT.1588

(32) As doth an hauk // that lysteth / for to pleye.   TC 1.671

(33) Knowe ich hire ought? // For my love, / tell me this.   TC 1.864

In (31–3), the subsidiary phrase boundary falls in midfoot. Hence, such lines tend to undermine the foot as a significant metrical unit. Nevertheless, it would be both unreasonable and undesirable to prohibit all trisyllabic words and phrases in iambic verse, and the 4//3/3 line accommodates such sequences with remarkable symmetry.

Another common variant in iambic verse is the 5/5 line:

(34) 'Lat be thi wepyng / and thi drerynesse, . . .'   TC 1.701

(35) 'No certes, brother', / quod this Troylus.   TC 1.773

(36) And ben converted / from hir wikked werkes   TC 1.1004

Despite the syllabic symmetry of such 5/5 lines, they are far less common than either 4/6 or 6/4 lines. This fact in itself lends support to those theories that treat the foot as a metrically significant unit, because the major subdivision within the line, the hemistich boundary, normally coincides with a foot boundary – as the line boundary always does. Similarly, in the prototypical 4//2/4 line as well as many of its variants (such as 4/2//4, 4//4/2, and 2/4//4), the subsidiary phrase boundary as well as the hemistich and the line boundaries coincide with foot boundaries. From a statistical point of view, then, Chaucer's verse tilts heavily towards iambic phrasing, towards lines such as (37), and away from ones such as (38), which is a headless line that could be scanned as regular trochaic pentameter:

(37) Unknowe, unkyst, and lost, that is unsought   TC 1.809
(38) Twenty wynter that his lady wyste   TC 1.811.

Chaucer's treatment of midline phrase boundaries suggests that a hierarchically structured prototype such as (12) is a more accurate model for his iambic pentameter than any simple sequence of WSWS positions can be. In Youmans (1989), I attempted to show in some detail the normative influence of the prototype (12) on Milton's verse. Using *Areopagitica* as a guide, I rephrased more than 7,300 lines of Milton's blank verse in his normal prose word order: the first four books of *Paradise Lost* (3,610 lines), all of *Paradise Regained* (2,070 lines), and the blank verse in *Samson Agonistes* (1,659 lines). I found 1,917 lines in this sample containing one or more syntactic inversions such as those in (39):

(39) Of Guardians bright, when he from Esau fled   PL 3.512
          bright guardians   fled from Esau

I scanned the original and the rephrased versions of these 1,917 lines, cataloguing the metrical effects of Milton's syntactic inversions wherever they occurred. For example, the first inversion in (39) prevents a violation of the MWC, whereas the second prevents violation of both the SMP and the MWC. In all, 1,105 of the 1,917 lines (56%) include syntactic inversions that prevent violation of the MWC, and no inversions have the opposite effect. Statisticians are rarely blessed by ratios this lopsided: 1,105 to zero. Hence, the evidence from Milton's inversions is overwhelming that the MWC or some comparable principle is strongly normative in his verse. The SMP is nearly as successful as the MWC, but Kiparsky (1977) accounts for all of the syntactic inversions that HK do, plus a few more. Consequently, I concluded that Kiparsky's theory describes Milton's metrical practice more accurately than do HK. In earlier articles (Youmans 1982, 1983), I reached the same conclusion for *Hamlet* and for Shakespeare's Sonnets.

Of course, there are other principles besides the MWC that govern Milton's verse. For example, 205 (10%) of Milton's inversions are not required by either the MWC or the SMP, but they do regularise the stress pattern, as in (40):

(40) In whom the fulness dwels of love divine,   PL 3.225
            of divine love dwells

Examples such as (40) illustrate that the alternating pattern [−stress]/[+stress] has a strong normative influence on Milton's verse. Somewhat more surprising are examples such as (41) and (42). In these lines, the inversions do not affect the number of stresses occupying odd and even positions in the line, but the inversions do shift weakly stressed or unstressed syllables away from final positions in lines and hemistichs:

(41) Temptation and all guile on him *to try*; [Strong closure]   PR 1.123
        To try temptation and all guile *on him*; [Weaker closure]

(42) So easily *destroy'd*, and still destroyes [Strong closure]   PL 3.301
        Destroy'd so eas*ily*, [Weak closure]

Of Milton's inversions, 140 (7%) have this effect, and only six have the opposite effect:

(43) Ascending by degrees magnif*icent* [Weak closure]   PL 3.502
            magnificent *degrees* [Strong closure]

This ratio, 140 to 6, implies that there is a significant normative tendency towards strong closure in Milton's lines and hemistichs. This tendency further corroborates the iambic prototype in (12), which locates the strongest stresses of the verse at the ends of hemistichs and lines. On the other hand, Milton not only allows variations from this norm but he occasionally prefers them, as countervailing inversions such as (43) attest.

Some of Milton's inversions imply that he also prefers regular metrical bracketing at the ends of his lines and hemistichs, as in the following examples:

(44) Was difficult, by humane steps *untrod* [Final iambic word]

                                                    PR 1.298

               untrod by *human steps* [Irregular final bracketing]

(45) Towards either Throne *they bow*, and to the ground [Iambic phrase]   PL 3.350

     They bow towards *either throne*, [Irregular final bracketing]

Forty-three (2.2%) of Milton's inversions have the same effect as the ones in (44) and (45); they do not change the stress patterning in the line, and they seem to have little metrical effect except to shift an iambic word or phrase into the final foot of the line or hemistich. Only 10 lines have the opposite effect, as in (46):

(46) Invincible: abasht *the Devil stood*, [Irregular final bracketing]

                                                    PL 4.846

               the Devil stood *abashed*, [Final iambic word]

This ratio, 43 to 10, suggests that Milton prefers regular iambic bracketing at the ends of his lines and hemistichs, although this normative tendency governing bracketing is not as strong as the one governing stress patterning.

Perhaps most surprising of all, there is even evidence that Milton prefers iambic words over iambic phrases at the ends of his lines and hemistichs:

(47) Before Messiah and his way *prepare*. [Final iambic word]

                                                    PR 1.272

               prepare *his way*. [Final iambic phrase]

Fifty-two of Milton's inversions (2.6%) have the same effect as the one in (47), while only 8 have the opposite effect. The evidence from Milton's other inversions demonstrates that his verse tends to become more regular at the right edges of lines and hemistichs; therefore, his preference for final iambic words over iambic clitic phrases implies that iambic words (even more so than iambic phrases) are the protypical occupants of iambic feet. At least for Milton, then, the foot appears to be a normative metrical constituent, and the prototype in (12) seems to be corroborated in remarkable detail. The next step is to see whether this same prototype applies to Chaucer's iambic pentameter verse.

Following the procedure of my earlier studies of Shakespeare (Youmans 1982 and 1983) and Milton (1989), I examined the standard word order in selections from Chaucer's prose, specifically his *Retraction* and the Prologue and Part I of *Treatise on the Astrolabe*. These samples include remarkably few deviations from the word order of Modern English prose. Some of these minor deviations, such as the placement of the negative particle, are also common in Shakespeare:

(48) Forget nat this, lite Lowys . . .   (*Astrolabe*)
     Don't forget this . . . [Twentieth-century English]

Such forms survive even to the present day as self-consciously literary constructions:

(49) Ask not what your country can do for you . . .   (J. F. Kennedy)
     Don't ask . . .

By far the most common deviation in Chaucer's prose from modern word order is illustrated by examples such as (50):

(50) Now *wol I* prey mekely . . .   (*Astrolabe*)
     Now I will . . . / I will now . . .

In sentences such as this, which begin with an introductory adverbial phrase, Chaucer typically inverts the subject and auxiliary verb. The same sort of auxiliary-movement transformation survives in Modern German: *Nun will ich beten*. The effect of this rule is to preserve the second position in canonical sentences for a verb. Chaucer often applies this rule to main verbs, too:

(51) Now *preye I* to hem alle that herkne this litel tretys . . .

                                        (*Retraction*)
     Now I pray . . . / I pray now . . .

This inversion rule seems to be optional rather than obligatory. Even in the case of auxiliary verbs, Chaucer occasionally follows the Modern English pattern:

(52) . . . for from hennesforthward *I wol* clepe the heyhte of anything . . .

                                             (*Astrolabe*)

Nevertheless, I assume that *wol I* rather than *I wol* is the standard word order for Chaucer in sentences such as (52).

Otherwise, Chaucer's normal word order is much the same as that in Modern English. Subjects normally precede, and complements follow, verbs. Attributive adjectives normally precede rather than follow nouns;

the few deviations are in phrases borrowed from French and Latin sources, as such examples as (53) make clear:

> (53) The whiche lyne . . . is cleped the Sowth Lyne, or elles the Lyne Meridional . . . Est Lyne, or elles the Lyne Orientale . . . West Lyne, or the Lyne Occidentale . . . (*Astrolabe*)

In (54) the systematic contrast between the native English pattern (*West line*) and the Romance pattern (*Line Occidental*) is obvious.

Using the *Retraction* and the *Treatise on the Astrolabe* as guides, I rephrased 5,200 lines of Chaucer's verse in normal prose word order: the 'General Prologue' to the *Canterbury Tales*, 'The Knight's Tale', and Part I of *Troilus and Creseyde*. Chaucer includes some syntactic inversions that extend over several lines of verse:

> (54) The double sorwe of Troylus to tellen,
> That was the Kyng Priamus sone of Troye,
> In lovynge, how his aventures fellen
> Fro wo to wele, and after out of joye,
> My purpos is . . .   TC 1.1–5
>
> My purpos is to tellen the double sorwe of Troylus . . .

I ignored all multiline inversions such as these. Most of the remaining syntactic inversions shift rhyming words to the end of the line:

> (55) The somer passeth, and the nyghtes longe [longe nyghtes]
> Encressen double wise the peynes stronge [stronge peynes]
>   A.KT.1337–8

Such inversions as these merely confirm the obvious, that rhymed verse is the normative prototype here. Hence, I have ignored these inversions, too, although this exclusion represents a loss of data, because the remaining syntactic inversions can give no direct evidence about the normative principles governing stress patterning and phonological bracketing at the ends of Chaucer's lines, where verse is normally constrained most strictly. The remaining inversions do provide some evidence about the end of the first hemistich, however, and by inference, any constraints governing the end of a hemistich are likely to apply with even greater force to the end of a line.

In the General Prologue to the *Canterbury Tales* approximately 44 per cent of the lines include syntactic inversions such as those in (55), compared with about 34 per cent of the lines in Shakespeare's sonnets. Hence, Chaucer's overall inversion rate is significantly higher than Shakespeare's. Considering only those lines containing syntactic inversions that have no effect on rhyme, I found 538 examples (10.3%) in the 5,200-line sample from Chaucer, compared with just 152 (7.1%) in the 2,155 lines of Shakespeare's sonnets. Hence, Chaucer's 'non-rhyme' inversions are also more frequent than Shakespeare's, reflecting an overall tendency of Chaucer's verse to be metrically more regular than Shakespeare's.

Hereafter, I will focus my discussion upon those 538 lines with syntactic inversions that do not affect the rhyme. Of these, 188 (35%) contain inversions that prevent violations of both the SMP and the MWC. (In these and all remaining scansions, I have marked only clear-cut stresses with *s*; other syllables in the line might also receive some stress, such as *erst* in (56) and *whan* in (57)):

```
         s                s                   s
(56)  That shapen was my deeth erst than my sherte.   A.KT.1566
        1    2 3    4    5 6    7    8    9   10
                    s            s
      That my deeth was shapen [Violates both the SMP and the MWC]
        1    2 3      4    5 6
          s                s          s
(57)  Whan hunted is the leon or the bere,   A.KT.1640
        1    2   3 4    5 67 8    9  10
          s
      Whan the leon is hunted [Violates both SMP and MWC]
        1     2 34
```

None of the stylistic inversions that I examined has the opposite effect; that is, none of them converts a metrically regular line into one that violates the SMP or the MWC. A few lines seem to be counterexamples, but an examination of a concordance to Chaucer (Tatlock and Kennedy 1963) demonstrates that these lines are not actually exceptions. One frequently cited example is the word *honour*, which shifts its stress to the second syllable in its trisyllabic variants, *honoure, honoured, honouren*. Hence, instead of being a counterexample, (58) is just one more line including a stylistic inversion that prevents a violation of the SMP and the MWC:

             s   s   s   s
(58) Of Trace honoured art and lord yholde,   A.KT.2374
      1   2   3 4   5 6 7   8   9 10

           s
art honoured [Violates both SMP and MWC]
3   4 5   6

A somewhat different example is the word *royal* (and its variants *roial* and *real*), which is stressed on the first syllable when it occurs before the noun it modifies:

(59) To speke of *roial* lynage and richesse,   A.KT.1829
(60) Retorned to his *real* paleys sone   TC 3.1534

However, when *royal* follows the noun it modifies, the main stress shifts to the final syllable, as in *blood royal*, which seems to have been a fixed expression for Chaucer:

             s   s
(61) The blood roial of Cadme and Amphioun –   A.KT.1546
           s   s
The roial blood [Equally regular stress patterns]

The shift in stress may be explained as an example of the rhythm rule, which still applies to words such as *thirteen* in phrases such as *thírteen rooms* (contrasting with *Room Thirtéen*). Alternatively, the phrase *blood royal* may have been influenced by French stress patterning as well as by French word order, as is *Casino Royále* today (contrasting with *Róyal Casino*). In either case, the systematic variation in the stress pattern for *royal* means that *estát royál* is metrically regular in (62), whereas *róyal estát* would violate both the SMP and the MWC:

               s   s   s
(62) For myn estat royal here I resigne   TC 1.432
      1   2 3 4   5 6   7   8 9 10

           s
myn royal estat [Violates both SMP and MWC]
    2   3   4

Apparent exceptions such as *honoured* and *royal* are typical. Upon closer examination, they prove to be consistent with the SMP and the MWC. In fact, the syntactic-inversion test turns out to be a very reliable indicator of Chaucer's stress patterns. Any word that is aligned consistently with, say, WS metrical positions and which is regularly moved by stylistic transformations from SW to WS position – such a word is almost certain to have been stressed WS by contemporary readers, whatever its stress pattern today.

In addition to the 188 syntactic inversions that prevent violations of the SMP and the MWC, there are another 40 inversions that prevent violations of the SMP and an extended version of the MWC (which constrains the positioning of clitic phrases as well as polysyllabic words):

```
                    s              s
(63)  As he that wys was and obedient,   A.GP.851
       1    2   3   4    5 6    7 8 910
                          s
      that was wys [Violates SMP and extended MWC]
        3    4   5
```

Another 59 lines include inversions that prevent violations of the MWC (in either its original or its extended version) but not of the SMP:

```
             s     s  s       s
(64)  Upon a steede bay trapped in steel   A.KT.2157
       1  2   3    4   5   6    7   8  9  10
      bay steede [Violates the MWC but not the SMP]
       4    5  6
```

The rephrased version of (64) does not violate the SMP, because the adjacent stresses in *bay steede* neutralise each other. However, the rephrased version of the line does violate the MWC, because the misaligned stress in *steede* is not preceded by a major phrase boundary such as [NP. In this respect, it contrasts with the word *trapped* in the same line, which occurs at the beginning of a participial phrase, bracketed by [S]. In traditional metrics, such metrical variations are called trochaic substitutions, and the MWC freely permits them at the left edges of major phrases. (Note that (64) is a 6/4 line. The trochaic substitution occurs in the third foot, immediately after the caesura.)

Syntactic inversions in lines such as the one in (64) might seem to offer clear evidence in favour of the MWC over the SMP, but HK can account for them merely by noting that the phrase *steede bay* conforms with the SWS iambic prototype, whereas *bay steede* does not. Hence, the stylistic transformation in the verse line decreases metrical tension. In support of this account, there are 38 additional lines that include inversions that do not prevent violations of either the SMP or the MWC but do bring the stress pattern into conformity with the WSWS proto-type:

```
        s       s       s           s
(65)  That lene he wex and drye as is a shaft    A.KT.1362
        1  2    3  4 5    6  7 8 9   10
      That he wex lene [Violates neither SMP nor MWC]
        1  2   3   4
```

Cable (1991 and this volume) points out that stress patterns similar to the one in *that he wex lene* are rare in Chaucer but common in Shakespeare:

```
(66)  When to the sessions of sweet silent thought
      I summon up remembrance of things past.    Son. 30
```

Cable argues that such sequences are common in Shakespeare because they represent a pattern of four rising stresses; hence, in a foot-based metre such as Shakespeare's, each foot is a perfectly regular WS iamb. By contrast, Cable claims, Chaucer's metre is based upon a regular alternation of rising *and* falling stresses, which makes such sequences of four rising stresses irregular and hence rare in his verse. Partly from this evidence, Cable concludes that the foot is not a significant metrical constituent in Chaucer's verse.

Stylistic inversions such as the one in (65) tend to support Cable's argument, and collectively Chaucer's syntactic inversions confirm that the alternating-stress principle is more strongly normative in Chaucer's verse than in Shakespeare's. Nevertheless, Chaucer does allow varia-tions – even radical ones – from his normal pattern, as lines such as (67) and (68) illustrate:

```
(67)  For with good hope he gan fully assente    TC 1.391
       1     2   3      4
(68)  For of good name and wysdom and manere     TC 1.880
       1  2  3     4
```

Metrically, the initial phrases *for with good hope* and *for of good name* are very similar to the one that was avoided in (65): *that he wex lene*. Furthermore, in (68) there is a stylistic transformation available that would bring the line into perfect conformity with the alternating-stress principle; namely, *for good of name*. Evidently, then, *for of good name* is a permissible metrical option rather than a desperate remedy. In addition, if the stress on the tenth syllable of (68) is promoted because of rhyme, then this line includes the same sort of sequence of four 'rising stresses' that Cable considers common in Shakespeare: -*dom and mànére*. If the stress-promotion theory is accepted, then such sequences are actually quite common at the ends of Chaucer's lines. Finally, most devastating of all to the alternating-stress principle are trochaic substitutions such as *fully* in (67) and *trapped* in (64). Such substitutions occur regularly (if infrequently) in Chaucer, especially after the fourth syllable (that is, in the third foot), just as they do in Shakespeare and Milton. No metrical theory that relies on a simple pattern of alternating stresses can account for such substitutions.

Examples (67) and (68) illustrate that with respect to phrases such as *for of good name* and *he gan fully assente* the difference between Chaucer on the one hand and Shakespeare and Milton on the other seems to be one of metrical style rather than metrical 'grammar'. That is, all three poets permit such phrases, although Chaucer uses them least frequently. Like Shakespeare and Milton, Chaucer also occasionally allows an Adjective–Noun sequence to occupy SW rather than WS position, as with *greet harm* in (69):

```
             s   s              s
(69) But greet harm was it, as it thoughte me,   A.GP.385
     1   2   3     4 5 6 7   8     9  10
             s   s
     But it was greet harm [End of hemistich is irregular]
     1 2  3    4     5
```

This is an instructive example, because one effect of the stylistic inversion in the verse line is to shift the irregular sequence *greet harm* away from the end of the hemistich. In 6/4 lines, and in 5/5 lines such as (69), position five seems to be governed quite strictly, whereas position three is freer, even including occasional violations of the SMP and the MWC. By contrast, in 4/6 lines, the fifth position follows a midline caesura, and hence trochaic substitutions are permitted, as with *lowely* in (70):

```
(70) Curteis he was, lowely, and servysable   A.GP.99
     1  2   3   4   5    6 7    8  9 10
```

As (70) illustrates, Chaucer, like later English poets, allows trochaic substitutions after midline caesuras as well as at the beginnings of his lines.

This digression into the permissible variations from the iambic-pentameter prototype may have obscured the fact that Chaucer's stylistic inversions do tend to corroborate Cable's central claim that the alternating-stress principle is strongly normative in Chaucer's verse. Of the 538 syntactic inversions I have examined, 325 (60%) have the effect of shifting stressed and unstressed syllables into their expected S and W metrical positions. Consequently, it is clear that the alternating-stress principle is normative for Chaucer, although it is equally clear that this principle is not a categorical rule for Chaucer or for any other major iambic poet.

An additional 47 (8.7%) of Chaucer's syntactic inversions have little metrical effect except to shift a stressed syllable from an odd-numbered position within the line to the beginning, where they are least disruptive to the metre:

        s   s   s
(71) *Two* woful wrecches been we, two caytyves   A.KT.1717
      1   2 3   4   5 6   7
                s   s   s
      We been *two* woful wreches
        1 2   3   4 5   6 7

Such lines illustrate the well-known freedom granted to the first position of iambic verse.

An additional 7 syntactic inversions affect the number of syllables in the line. In (72) the rephrased version of the line loses a final *-e* to elision, unmetrically reducing the number of syllables:

(72) And *softe* taak me in youre armes tweye,   A.KT.2781
      1   2 3 4   5 6 7 8   9   10
      And taak me *softe* in   [Final *-e* is followed by a vowel; hence, it
      1   2   3 4 5   is silent.]

Lines such as (72) are further evidence that Chaucer intended his final *-e*'s to be pronounced when required by the metre. Such critics as Southworth (1962) have occasionally disputed this claim. Barber and Barber (1990) have now offered convincing statistical evidence refuting Southworth. After counting the number of syllables in thousands of lines from the *Canterbury Tales*, the authors found that, on the average, the number of final scribal *-e*'s is inversely proportional to the number of other syllables in the line. Hence, by purely statistical arguments, the

Barbers demonstrate that roughly 75 per cent of scribal final -*e*'s (not followed by a vowel) should be counted as syllables. Stylistic inversions such as the one in (73) tend to corroborate this conclusion, as, indeed, do the overwhelming majority of Chaucer's other inversions, since it would be pointless for him to align his stressed syllables meticulously with even-numbered positions in his lines if he varied the number of his syllables more or less at random as Southworth's theory implies.

Altogether, 379 (70%) of Chaucer's syntactic inversions tend to bring his lines closer to the iambic prototype in (12). Only 27 (5%) of his inversions have the opposite effect. Of these, 9 follow the pattern of (73) and (74):

> (73) Short was his gowne . . . [His gowne was short]   A.GP.93
> (74) Whit was his berd . . . [His berd was whit]   A.GP.332

Cable (1991) contends that inverted first feet are accommodated more readily within a metre based upon iambic feet than one based upon alternating stresses. He notes that Chaucer and Gascoigne have a smaller proportion of inverted first feet than do later iambic poets, and he takes this as further evidence that Chaucer and Gascoigne wrote alternating rather than foot metre. However, lines such as (73) and (74) demonstrate that, for Chaucer, initial metrical inversions are not only permissible but sometimes desirable options. Chaucer places no categorical constraint upon these inversions. He even begins lines with trochaic words occasionally, and in one case, such an initial trochee results from a stylistic inversion:

> (75) Swelleth the breast of Arcite, and the soore   A.KT.2743
>   The breast of Arcite swelleth [Rephrased version is metrically more regular]

Another stylistic transformation results in an inverted foot after the caesura:

> (76) That Calkas, traitour fals, fled was and allyed   TC 1.87
>   was fled   [Rephrased version is more regular]

Examples such as (75) and (76), coupled with numerous other examples of inverted feet, as in (64), (67), and (70), illustrate that Chaucer placed no greater categorical constraints on such inversions than did Shakespeare and Milton. Stylistically, his verse is more regular than

theirs, but all three poets are remarkably similar in the metrical variations that they allow. Hence, a hierarchically layered metrical prototype
such as (12) seems to apply to Chaucer's verse as well as to
Shakespeare's and Milton's, and any description of Chaucer's metre
that relies upon a simple pattern of alternating strong and weak positions (such as HK) or alternating stresses (such as Cable 1991) will prove
to be at least partly inadequate.

13 Chaucer, Gower, and the history of the hendecasyllable

Martin J. Duffell

I shall begin by giving a brief account of the history of the Romance hendecasyllable up to the time of Chaucer, because I know of no publication in which a reliable account of this subject is available in English. The information can be found in French, Spanish, and Italian, in the works of Thomas (1904), Saavedra Molina (1946), and Avalle (1963), respectively. But Preminger et al. in the *Princeton Encyclopaedia of Poetry and Poetics* (1975) give a long-discredited view of the early history of the Romance hendecasyllable. Preminger et al. (1975: 186) state that the French *vers de dix* and the Italian *endecasillabo* evolved separately. The case for independent evolution is based entirely on the Ferrarese inscription: this is a poem of four lines which Baruffaldi (1713) claimed to have seen on the cathedral of Ferrara just before its demolition. The inscription commemorates the completion of the cathedral in 1135 and would make these the only surviving Italian *endecasillabi* which are too early to be derived from the Provençal *vers de dix*. The lines are very like those of Trecento poets, which in itself should have aroused suspicions. Monteverdi (1963), by a detailed investigation of Baruffaldi's papers and correspondence, proved them to be forgeries more than ten years before the first edition of the *Princeton Encyclopaedia* was published.

Dante, in Book 2 of his *De vulgari eloquentia*, writing within a century of the composition of the first surviving *endecasillabi*, has no doubts that the French line of ten syllables is exactly the same metre as the Italian line of eleven. But before tracing how one evolved into the other, I need to do two things. The first is to disambiguate the terminology of the subject; the second is to clarify the definitions of verse and metre which underlie my explanation.

French and Portuguese metrists count the syllables in a line only as far as the last accented syllable, while Italian and Spanish metrists count to the last accented syllable and add one, whether the eleventh (or indeed a twelfth) is present or not. Thus, what to a French reader is a *décasyllabe*, and to a Portuguese is a *decassílabo*, is an *endecasillabo* to an Italian and an *endecasílabo* to a Castilian. Just to be different, the English metrist counts five pairs of syllables and calls the line a *pentameter*, which was the Greek word for a line of twenty syllables (if it had an iambic rhythm). To avoid inconsistency and save space, I shall here use the abbreviation *X(I)* for the term *(hen)decasyllable/pentameter*. I shall, however, find it useful to adopt the French metrists' convention of suffixing an M (Masculine) or an F (Feminine) to the number of syllables in a line up to the last accent. An *X(I)* is thus a line which normally contains 10M/F syllables.

My account of the early history of the Romance *X(I)* depends upon the recognition of two definitions of verse; the first is musicological, noted by Gross (1979: 269): metre is low-grade musical material. This is to say that it is rhythmic but not tonic, or at least only in the most rudimentary way. The other members of this class are percussion and dancing. For some years I have been trying to change the solemn image of metrics by calling it 'word-dancing', but unfortunately this hasn't caught on. The second is the linguist's definition given by Lotz (1960: 135): verse is numerically regulated phonetic material, i.e. language containing a pattern. The patterns of Romance and English verse are based on two linguistic features, syllable count and accentuation. No Romance verse is purely syllabic like Japanese *haiku*: French syllabic metres contain mandatory positions for accented syllables. Similarly, even OE strong-stress metres are not purely accentual: the number and position of their unstressed syllables are regulated to some extent, as writers from Sievers (1885) to Russom (1987) and Cable (1991) have shown. The history of the Romance *X(I)* can be seen as the story of a gradual change in the relative importance of the two patterning features, syllable count and accent.

The earliest surviving Romance *X(I)*s are in the French *Vie de Saint Alexis* (*VSA*), which was composed soon after the year 1020. The *VSA*, has strongly divided lines of 4 + 6 syllables, and the last syllable of each hemistich must be accented (see also Youmans, this volume). Its rhythm is *de-de-de-**da**-de-de-de-de-de-**da***, a rhythm reminiscent of Beethoven. In the *VSA* the last syllable of each hemistich could be followed by an unaccented syllable which was not included in the syllable count. It is easy to see that an echo following the last strong beat in each group interferes minimally with the rhythm: *de-de-de-***da**-*eh de-de-de-de-de-***da**-*eh*. The earliest French *vers de dix* could thus have between ten and twelve actual syllables: to be more accurate, it is a 4M/F + 6M/F line rather than a *décasyllabe* of 10M/F.

Other types of *X(I)* were composed in French during the eleventh and twelfth centuries in which the hemistich formula was 6 + 4 or 5 + 5 (cf. again Youmans, this volume), and again each hemistich could be M or F. But no poem was composed in *X(I)*s which mixed different hemistich formulas, 4 + 6 and 6 + 4 or 5 + 5; and the first of these was by far the most popular.

The first *X(I)*s had been employed in epic or religious narrative. By the twelfth century the metre was being employed for lyric works, particularly by the Provençal troubadours. The earliest surviving *X(I)*s in Provençal are in the *Boecis*, dating from very soon after the *VSA*, and have a similar 4 + 6 hemistich formula. The twelfth-century troubadours also employed the 4 + 6 *X(I)*, but their *sirventés* were composed to fit predetermined music, and they had no compunction in wrenching phrases of 3F syllables like their favourite, *Bella domna*, so that they fitted the pattern *de-de-de-***da**. This was called a *lyric caesura* and served as a precedent both for mixing different types of caesura in the same poem and for counting an unaccented syllable at the end of the first hemistich in the syllable count. The troubadours thus developed a unified line of 10M/F syllables with a mobile caesura (after the fourth, fifth, sixth, or seventh syllable).

The twelfth century in Provence was followed by the Albigensian Crusades, in which the pope's thugs descended from the North and extinguished the rich political, social, and cultural life of the South. The brutal victory of the Church and the North made French the language of the whole of France and ensured that the strongly divided French line of 4 + 6 syllables became the *décasyllabe* of subsequent centuries. The reasons for this are probably linguistic. French scholars agree that word stress was much stronger in Old French than it is in the modern language, where it has been reduced to the potential of final syllables of words to become prominent in delivery whenever they coincide with phrase accent (Pulgram 1964: 132–33). Elwert (1965: 23) gives an explanation of why this came about which suggests that French word stress weakened gradually but steadily.

The *X(I)* of 10M/F syllables with mobile caesura was carried by Provençal influence and refugees to two foreign courts and to two languages with much stronger word stress than French or Provençal. These were the Italian-speaking court of Frederick II in Palermo, and the Castilian court, where traditionally lyrics were always composed in Galician-Portuguese. Because of their stronger word stress, these languages proved a fertile field for this type of *X(I)*.

A ten-syllable line causes rhythmic and psychological problems. A tap-dancer finds little difficulty in dancing a series of fours or sixes or of sixes and fours, but a series of tens is much more difficult: almost certainly he will get nines and elevens mixed in, if not make grosser errors. Modern psychologists have long recognised that human senses can only discriminate rapidly between a limited number of levels (e.g. beats, taps, or syllables). That number, as Miller (1956) shows, is approximately seven. French poets could, therefore, generate a series of fours and sixes effortlessly and endlessly, but not a series of tens. It is not surprising that traditional French metrists, such as Brandin and Hartog (1904: 10), claim that a line longer than nine syllables must contain a caesura. This is not a convention, but a psychological necessity, providing that the metrical pattern is based only on a series of taps or beats (syllables).

For languages in which word stress is strong and clearly discernible, there is a solution to the problem of generating lines of 10M/F syllables easily. The solution is to regularise the position of stressed syllables, and this can be done in two ways. The first is to place the stressed syllables in positions 2, 4, 6, 8, and 10. This is called duple time and can be exemplified by Keats'

(1) A thing of beauty is a joy forever (10F)

This produces a line of five prominence peaks, and, as I have noted, the mind can readily recognise a series of fives. It can also easily recognise a series of fours; hence the alternative solution. This is to place stressed syllables in positions 1, 4, 7, and 10; it is called triple time. It can be exemplified by Keats'

(2) How many bards gild the lapses of time (10M)

This line is clever in two ways. First, it is mimetic: Keats lapses into triple time for this line in what is a duple-time poem. Second, the ancient bards with whom Keats was most familiar were Virgil, Ovid, and (indirectly) Homer, all of whom composed in triple time (dactylic hexameter).

Another type of $X(I)$ with five prominence peaks in it has stressed syllables in positions 2, 4, 6, 7, and 10; it breaks from duple into triple time and is called by Spanish metrists a *fragmento adónico*. An English example is the following line from Tennyson's *Ulysses*:

(3) Much have I seen and known; cities of men (10M)

This line has an inversion at syllables 1–2 in addition to the inversion at syllables 7–8, which makes it a *fragmento adónico*. Tennyson is a much more metrically sophisticated poet than Keats. In this line he has made the first six syllables a perfect quantitative dactylic hexameter to the penthemimeral caesura, like the line of Homer (*Odyssey*, I.3) of which it is an almost literal translation:

(4) Pollōn d'anthrōpōn iden astea kai noon egnō

These are the three basic variants of the unified Romance $X(I)$ of 10M/F syllables: duple time, triple time, and *adónico*. There are, as Pighi (1970: 414) points out, 512 theoretical accentual variants of the $X(I)$, but most of the others are variations of these three with one or two of the stressed syllables missing. A single missing or misplaced stress does not interfere with our perception of the pattern, nor do two missing stresses, providing they occur early in the line and the basic rhythm is soon restored. The remaining variants have consecutive stresses which make them ambiguous in rhythm; they represent a small minority of lines in the work of the most technically proficient poets.

Italian and Galician-Portuguese poets developed the $X(I)$ with variable caesura, using all three of the basic rhythmic patterns. The latter preferred triple time to duple for the majority of their lines, although they used both freely. This preference probably derives from the Galician love of triple-time dance music and its rhythms; Galician folk dances, played on the local bagpipe, sound very different from the waltz or the polonaise, but their rhythm is the same. Ker (1898: 120) notes that English 'tumbling' verse of the sixteenth century shares the same rhythm. In Spain a metre derived from the triple-time $X(I)$ dominated long-line verse from the end of the fourteenth century to the beginning of the sixteenth. It was called *arte mayor* and again had an English equivalent in the Scottish and Border ballads; the ballad *Lord Rendal* is in *arte mayor* metre.

Italian taste in the Duecento and Trecento preferred the duple-time $X(I)$ of 10F syllables, the F(eminine) line, because of the plethora of proparoxytone words in Italian word stocks. The inventor of the sonnet, Giacomo da Lentini (fl. 1230–50), composed poems in which an overwhelming majority of lines were in duple time. But later poets, such as Cavalcanti, Dante, Petrarch, and Boccaccio, preferred variety. While a majority of their lines were duple time, there was always a substantial minority which were triple time or *adónicos*. Saavedra Molina (1946: 68) states that there are 1,229 triple-time lines in the *Divina Commedia* (9%) and 8,771 duple-time (61%). The variety of rhythms in the Italian $X(I)$ leads most Italian metrists to insist that Italian verse is syllabic; and, indeed, Dante himself in the *De vulgari eloquentia* describes the *endecasillabo* entirely in syllabic terms.

This historical sketch brings us up to the time of Chaucer. It shows clearly that if Chaucer composed iambic pentameters – monorhythmic duple-time $X(I)$s – then he was the first poet to do so. Most of the scholars who think Chaucer wrote iambic pentameters do not seem to realise the importance of the claim they are making. Chaucer transformed the *endecasillabo* into the iambic pentameter by excluding triple-time lines and using *adónicos* only for special effects. Windeatt (1984: 59) notes that many lines in Chaucer's *Troilus and Criseyde* are modelled on the lines of Boccaccio's *Filostrato* which they translate: they match stress for stress. But if Chaucer was so aware that many of Boccaccio's lines are in duple time, he could hardly have missed the obvious fact that many are in triple time. *Filostrato*, Book I, begins:

(5) Alcun di Giove sogliono il favore
     ne'lor principii pietosi invocare,
     altri d'Apollo chiamano il valore;
     io di Parnaso le Muse pregare
     solea ne'miei bisogni, ma Amore
     novellamente m'ha fatto mutare

Lines 2, 4, and 6 are triple-time $X(I)$s. It was Chaucer's exclusion of such lines from his verse that transformed the *endecasillabo* into the iambic pentameter.

Such scholars as Southworth (1954), Lewis (1939), and Ian Robinson (1971), who have denied that Chaucer's long-line metre is iambic pentameter, do not seem to realise that his would have been the first in

Europe. If Chaucer did not invent the iambic pentameter, then they must concede that Robert Henryson or some unknown intermediate poet did. In view of the strong French influence shown in Henryson's verse, this hardly seems likely.

The argument against Chaucer's metre's being any sort of $X(I)$ has always depended on the denial that final -*e* is syllabic in his verse. But the arguments for a syllabic final -*e* brought by Samuels (1972) and Windeatt (1977) are overwhelming. There are, moreover, equally strong arguments which neither Samuels nor Windeatt mentions. I have analysed many hundreds of Chaucer's lines which have the same scansion in the Hengwrt and Ellesmere MSS and which contain neither a midline final -*e* nor a word such as *pardoner* or *frankeleyn* which may contain either two syllables or three. Such lines all contain exactly ten syllables to the last stress; this cannot be a coincidence. There is further evidence: Chaucer's contemporary John Gower composed octosyllables in both French and English which appear to be based on exactly the same pattern; both are very strict in their syllable count, providing final -*e* is syllabic in both. There is no good reason for doubting that this is the case.

There is, I believe, a linguistic reason why Chaucer, composing English $X(I)$s, should have invented iambic pentameter more than a century before Garcilaso de la Vega (1501–36) did in Spanish, or Torquato Tasso (1544–95) in Italian. A clue as to why this was so is found in the *Cinkante Balades* of John Gower and the difference between Gower's French $X(I)$s and those of every French poet before and after him.

Most editors and commentators make some mention of Gower's use of *décasyllables* with variable caesura. None, however, emphasises sufficiently how remarkable these lines are in a metrical context. They have no parallel in the $X(I)$s of French poets of the fourteenth or fifteenth century, as an examination of the $X(I)$s of Machaut, Granson, Froissart, Chartier, Charles d'Orleans, or Villon will quickly show. All composed $X(I)$s with a fixed caesura after syllable 4, lines of 4 + 6 syllables, for the rhythmic and psychological reasons I have explained. Gower's French $X(I)$s were Italian *endecasillabi* in the French language, an amazing phenomenon when we consider the subsequent history of the French $X(I)$.

In the 1530s, as Jasinski (1970) explains in the greatest detail, Italian influence swept into French literature in the form of the Italianate sonnet, in the fashion of Petrarch but more directly influenced by Pietro Bembo (1470–1547). Saint-Gelais, Marot, Ronsard, and Du Bellay are four of the best-known of the many French poets who composed Italianate sonnets in the mid sixteenth century. They imitated the verse-form, style, vocabulary, themes, and sentiments of the Italians; but one thing they did not imitate: the variable caesura. They preserved the strongly divided French $X(I)$ in the most Italianate of their poems, even in the French translation of part of Petrarch's *Canzoniere* which appeared in Paris in 1548 (see Jasinski 1970: 50).

The reason why poets such as Ronsard did not attempt to compose in $X(I)$s with Italian variable caesura was almost certainly the weakness of French word stress. This would have prevented either the French poet or readers perceiving the pattern in such lines as four or five prominence peaks. In fact, Ronsard's $X(I)$s are an almost equal mixture of lines in which word stress occurs on every second syllable (duple time) and on every third syllable (triple time). Ronsard did not impose a single domi-nant accentual pattern on his lines, not even on a significant majority of his lines, as Petrarch and Bembo had done on theirs.

All this makes Gower's adoption of variable casura not just remark-able but unique in French. Gower's French also differed from that of the French poets I have named in that it was not Francien, the French of Paris, but Anglo-Norman, the French of Stratford-atte-Bowe. Opening Macaulay's edition of Gower at random, we find (pp. 356–57) numer-ous Anglo-Norman forms which distinguish the language from Francien: *assetz, hure, plure, toutz, mieulx, ailors, auns, consail, averai, serra, deinz, noun, vein, char*. There is one other feature of Anglo-Norman which I would hypothesise from an analysis of Gower's remarkable $X(I)$s. That is strong word stress, more like that of English than of French.

The first reason for hypothesising strong word stress is that Gower, unlike French poets before and after him, was somehow able to manage $X(I)$s with variable caesura without losing count of the syllables. The second reason is that Gower's $X(I)$s, like those of Petrarch, are pre-dominantly in duple time. The percentages of duple-time lines in various poets' work are as follows:

(6)					
Boccaccio	70	Thibaud IV	56	Orleans	60
Petrarch	79	Machaut	61	Villon	48
Gower	78	Froissart	60	Ronsard	50

I have already explained that Chaucer invented the iambic pentameter by excluding triple-time lines; in my own analysis, 97 per cent of his *X(I)*s are in duple time, about the same proportion as Garcilaso de la Vega's or Tasso's lines. Gower, like Petrarch, did not settle for this level of rhythmic monotony, but he was able to use the number of prominence peaks in the line in order to solve the problems presented by a variable caesura and a unified line of 10M/F syllables, as Petrarch had in Italian.

This predicates an Anglo-Norman with strong word stress, at least as strong as that of Italian, perhaps as strong as that of English. Gower often composed a series of lines in duple time or even a whole poem; 'Balade XXXV' by Gower is as iambic as Chaucer's *Troilus* or the *Canterbury Tales*. Macaulay notes that Gower (1330–1408) composed love poems of some kind in his early life, but argues that the *Balades* are late works. It is, therefore, disputable whether 'Balade XXXV' is earlier or later than Chaucer's first *X(I)*s in the *ABC*. In either case it is likely that the strong–weak alternating structure of the English and Anglo-Norman languages made an entirely duple-time *X(I)* acceptable to English ears long before it became the norm in Italian and Spanish. To illustrate its similarity to Chaucer's English metre, I give the last ten lines of Gower's 'Balade XXXV':

(7) O com nature est pleine de favour
     A ceos oiseals q'ont lour eleccion!
     O si jeo fuisse en droit de mon atour
     En ceo soul cas de lour condicioun!
     Plus poet nature qe ne poet resoun
     En mon estat tresbien le sente et voie:
     Qui soul remaint ne poet avoir grant joie.

     Chascun Tarcel gentil ad sa falcoun,
     Mais j'ai faili de ceo q'avoir voldroie:
     Ma dame, c'est le fin de mon chancoun,
     Qui soul remaint ne poet avoir grant joie.

14 Libertine scribes and maidenly editors: meditations on textual criticism and metrics

Hoyt N. Duggan

> You say tomato, and I say tomato.
> You say potato, and I say potato.
> Tomato, tomato, potato, potato,
> Let's call the whole thing off.
> Ira Gershwin

John Dryden's account of Chaucer in his *Preface to Fables Ancient and Modern* is marked by the conviction that something is seriously wrong with Chaucer's verse. Though granting it the 'rude Sweetness of a Scotch Tune', he bluntly faults it as 'not harmonious to us'. With bluff common sense, Dryden trusts the ocular proof of Speght's printed text, insisting

> that common Sense (which is a Rule in every thing but Matters of Faith and Revelation) must convince the Reader, that Equality of Numbers in every Verse which we call *Heroick*, was either not known, or not always practis'd, in *Chaucer's* Age. It were an easie Matter to produce some thousands of his Verses, which are lame for want of half a Foot, and sometimes a whole one, and which no Pronunciation can make otherwise. Dryden (Watson 1967–8: 281)

The received text of Dryden's day, Speght's second edition of 1602, will go far to explain Dryden's account of Chaucer's metre:

> When that Aprill with his shours sote,
> The drought of March had pierced to the rote,
> And bathed euery vaine in suche licour,
> 4 Of which vertue engendred is the flour:
> When Zephirus eke with his sote breath,
> Espired hath in euery holt and heath,
> The tender croppes, and that the yong sonne

8   Hath in the Ram halfe his course yronne,
     And small foules maken melodie,
     That slepen all night with open eie:
     So priketh hem nature in her courage,
12   Then longen folke to goe on pilgrimage,
     And palmers to seeken straunge strondes,
     To serue hallowes couth in sundry londes:
     And specially fro euery shires end
16   Of Englond, to Canterburie they wend,
     The holy blisful martir for to seeke,
     That hem hath holpen when they were seeke.

Scanning the passage, you, like Dryden, may think it 'not worth confuting [that] there were really Ten Syllables in a Verse where we find but Nine'. Perhaps Dryden's opinion of Chaucer's metrical competence may appear to err on the side of generosity. Imagine scanning these lines in ignorance of the syllabic status of final -e or of variable word stress in Chaucer's language, as Dryden did, since in the late seventeenth century philology was an unborn discipline. Philological ignorance and textual errors – the printer's loss of medial -e- in *shour(e)s* (line 1) or the defective *small* for *smale* (line 9), the unauthentic and unmetrical *that* in line 7, the inversion of *his halfe* in 8, the omitted *the* in 10, the omitted metrical filler *for* in 13, the disyllabic form *Englond* in 16, the omitted *that* of 18 – construct Dryden's commonsense view that 'Equality of Numbers . . . was either not known, or not always practis'd, in *Chaucer's* Age'. Of the first eighteen verses in Speght's edition, half are metrically defective because of defects in the text (1, 6, 7, 8, 9, 10, 13, 16, 18). Another four are metrical only to the reader who knows to discard the customary seventeenth-century word stresses (3, 4, 11, 12), and another four (2, 3, 5, 14) are metrical only if one knows to make an inflectional ending syllabic.[1] Only lines 6 and 17 are unambiguously regular to a reader untrained in ME. A defective text and ignorance of ME generated Dryden's defective account of the metre.

Three-quarters of a century later, Thomas Tyrwhitt, better informed about ME, constructed an accurate theory of Chaucer's metre and thus began the process of modern editing. Tyrwhitt dismissed apparent metrical ineptness as the function of a bad text, realising that no extant manuscript – and certainly no printed text – accurately reflected what Chaucer had written. He succinctly stated the basis for textual and metrical investigation when he imagined how a 'sensible critic in the Augustan age' would have addressed a poem by Ennius:

When he found that a great proportion of verses were strictly conformable to the ordinary rules of Metre, he would, probably, not scruple to conclude that such a conformity must have been produced by art and design, and not by mere chance. On the other hand, when he found, that in some verses the number of feet, to appearance, was either deficient or redundant; that in others the feet were seemingly composed to too few or too many syllables, of short syllables in the place of long or long in the place of short; he would not, I think, immediately condemn the old Bard, as having all at once forgotten the fundamental principles of his art, or as having wilfully or negligently deviated from them. He would first, I presume, enquire, whether all these irregularities were in the genuine text of his author, or only the mistakes of Copyists: he would enquire further, by comparing the genuine text with other contemporary writings and monuments, whether many things, which appear irregular, were not in truth sufficiently regular, either justified by the constant practice, or excused by the license of the age: where authority failed, he would have recourse (but soberly) to etymology and analogy; and if after all a few passages remained, not reducible to the strict laws of Metre by any of the methods abovementioned, if he were really (as I have supposed him) a sensible critic, he would be apt rather to expect patiently the solution of his difficulties from more correct manuscripts, or a more complete theory of the author's versification, than to cut the knot, by deciding peremptorily, that the work was composed without regard to metrical rules. (1822: I, 76–7)

Tyrwhitt, precociously aware of the usefulness of patterns of avoidance, noted Chaucer's use of syncope, apostrophe, syneresis, etc. to avoid excess syllables in a line. Observing the prevailing regularity of Chaucer's verse, Tyrwhitt expressed astonishment that others had denounced Chaucer for failing to achieve what 'every Balladmonger in our days, man, woman, or child, is known to perform with the most unerring exactness, and without any extraordinary fatigue' (p. xli).

Unhappily, the eighteenth-century discovery that Chaucer's text required emendation in the light of metrical theory was not generalised to the works of others, perhaps on the assumption that they were lesser poets, writing 'in the Infancy of our Poetry'. English textual critics, never caught up in the French and German 'scientific' interventionism of the last century (Foulet and Speer 1979: 8–19), showed instead a propensity to preserve manuscript readings wherever possible and provided parallel texts or, for poems surviving in multiple copies, 'best' text editions. Although not completely detrimental in effect upon English medieval texts, this cultural commitment to conservative editing has nevertheless produced a few curious, not to say retrograde, stances upon text and metre.

About ninety years ago C.S.Northup correctly characterised the metre of the *Pearl* as iambic tetrameter, in a pioneering study that has been refined by a succession of scholars, including Sir Israel Gollancz, Oliver F. Emerson, and Marie Borroff. Unfortunately, however, the impact of their scholarship upon recent editions of the poem has been slight. Instead, in the six editions published since Gordon's in 1953, the text has deteriorated, and the accompanying characterisations of the metre and language have become progressively less accurate.

Pearl survives in a single manuscript, our only witness to what the poet wrote. And it is not a *direct* witness. Its readings have been mediated by the work of the scribe who copied it and by an indeterminable number of scribes who wrote at indeterminable intervals between the composition of the poem and the date of the manuscript. Though the scribe perhaps made his copy within a decade or two of the composition of *Pearl*, more than half a century may have elapsed (Davis 1968: xxv–xxvi). I think it unlikely that the extant manuscript was copied directly from the poet's original; in fact, we cannot know how many scribes intervened in the textual traditions of these poems. Nor can we know in any useful detail how a succession of such copyists affected the texts and their metrical structures (Benskin and Laing 1981).

At least when we approach the text of *Pearl* we may reasonably entertain scepticism as to whether the immediate scribe's work accurately reflects the poet's original words and forms, especially his spellings. After all, this scribe's propensity to error is evident in the three other poems of the manuscript; and we need not subscribe to Emerson's 'exceedingly bad copyist' (1922: 52) to know that editors who reproduce the manuscript 'wherever possible' (Vantuono 1984: xiv) and without regard to probability must incorporate into their texts errors and misrepresentations of the poet's intentions (Duggan 1990a).

In Henry Savage's (1956) review of Gordon's edition, we can observe the beginnings of the present sorry state of affairs. Citing Emerson's views with evident contempt, Savage enunciates 'the rule that what an author (or scribe) wrote down in a unique medieval manuscript is not to be changed without overwhelming evidence against leaving it as it stands' (p. 126). Savage scornfully rejects Emerson's view that 'it should be our purpose to restore these poems in their original form, so far as that may have been distributed by an unreliable copyist, and with such light as a knowledge of the language of the time may throw upon the poet's probable accuracy' (Emerson 1922: 61). Emerson's goal, so far as I can tell an unexceptionable one, is dismissed as 'throw[ing] away the canons of good editorship'.[2]

Since Gordon, all editors of *Pearl* have followed, more or less rigorously, Savage's noninterventionist view of things. The result, predictably, has been increased fidelity to the MANUSCRIPT and infidelity to the POEM. Substituting the Cotton Nero scribe for the poet, the two most recent editors, Charles Moorman and William Vantuono, have confused the metre of the *Pearl* with that of the alliterative long line. Both editors ignore problems of form, sense, and grammar in defence of every possible manuscript reading, constructing a perverse metrical theory to support bad editorial practice.

In this chapter I can address but four of the many factors contributing to our confusion about the metre of *Pearl*. First, we lack an authoritative statement of the metrical rules that governed the composition of foot-counted, four-stress poetry in Middle English.[3] Second, we lack consensus on the state of final etymological and grammatical -*e* in the poet's dialect.[4] Third, and perhaps most debilitating, the texts upon which our analyses must rest often better represent scribal error and sophistication than final authorial intentions. Finally, many modern editors, by temperament and training committed to naive empiricism, confuse the document with the poem and thus find themselves in Dryden's shoes. They perceive in *Pearl* a poem composed in half-lines of no discernible shape, with the full line varying between seven and fourteen syllables and with unpredictable alternations of iambic, trochaic, anapaestic, pyrrhic, and spondaic feet (and compare Osberg, this volume).

The rhythmic patterns of *Pearl* are quite unlike those of the alliterative long line. Alliterative poets avoided alternating rhythms, whether iambic or anapaestic, in their b-verses (Cable 1989; Duggan 1986a, 1988b). In *Pearl*, on the contrary, over 90 per cent of the last two feet in any line are regular iambs as they stand in the manuscript. Moreover, alliteration and metrical stress coincide in the alliterative long line. Clearly, they do not coincide in *Pearl*, as we may see in its first line: 'Perle, pleasaunt to princes pay'. Only those who take the distribution of syllables in the alliterative line to be without rule can speculate that the *Pearl* line originated in alliterative verse (see also McCully and Hogg 1994).

If its metre is not that of the alliterative long line, what can it be? That the verseform steadily has four stressed syllables per line requires no proof or elaboration. Nor, in spite of Gordon's claim to the contrary, should it need proof that the majority of lines consist of alternating iambic feet. The fundamentally iambic form of most verses is readily seen in those verses in which syllable count or stress assignment are not at issue:

27   Blomez blayke and blwe and rede
29   Flor and fryte may not be fede
30   þer hit doun drof in moldez dunne
33   Of goud vche goude is ay bygonne
320   þy corse in clot mot calder keue
371   Of care and me ȝe made acorde

In the text as now available, however, lines remain where too few or too many syllables appear. One explanation – so far a compelling one to students of ME – is that the poet, though content to write regular iambic tetrameter verse most of the time, did not intend to restrict himself to the form. If we, like Savage and Vantuono, confuse the poet with the immediate scribe and attach authority to scribal spellings and scribal choice from among synonyms or doublet forms, we will be drawn inevitably to that explanation. However, evidence both from *Pearl* and from the other poems in the manuscript shows that this scribe's spellings and forms are not those of the poet. For instance, the scribe demonstrably in *Cleanness*, *Patience*, and *Gawain* wrote *oþer* where the poet had written *or*. Each of the following b-verses is unmetrical as it stands but would be metrical with synonymous *or*:

GGK 1255b	. . . oþer golde þat þay hauen
GGK 1772b	. . . oþer lodly refuse
GGK 1956b	. . . oþer dronken ben oþer
Pat. 432b	. . . oþer demed þe ȝet
Pat. 463b	. . . oþer Ermonnes hillez
Cleanness 417b	. . . oþer myry bawelyne
Cleanness 1047b	. . . oþer byten in twynne
Cleanness 1092b	. . . oþer ordure watz inne

Fully twenty-three lines in *Pearl* that appear to have anapaestic feet are metrically regular if the correct synonym *or* is supplied:

> 118   Watz emerad, saffer, [or] gemme gente
> 141   By onde þe broke by slente [or] slade
> 359   For marre [or] madde, morne and myþe
> 491   [Or] ellez a lady of lasse aray[5]

Similarly, dozens of apparent instances of disyllabic occupancy of a thesis become regular if a scribal disyllabic form is replaced with the appropriate monosyllabic doublet. For instance, *syþen* is written for *syn* and *wheþer* for *wher*, while the monosyllabic forms *ner*, *ere*, and *o're* are invariably spelled as disyllabic *neuer*, *euer*, and *ouer*:

(1)   The manuscript reads *neuer*:
> 71   For wern [ner] webbez þat wyȝ ez weuen
> 376   I wyste [ner] quere my perle watz gon
> 484   þou cowþez [ner] God nauþer plese ne pray[6]
> 571   And þe fyrste þe laste, be he [ner] so swyft[7]

(2)   The manuscript reads *neuer*:
> 852   In honour more and n[au]þelesse
> 864   And neuer onez honour ȝet n[au]þeles
> 876   þat lote, I leue, watz n[au]þeles
> 888   Her songe þay songen n[au]þeles
> 900   Fro þat maskelez mayster n[au]þeles

(3)   The manuscript reads *euer*:
> 144   And [ere] me longed ay more and more
> 153   And [ere] me poȝt I schulde not wonde
> 180   And [ere] þe lenger þe more and more
> 200   þat [ere] I seȝ ȝet with myn [ene][8]

(4)   The manuscript reads *syþen*:
> 13   [Syn] in þat spote hit fro me sprange
> 245   [Syn] into gresse þou me aglyȝte
> 1207 And [syn] to God I hit bytaȝte

(5)   The manuscript reads *ouer*:
> 138   Watz þer [ore] gayn þo bonkez brade
> 318   þou wylnez [ore] þys water to weue
> 324   Er [ore] þys dam hym Dryȝtyn deme
> 1166 [Ore] meruelous merez, so mad arayde[9]

The mere existence of syllabic and stress doublets in ME and the poet's dialect does not itself prove that the poet would have selected those forms. Other kinds of evidence must be adduced to show that the poet chose forms to make his verse metrically regular. Fortunately, some inferential evidence is available in the poet's use of stress doublets, of metrical fillers, and of final historical -*e*. The accumulated evidence shows that the poet wrote a much more regular form of iambic tetrameter verse than the manuscript or any modern edition suggests.

The immediate scribe did not take final -*e* to be sounded. Graphemic analysis shows that his practice in this respect is not chaotic but subject to rule.[10] As for the poet himself, conclusive evidence exists both within the poem and in the other poems of the manuscript that he did not habitually sound such -*e*'s either within the verse or at verse ends. However, he occasionally used historically motivated forms when the metre demanded them (Borroff 1962: 140–60, 182–9; Duggan 1988b). The rhyme evidence shows unambiguously that the poet did not routinely sound final -*e* (Borroff 1977: 33–5). Within the line, corroborative evidence for the loss of -*e* appears in monosyllabic weak or plural adjectives when the metre suggests the silencing of a historical -*e*.[11] Note that in these cases, assuming for the moment that a monosyllabic thesis is more probable than a disyllabic one, the metrical evidence suggests that the poet as well as the scribe did not consistently sound weak and plural adjective inflections.

On the other hand, continuing to assume metrical regularity that demands one obligatory unstressed syllable between ictuses, we will discover a substantial number of lines which are metrically regular only because an etymological -*e* is inscribed.[12] Another set of lines, somewhat smaller, is metrically regular because a historically motivated inflectional -*e* is present.[13]

Other evidence that the poet intended to write regular iambic tetrameter can be inferred from his use of metrical fillers. Pre-Romantic poets, even the most accomplished – one thinks of Chaucer and Shakespeare – used metrical fillers or selected from among doublet forms to achieve regular metrical patterns. They selected *for to* as the marker of the infinitive rather than *to* alone, or they used meaningless intensifiers like *full*, *well*, and *so* to make their lines metrically regular. The *Gawain* poet, justly recognised as a verbal artist of extraordinary power, used even more metrical fillers than some lesser poets. For instance, to achieve metrically regular b-verses, the *Gawain* poet in *Cleanness* used *ful* in thirty-seven lines, sometimes twice in a single verse.[14]

The *Pearl* poet's practice is consonant with that of the *Cleanness* poet in regard to *ful* as a metrical filler. In forty lines, *ful* appears to avoid clashing stress, providing the thesis in positions 3, 5, and 7.

> 28   þer schynez *ful* schyr agayn þe sunne
>
> 42   Schadowed þis wortez *ful* schyre and schene
>
> 531   He seȝ þer ydel men *ful* stronge[15]

The *Pearl* poet also uses *for to* in place of *to* alone, apparently for the sole purpose of achieving an iambic foot:

> 99   þe derþe þerof *for to* deuyse
>
> 333   Now rech I neuer *for to* declyne
>
> 403   My Lorde ne louez not *for to* chyde
>
> 613   Bot now þou motez me *for to* mate
>
> 1118   To much hit were of *for to* melle
>
> 1129   Delit þe Lombe *for to* deuise

Similarly, the semantically lightweight intensifier *so* appears in fifty-three lines, always to avoid clashing stress:

> 2   To clanly clos in golde *so* clere
>
> 5   So rounde, *so* reken in vche araye
>
> 190   So smoþe, *so* smal, *so* semé slyȝt[16]

The poet's choice of doublet forms of the related adverbials *als* and *also* appears to have been motivated by considerations of metre:

> 685   The ryȝtwys man *also* sertayn
>
> 765   He gef me myȝt and *als* bewté
>
> 1071   And *also* þer n[']is neuer nyȝt
>
> 822   Lo, Godez Lombe *as* trwe *as* ston

Rarely do the adverbial intensifiers *al* and *ay* contribute as much to meaning as to metre:

> 16   And heuen my happe and *al* my hele
>
> 86   Garten my goste *al* greffe forȝete
>
> 518   So watz *al* samen her answar soȝt
>
> 540   þe day watz *al* apassed date.[17]
>
> 33   Of goud vche goude is *ay* bygonne
>
> 101   I welke *ay* forth in wely wyse

132   Hyttez to haue *ay* more and more
596   þou hyȝe kyng *ay* pertermynable
684   þe innosent is *ay* saf by ryȝt[18]

   The poet's choice of fillers and of doublet forms for metrical purposes provides the clearest evidence of his intention to avoid clashing stress. However, a significant number of apparently anapaestic feet occur, several already quoted above. The evidence more strongly supports the hypothesis that one unstressed syllable must appear between ictuses than the hypothesis that the poet avoided triple rhythms. The occasional appearance of triple rhythms in a verseform predominantly duple is an old problem for English metrists, and I do not pretend to propose a definitive solution here. However, as we have seen, the poet's forms differed frequently from those suggested by the scribe's spellings. If the linguistic features common to English verse apply to *Pearl*, most of the apparently extrametrical syllables in the present editions of *Pearl* simply disappear. That is, if we permit the *Pearl* poet the use of stress doublets, the syncope, the elision, the syneresis, the contraction, and the very occasional apocope that we permit Chaucer and Gower or the poets of the alliterative revival (Duggan 1988b, 1990b), only a few remaining lines will depart from regular iambic tetrameter.

   Regular iambic tetrameter, however, does not demand the monotonous alternation of iambic feet. True, tetrameter verse tends towards greater rhythmic sameness than pentameter, but in English the regular alternation of identical iambic feet is not required to establish either form. Headless lines lacking the unstressed initial syllable are common in *Pearl* and in other poems written in iambic tetrameter: about 7 to 15 per cent in *Pearl*, Chaucer's *The Book of the Duchess*, and other poems like *Octavian* and *Kyng Alisaunder*. Epic caesura occurs with greater frequency in *Pearl* than in *The Book of the Duchess* or *Cursor Mundi*, but perhaps no more than in other popular poems composed in the four-stress line. Predictably, disyllabic occupancy occurs more often in the first foot than in the second, and again we must remember that scribal spellings often misrepresent what the poet wrote.

   The pervasiveness of the epic caesura in *Pearl* contributes to the illusion that its metre is based on that of the alliterative line, that it shares with the long line an obligatory caesura before the penultimate stress, that it, in short, like the other three poems in the manuscript, is composed in half-lines. It would be easy to cite many lines in *Pearl* in which

a syntactic juncture occurs after the second stress and appears to coincide with metrical caesura, e.g.:

5   So rounde, so reken   in vche araye

14 Ofte haf I wayted   wyschande þat wele

22 To þenke hir color   so clad in clot

25 þat spot of spysez   mot nedez sprede

Examples may readily be multiplied, since – depending upon what one
decides about syncope of unstressed syllables in words like *neuer*, *euer*,
skyllez, *myrþez*, *called* (all words with monosyllabic forms in Middle
English) – epic caesura appears in 5 to 10 per cent of its lines.

As we have noted, epic caesura, though it appears less frequently in
Chaucer's *Book of the Duchess* than in *Pearl*, is well attested in
Chaucer's tetrameter verse and in other four-stress poems:

BD 113   Or how he fareth,   or in what wise

BD 134   To do hir erande   and he come nere

BD 136   Go bet quod Juno   to Morpheus

BD 147   And shewe hire shortly   hit ys no nay.

Though such lines superficially resemble the half-lines of alliterative
verse – the metrical caesura corresponds with syntactic juncture, and
each half-line is a metrical phrase – the resemblance is accidental. Other
verses show clearly that the full line – not the half-line – is the fundamental metrical unit. That is, the syntactic integrity of the colon in ME
alliterative verse (and in the verses cited above) is frequently violated in
Pearl. Lyric caesura appears in many lines where metrical and syntactic
units are not coterminous:

x   x   / x / x   /   x   /

7   Queresoe[']er I jugged   gemmez gaye

x /   x   /   x   / x   /

8   I sette hyr sengeley   in syngl[e]re

x   /   x   / x   /   x   /(x)

98   þat fryth þer fortwne   forth me ferez

x   x   /   x   / x   / x   /

113 In þe founce þer stonden   stonez stepe

/   x   x   /   x   / x   /

202 Dubbed with double   perle and dyȝte

```
        x  /  x  /  x      /  x  /
260  As in þis gardyn   gracios gaye¹⁹
        x   /   x  /     x  /  x  /
295  þou says þou trawez me   in þis dene
        x  /  x   /  x   /  x  /
351  þy mendez mountez   not a myte
        x  / x   /  x    /   x  /
388  þaȝ I hente ofte   harmez hate
        x     /     x  / x    /  x   /
438  And speke me towarde   in þat space
        x   /  x   /  x    /  x /
489  Of countes, damysel,   par ma fay
        x    /  x   /  x  /  x     /
497  As Mathew melez   in your messe²⁰
         x  /     x  / x   /   x  /
506  þe lorde ful erly   vp he ros
        x  / x  /   x     /  x  /
507  To hyre werkmen   to hys vyne
```

Yet other lines show what would be the caesura occurring after the syntactic juncture:

```
        x  /     x     /  x  /  x  /
 85  Th'adubbement   of þo downez dere
        x     /     x    /  x  / x /
238  And haylsed me   wyth a lote lyȝte²¹
        x   /    x     /   x  /   x     /
411  þow wost wel   when þy perle con schede
        x  / x    / x    /  x  /
418  Hys lef is.   I am holy hysse
        x    /    x  /  x  /   x  /
516  Ne knawe ȝe   of þis day no date?
        x    /      x  /   x  /  x  / x
544  And fyrre,   þat non me may reprené
        x  / x     /  x     /   x    /
737  For hit is wemlez,   clene, and clere.
```

A few other verses have two syntactic junctures, and the metre moves regularly without reference to either:

```
        x   /     x  / x  /   x     /
525  þay wente   into þe vyne   and wroȝte
```

```
      x    /     x /    x  /      x  /
530  On our  byfore þe sonne  go doun
       /    x  /  x     /     x   /
569  þus schal I   quod Kryste  hit skyfte
```

Gordon asserts that the poet, who from time to time produces two stresses with a single word, does not do so in the second and third stressed positions. He is willing to generalise on this basis that 'the line in *Pearl* is probably more truly understood as a modification of the alliterative line than as a basically French line assimilated to the alliterative tradition' (1953: 91). If Gordon's description were correct, the medial caesura would be a categorical metrical constraint rather than a statistical norm. As a matter of fact, a few lines appear in which a compound word or an inseparable noun phrase occupies the middle stresses:

```
        /   (x) x    /   x  /   x    /
202   Dubbed with double perle and dyȝte
        x / x / x    /    x   /
531   He se þer ydel men ful stronge
        x /    x   / x   /    x / (x)
719   To suche is heuenryche arayed²²
        /  x  x   /   x   /    x    /
1093  Ryȝt as þe maynful mone con rys
```

More to the point, other poems generally taken to be written in iambic tetrameter also manifest very few such verses.²³ Though the point is of interest to the metrist and student of style, the practice does not distinguish *Pearl* from poems like *Hauelok the Dane*, *Cursor Mundi*, *Sir Orfeo*, and *The Book of the Duchess*. Certainly it does not prove half-line structure.

Little space remains in which to discuss apparent instances of clashing stress. Clashing stress appears in several lines because a historically justified final -*e* is omitted in the manuscript. In square brackets I have supplied the historically justified inflectional or etymological *e*'s that make each verse metrical:

```
 17   þat dotȝ bot þrych my hert[e] þrange²⁴
 68   Where rych[e] rokkez wer to dyscreuen
122   Of wod and water and wlonk[e] playnez
225   I hope no tong[e] moȝt endure
286   þat hatȝ me broȝt þys blys[se] ner
```

381   þa cortaysly ȝe carp[e] con
486   And quen mad on þe fyrst[e] day
564   Wy schalte þou þenne ask[e] more
586   þat swange and swat for long[e] ȝore
678   Lorde, quo schal klymbe þy hyȝ[e] hylle
683   þer schal hys step[e] stable stylle
825   Hymself ne wroȝt[e] neuer ȝet non[25]
999   Jasper hyȝt þe fyrst[e] gemme
1036 þe portalez pyked of rych[e] platez.
1046 þe self[e] God watȝ her lompe-lyȝt[26]

The fit between the independent systems of grammar and metre lends credence to the theory that the poet used doublet forms. My case would be weakened if it were possible to find numerous lines with clashing stress for which no historically motivated -e is available. I find none.

We have, in less than a half-century, moved from a time when editors who assumed that poets cared about the formal features of their work frequently intervened – perhaps too frequently – in the text of *Pearl*, to the present state of affairs when good editors like Malcolm Andrew and Ronald Waldron (1978) appear to pay little attention to matters of metre and rhyme, and when incompetent editors simply transcribe the manuscript. Ours has not been, thus far, a golden age of textual criticism or metrical theory, and it is entirely possible that the scholars at the end of the last century who both perceived and assumed regularities in the text better served the *Pearl* poet than more recent conservative editors who have tended to serve the scribe of MS. Cotton Nero A.x.

If one approaches the metrical structures of *Pearl* with the assumption that scribal spellings are just that and no more, if one assumes that a degree of scribal dialect translation is rather more likely than letter-by-letter transcription, if one assumes the occasional scribal omission and insertion of words – if, in short, one assumes that the Cotton Nero A.x. scribe (and the unknown number of scribes whose work separates us from the poet's original) was like other scribes who copied ME texts, we can then approach the poem in search of its underlying metrical regularities. Once free from the unscholarly assumptions that spellings are authorial and phonemic and that metrically anomalous lines represent precisely what the poet wrote, we can determine the statistical regularities and analyse the statistically unusual verses to determine whether their divergences from a statistical norm are explicable by reference to features of the language such as inflectional endings, possible elision, syncope or apocope, the presence or absence of syntactic disjuncture, and metrical position within the line. We must also consider whether the scribe has not, in some instances, licentiously had his way with the poet's text and whether we can or ought to attempt to remedy his assault.

Editors of ME poems rarely have autograph copies to edit. When poems survive only in copies written in a dialect different from the poet's own, we have thought it necessary to edit for words alone and to reproduce the spellings as they are preserved in the scribe's dialect without reference to the poet's probable forms. In future, good editorial practice will require that we edit for syllables as well as words when the *usus scribendi* of the poets can be shown to differ from that of the immediate scribes. 'Conservative' scholars will doubtless accuse such editors of 'rewriting the poem'. The ensuing debate ought to revolve around an essential question: what is it that the editor attempts to conserve? A document? Or a poem? I submit that it is the proper task of librarians to conserve documents and of editors to conserve poems.

Notes

1 Ignorance on this head continued into the next century, when John Urry, whose posthumously published edition did much to put emendation *metri causa* in ill odour, put -*en* (which he sensibly spelled -*in* when he took it to be syllabic) on singular forms of the verb. Urry left an otiose *that* in *Gen. Prol.* 7 and did not supply the -*e* on the weak adjective in the phrase *the yonge Sunne*. Alderson cites prefatory material in the Gavin Douglas edition of 1710 to the effect that 'verb endings were "promiscuously" used in earlier English' (1970: 113). Alderson's account of Urry's editorial method shows that Urry was the first to grasp the principles of Chaucerian metrics. Imitations of Chaucer by seventeenth- and eighteenth-century poets make clear how ignorant most literary men were of ME grammar. For examples and discussion, see Spurgeon (1925: I. xlviiiff.).

2 Savage's retrograde notion, though fitting nicely into the mid-century Anglo-American climate of naive empiricism, derived its force from a logically unnecessary extension of Joseph Bédier's devastating attack on both Lachmannian recension and the distributional recensionist model of Henri Quentin. Bédier argued persuasively that editors of medieval vernacular texts should drop the pretence of scientific or 'critical' reconstruction. He also argued that they should select the best of the surviving

manuscripts and that they should print its readings where they were not obviously in error. Eugene Vinaver expressed what was to become the dominant attitude among Anglo-American editors of medieval texts, vigorously asserting that an editor ought not emend *any* manuscript reading that is *possibly* authorial. Mere probability is no basis for emendation: 'For it *is* right to preserve a reading as long as it is *possible* that it comes from the original, and it is wrong to replace it by what is merely *probable*. "Impossible" readings are those which can be shown to result from scribal errors; such readings it is our duty to correct. "Improbable" readings may or may not be due to the author, and those we have *obviously* no right to alter' (1939).

3 E. V. Gordon (1953: 89–90), like Tarlinskaja (1973), accepted the false notion that ME tetrameter verse is a hybrid form of the OE alliterative line and the French octosyllabic couplet:

> Most rhymed Middle English verse (apart from Chaucer, Gower, and many of the lyrics) descends from the rhythms of the old alliterative line modified in varying degrees by adaptation to rhyme-schemes. *Pearl* is even nearer than most rhymed verse to the alliterative cadences, possibly because the author was accustomed to compose unrhymed alliterative verse also. The chief effect of this close relationship is that the line is not measured, has not a fixed number of syllables, like the lines of French verse, nor is it systematically iambic or anapæstic, as the modern reader tends to make it. The essential basis of the line consists of four stresses ('lifts'), around which are are arranged unstressed elements ('dips'), varying in number from three to five. The position of the dips and the number of syllables in them is variable, the old rhythmic variety of the alliterative line being inherited and only slightly reduced by the addition of rhyme. Thus we find dips between the lifts consisting of one, two, or three syllables; or there may be no dip at all between the lifts, and we then have the 'clashing' of stresses familiar in OE poetry.

For recent studies of ME four-stress verse, see Minkova (1990), Smithers (1983), and Tarlinskaja (1976a, b). None is definitive.

4 For final -*e* in Chaucer, see Burnley (1982), Cowan (1987), Donaldson (1948), Guthrie (1988a), and Samuels (1972). For Hoccleve, see Jefferson (1987), and for eME, Smithers (1983). For Langland, see Duggan (1990b) and Samuels (1985, 1988). For ME alliterative verse in general, see Borroff (1962) and Duggan (1988b). See also Minkova (1984a, b, 1985, 1990).

5 The same is true in lines 130, 211, 380, 448, 463, 464, 466, 567, 592, 604, 606, 608, 679, 724, 726, 952, 1060, 1200, and 1201.

6 Manuscript *nauper* is substituted by the scribe for synonymous *nor*.

7   The same error appears in lines 631, 667, 699, 724, 750, 812, 825, 845, 889, 899, and 1057.

8   The same error occurs in lines 239, 261, 328, 349, 416, 591, 600, 666, 668, 698, 890, 959, 1030, 1062, 1066, and 1132.

9   See also lines 454, 473, 773, and 1205.

10 Scribal <-e> tends to appear under the following conditions in this manuscript:

(1) After monosyllabic stems ending in a consonant cluster (e.g. *golde* < OE *gold*; *grounde* < OE *grund*; *breste* < OE *bréost*; *corne* < OE *corn*; *honde* < OE *hond*; *towarde* < OE *tóweard*; *ofte* < OE *oft*; *foreste* < OF *forest*). The spelling *fonte* at line 327 for the past participle of *findan* suggests that the *e* is motivated by the combination of vowel plus consonant cluster rather than a survival of inflectional *-en*, since the *e* would have had to be reduced to zero for final *-d* to have become *-t* (Gordon 1953: xlvi, 93, 95). This is only a tendency and not universal in the manuscript. Counterinstances are *rert* 591, *bycalt* 1163, *flonc* 1165. For others, see Gordon (1953: xlvi).

(2) Following a single consonant to indicate the length of the tonic vowel (e.g. *oute* < OE *út*; *sede* < OE *séd*, etc.). The point is that for this scribe, final *e* had other functions in his writing system than to express grammatical function.

11 The following lines suggest that a historically possible *-e* was not in fact sounded:

> 15   þat wont watz whyle *deuoyde* my wrang (inf.)
> 50   For *care* ful colde þat to me caȝt (etym. < OE *cearu*)
>   x /   x /   x / x   /
> 87   So *frech* flauorez of frytez were (pl. adj.)
> 284 And wony wyth hyt in *schyr* wodschawez (pl. adj.)
> 597 Now he þat stod þe *long* day stable (wk adj.)

12 A metrically required and scribally written etymological *-e* appears in the following words: *stylle* < OE *stille*, 20; *faste* < OE *fæste*, 54 (stressed here, unstressed *faste* is monosyllabic in 150); *tonge* < OE *tunge*, 100; *gemme* < OF 118, 289; *herte* < OE *heorte*, 128; *tenþe* < OE *ten* + ordinal *-þa*, 136; *bytwene* < OE *betwéonan*, 140; *mote* < OF, 142; *nwe* < OE *néowe*, 155; *fayre* < OE *faeger*, 169, 177; *herte* < OE *heorte*, 176; *sute* < OF *su(i)te*, 203; *bryme* < OE, 232; *kynde* < OE *gecynde*, 276. In 335 *perle* < OF in the phrase *of perle myne* is an emendation from manuscript *perleȝ*, but the *e* is metrically required.

13 For instance, in *fyrce* (pl. adj.) 54; *fyrre* (wk adj.) 148; *wynne* (pl. adj.) 154; *aske* (inf.) 316; *oȝte* (pret. impersonal) 341; *for soþe* (petrified dat.) 292 (Gordon is correct to note that the dat. sing. is rarely written with *-e*); *hyȝe* (wk adj.) 395.

14 *Ful* appears as a b-verse metrical filler in *Cleanness* 20, 26, 27, 73, 146, 175, 221, 321, 364, 407, 414, etc.

15 See also lines 50, 80, 159, 162, 179, 182, 183, 307, 354, 387, 393, 412, 454, 460, 499, 506, 691, 716, 748, 807, 833, 834, 860, 868, 879, 880, 882, 894, 1023, 1024, 1076, 1077, 1078, 1079, 1098, 1135, 1177, 1202, and 1204. The appearance of *ful* as metrical filler in a number of verses supports the hypothesis that many inflectional syllables had been syncopated in the poet's speech, e.g. 28, 307, 691, etc.

16 See also lines 6, 19, 22, 72, 74, etc.

17 See also lines 204, 210, 257, 280, and 386.

18 See also lines 44, 56, 144, 156, 342, 408, 573, 696, 720, 956, 1189, and 1195.

19 The endings *-io(u)n* and *-io(u)s*, normally productive in Chaucer's verse of two syllables, in *Pearl* are usually made monosyllabic by syncope. Northerly dialects were presumably more advanced than southern in this respect as in many others. See Dobson (1968: II, §§270, 276, 292, 387).

20 Northup (1897: 329) suggests emendation to *your[e]* on the ground that it modifies a dative, but the verse is regular with the stress falling on *in*. Cf. 1004.

21 This verse is not straightforward, since *lote*, which must be disyllabic to avoid clashing stress, is derived from monosyllabic ON *lát*. Citations in *MED* are not entirely conclusive, but spellings with *-e* in *Ormulum* and *The Owl and the Nightingale* suggest it had become disyllabic in some ME dialects.

22 Line 787 requires emendation to be metrical: 'As in þe Apocalyppez hit is sene'. If all the written syllables were sounded, the line would have eleven. However, elision of *þ'Apocalypse* is probable, and *hit* is otiose.

23 My sample is small – 300 lines from *Cursor Mundi* 25001–300, *The Owl and the Nightingale* 801–1100, *Sir Orfeo* 201–500, *Kyng Alisaunder* 7451–750, *Hauelok the Dane* 2301–600, *The Book of the Duchess* 801–1100 – but the rate of occurrence of similar lines ranges from 1 in 300 lines (*Owl and Nightingale*) to as many as 7 (*Cursor Mundi*). A brief look at *The House of Fame* suggests that at least one version of Chaucer's tetrameter line incorporates many more such verses.

24 Note that *-e* is historically justified on the infinitive *þrych*, but in view of the evidence that the inflected forms were not steadily retained by the poet, there is no reason to add it where it is not metrically motivated.

25 If *neuer* were stressed on the second syllable, the verse would be metrical, but given the evidence in the manuscript for *neuer* representing monosyllabic *n'er* in such positions, it is rational to think that the verb inflection was deleted by the scribe.

26 Cf. 1076. Though Northup suggested emendation of the following verses, it is not necessary. Stress assignment in iambic tetrameter verse is a func-

tion of syllabic position as well as word class, and each verse may be
scanned regularly without distortion of word or phrasal stress:

```
        /   x   /  x /  x  /
616   Am not worþy so gret fere
        / x   /   x  x  / x   /
635   3ys and pay hym at þe fyrst fyne
        x   /   x  / x  /  x    /
776   For Kryst han lyued in much stryf
        x   /  x  x / x  /  x  /
995   As derely deuysez þis ilk toun
        x   / x  /    x  / x /
1076  And þe self sunne ful fer to dym.
```

Though I take each of these scansions to be possible, I do not know how
probability is to be established, and Northup's suggested emendations
may be correct.

References

Abercrombie, D. 1965. *Studies in phonetics and linguistics*. London: Oxford University Press. (Contains papers 'A phonetician's view of verse structure' and 'Syllable quantity and enclitics in English'.)
1976. '"Stress" and some other terms'. *Work in Progress* 9. 51–9. University of Edinburgh, Department of Linguistics.
Abercrombie, L. 1923. *Principles of English prosody*. London: Secker.
Adams, C. 1979. *English speech rhythm and the foreign learner*. The Hague: Mouton.
Adams, V. 1973. *An introduction to modern English word-formation*. London: Longman.
Alderson, W. L. 1970. *Chaucer and Augustan scholarship*. (University of California Publications 35). Berkeley and Los Angeles: University of California Press.
Alexander, M. 1983. *Old English literature*. London: Macmillan.
Alexis. 1933. *'La vie de Saint Alexis', poème français du XIe siècle*. Ed. J.-M. Meunier. Paris: Droz.
Allen, W. S. 1973. *Accent and rhythm*. Cambridge: Cambridge University Press.
Anderson, J. J., ed. 1969. *Patience*. Manchester: Manchester University Press.
1977. *Cleanness*. Manchester: Manchester University Press.
Anderson, J. M., & C. Jones. 1977. *Phonological structure and the history of English*. New York and Oxford: North-Holland.
Andrew, M., & R. Waldron, eds. 1978. *The poems of the 'Pearl' manuscript*. London: Edward Arnold.
Atkins, H. G. 1923. *A history of German versification*. London: Methuen.
Attridge, D. 1974. *Well-weighed syllables: Elizabethan verse in classical metres*. Cambridge: Cambridge University Press.
1982. *The rhythms of English poetry*. London: Longman.
Avalle, D'Arco S., ed. 1960. *Poésie* [Peire Vidal]. 2 vols. Milan: Ricciardi.
1963. *Preistoria dell'endecasillabo*. (Prolusione letta nell' Univ. di Torino). Milan: Ricciardi.
Baker, S. 1960. 'English meter *is* quantitative'. *College English* 21. 309–15.

Barber, C., & N. Barber. 1990. 'The versification of *The Canterbury Tales*: a computer-based statistical study'. *Leeds Studies in English* **20**. 81–101.

Baruffaldi, G., the Elder, et al. 1713. *Rime scelte de' poeti ferrarese antichi e moderni*. Ferrara: Authors.

Bauer, L. 1983. *English word-formation*. Cambridge: Cambridge University Press.

Baum, P.F. 1922. *The principles of English versification*. Cambridge, Mass.: Harvard University Press.

1930. 'The character of Anglo-Saxon verse'. *Modern Philology* **28**. 143–56.

1948–9. 'The meter of the *Beowulf*'. *Modern Philology* **46**. 73–91, 145–62.

Bédier, J. 1928. 'La tradition de lai de l'ombre: réflexions sur l'art d'éditer les anciens textes'. *Romania* **54**. 161–96, 321– 56.

Beissner, F. 1946. *Stuttgarter Hölderlin-Ausgabe*, vol. 1.1: *Gedichte bis 1800. Text*. Stuttgart: Kohlhammer.

Bembo, Pietro. 1966. *Prose, rime*. Ed. Carlo Dionisotti. 2nd edn. Turin: Unione Tipografico Editrice Torinese.

Bennett, J.A.W., ed. 1968. *Selections from John Gower*. Oxford: Clarendon Press.

Bennett, J.A.W., & G.V. Smithers. 1966. *Early Middle English verse and prose*. Oxford: Clarendon Press.

Benskin, M., & M. Laing. 1981. 'Translations and *Mischsprachen* in Middle English manuscripts'. In Benskin & Samuels, eds. 55–106.

Benskin, M., & M.L. Samuels, eds. 1981. *So meny people longages and tonges: philological essays in Scots and mediaeval English presented to Angus McIntosh*. Edinburgh: Middle English Dialect Project.

Benson, L.D. 1966. 'The literary character of Anglo-Saxon formulaic poetry'. *PMLA* **81**. 334–41.

General ed. 1987. *The Riverside Chaucer*. 3rd edn. Boston: Houghton Mifflin.

Bethurum, D. 1971. *The homilies of Wulfstan*. 2nd edn. (1st edn 1957). Oxford: Clarendon Press.

Bevington, D., ed. 1980. *The complete works of Shakespeare*. 3rd edn. Glenview, Ill.: Scott, Foresman.

Blake, N.F. 1977. *The English language in medieval literature*. London: Methuen.

Blanchemain, P., ed. 1873. *Oeuvres complètes*. 2nd edn. 3 vols. Paris: Daffis.

Bliss, A.J. 1958. *The metre of 'Beowulf'*. Oxford: Basil Blackwell.

1962. *An introduction to Old English metre*. Oxford: Basil Blackwell.

ed. 1966. *Sir Orfeo*. 2nd edn. Oxford: Clarendon Press.

1967. *The metre of 'Beowulf'*. 2nd edn. Oxford: Basil Blackwell.

1972. 'The origin and structure of the Old English hypermetric line'. *Notes and Queries* **18**. 442–9.

Blockley, M., & T. Cable. 1990. 'Kuhn's Laws, Old English poetry, and the New Philology'. MS, University of Texas at Austin.

Boccaccio, Giovanni. 1970. *Opere minori in volgare*, vol. 2: *Filostrato, etc.* Ed. Mario Marti. Milan: Rizzoli.

Bolinger, D. L. 1958. 'A theory of pitch accent in English'. *Word* **14**. 109–49.

1962. 'Binomials and pitch accent'. *Lingua* **11**. 34–44.

1972. 'Accent is predictable (if you're a mind-reader)'. *American Speech* **33**. 5–20.

1986. *Intonation and its parts: melody in spoken English*. Stanford: Stanford University Press.

Boomsliter, P. C., Warren Creel & George S. Hastings. 1973. 'Perception and English poetic meter'. *PMLA* **88**. 200–8.

Borroff, M. 1962. *'Sir Gawain and the Green Knight': a stylistic and metrical study*. New Haven: Yale University Press.

1977. *'Pearl': a new verse translation*. New York: Norton.

1986. 'Reading the poem aloud'. In Miriam Y. Miller & Jane Chance, eds., *Approaches to Teaching 'Sir Gawain and the Green Knight'*. New York: Modern Language Association, 191–8.

Brandin, Louis M., & W. G. Hartog. 1904. *A book of French prosody*. London: Blackie.

Brereton, Geoffrey, ed. 1961. *The Penguin book of French verse*, vol. 1: *To the fifteenth century*. Introduced and ed. B. Woledge. Harmondsworth and Baltimore: Penguin.

Breuer, D. 1981. *Deutsche Metrik und Versgeschichte*. Munich: Wilhelm Fink.

Bridges, R. 1901. *Milton's prosody*. Oxford: Oxford University Press.

Brie, F. 1907. 'Zwei frühneuenglische Prosaromane'. *Archiv* **118**. 318–28.

Brink, Bernhard A. K. ten. 1901. *The language and metre of Chaucer*. 2nd edn, rev. Friedrich Kluge, trans. M. Bentinck Smith. London: Macmillan.

Brogan, T. V. F. 1981. *English versification, 1570–1980*. Baltimore and London: Johns Hopkins University Press.

Brook, G. L. 1964. *The Harley lyrics: the Middle English lyrics of Ms Harley 2253*. 3rd edn. Manchester: Manchester University Press.

Bunt, G. H. V., ed. 1985, *'William of Palerne': an alliterative romance*. (Mediaevalia Groninga **6**). Groningen: Bouma's Boekhuis.

1990. 'Localizing *William of Palerne*'. In J. Fisiak, ed., *Historical linguistics and philology*. (Trends in Linguistics. Studies and Monographs **46**). Berlin and New York: Mouton de Gruyter, 73–86.

Burnley, D. 1982. 'Inflexion in Chaucer's adjectives'. *Neuphilologische Mitteilungen* **83**. 169–77.

Butt, J. 1961. *The Twickenham edition of the poems of Alexander Pope*, vol. 1: *Pastoral poetry and 'An Essay on Criticism'*. Ed. E. Audra and Aubrey Williams. London: Methuen; New Haven: Yale University Press.

Cable, T. 1974. *The meter and melody of 'Beowulf'*. (Illinois Studies in Language and Literature **64**). Urbana–Champaign: University of Illinois Press.

1981. 'Metrical style as evidence for the date of *Beowulf*'. In Chase, ed., 78–82.

1988. 'Middle English meter and its theoretical implications'. *Yearbook of Langland Studies* **2**. 47–69.

1989. 'Old and Middle English prosody: transformations of the model'. In Patrick J. Gallacher & Helen Damico, eds., *Hermeneutics and medieval culture*. Albany: State University of New York Press, 201–11.

1991. *The English alliterative tradition*. Philadelphia: University of Pennsylvania Press.

Campbell, A. 1959. *Old English grammar*. Oxford: Oxford University Press.

Cassidy, F.J., & R. Ringler. 1971. *Bright's Old English grammar and reader*. 3rd edn. New York: Holt, Rinehart & Winston.

Catford, J. 1966. 'English phonology and the teaching of pronunciation'. *College English* **27**. 605–13.

Cavalcanti, Guido. 1967. *Rime*. Ed. Giulio Cattaneo. Turin: Einaudi.

Cawley, A.C., ed. 1962. *Pearl, Sir Gawain and the Green Knight*. London: Dent.

Cawley, A.C., & J.J. Anderson, eds. 1976. *Pearl, Cleanness, Patience, Sir Gawain and the Green Knight*. London: Dent.

Chambers, R.W. 1932. *On the continuity of English prose from Alfred to More and his school*. (EETS). Oxford: Oxford University Press.

Champagne, Thibaud de (King of Navarre). 1961. In *The Penguin book of French verse*, vol. 1: *To the fifteenth century*, ed. Brian Woledge. Harmondsworth: Penguin, 151–5.

Champion, P., ed. 1923–7. *Poésies* [Charles D'Orleans]. 2 vols. Paris: Honoré Champion.

Chartier, Alain. 1949. *'La belle dame sans mercy', et les poésies lyriques*. Ed. Arthur Piaget. 2nd edn. Lille: Librairie Giard; Geneva: Droz.

Chase, C., ed. 1981. *The dating of 'Beowulf'*. Toronto: University of Toronto Press.

Chatman, Seymour. 1960. 'Comparing metrical styles'. In Sebeok, ed., 149–72.

1965. *A theory of meter*. The Hague: Mouton.

ed. 1971. *Literary style: a symposium*. (International Symposium on Literary Style, Bellagio 1969). Oxford: Oxford University Press.

Chatman, Seymour, & Samuel Levin. 1969. *Essays on the language of literature*. Boston: Houghton Mifflin.

Chaucer, Geoffrey. *See* Benson, Furnivall, I. Robinson, Speght, Tyrwhitt, Windeatt.

Chomsky, Noam. 1957. *Syntactic structures*. The Hague: Mouton.

Chomsky, Noam, & M. Halle. 1968. *The sound pattern of English*. New York: Harper & Row.

Classé, André. 1939. *The rhythm of English prose*. Oxford: Basil Blackwell.

Cooper, G., & L. Meyer. 1960. *The rhythmic structure of music*. Chicago: University of Chicago Press.

Cosmos, Spencer. 1976. 'Kuhn's law and the unstressed verbs in *Beowulf*'. *Texas Studies in Literature and Language* **18**. 306–28.

Couper-Kuhlen, E. 1986. *An introduction to English prosody*. London: Edward Arnold.

Cowan, Janet M. 1987. 'Metrical problems in editing *The Legend of Good Women*'. In Derek Pearsall, ed., *Manuscripts and texts: editorial problems in later Middle English literature*. Cambridge: D. S. Brewer, 26–33.

Creed, R. P. 1966. 'A new approach to the rhythm of *Beowulf*'. *PMLA* **81**. 23–33.

   1990. *Reconstructing the rhythm of 'Beowulf'*. Columbia: University of Missouri Press.

Crook, Eugene J. 1974. *Richard Jordan's handbook of Middle English grammar: phonology*. The Hague: Mouton.

Danielsson, Bror. 1948. *Studies on the accentuation of polysyllabic Latin, Greek and Romance loan-words in English*. Stockholm: Almqvist & Wiksell.

Dante Alighieri. *See* Howell, Petrocchi.

Dauer, R. M. 1983. 'Stress-timing and syllable-timing reanalysed'. *Journal of Phonetics* **11**. 51–62.

Daunt, M. 1946. 'Old English verse and English speech rhythm'. *Transactions of the Philological Society*. 56–72.

Davis, Norman, ed. 1968. *Sir Gawain and the Green Knight*. Oxford: Clarendon Press.

de Bendittis, L., ed. 1965. *Rime per Lucrezia Bendidio* (Tasso, Collezione di poesia **18**). Turin: Einaudi.

DeFord, Sara. 1967. *The Pearl*. Northbrook, Ill.: AHM.

Dickins, Bruce, & R. M. Wilson, eds. 1952. *Early Middle English texts*. Cambridge: Bowes & Bowes.

Dionisotti, C., ed. 1966. *Prose, rime*. 2nd edn. Turin: Unione Tipografico Editrice Torinese.

Dobbie, Elliot V. K. ed. 1953. *'Beowulf' and 'Judith'*. Anglo-Saxon Poetic Records **4**. New York: Columbia University Press.

Dobson, E. J. 1968. *English pronunciation 1500–1700*. 2nd edn. 2 vols. Oxford: Clarendon Press.

Dogil, G. 1984. 'On the evaluation measure for prosodic phonology'. *Linguistics* **22**. 281–311.

Donaldson, E. Talbot. 1948. 'Chaucer's final -e'. *PMLA* **43**. 1101–24.

   1966. *'Beowulf': a new prose translation*. New York: Norton.

Donoghue, Daniel. 1987a. *Style in Old English poetry: the test of the auxiliary*. New Haven: Yale University Press.

1987b. 'On the classification of b-verses with anacrusis in *Beowulf* and *Andreas*'. *Notes and Queries* **232**. 1–5.

Dresher, B. Elan, & A. Lahiri. 1991. 'The Germanic foot: metrical coherence in Old English'. *Linguistic Inquiry* **22**. 251–86.

Dryden, John. *See* Watson.

Du Bellay, Joachim. 1968. *Poésies*. Ed. S. de Sacy. (Le livre de poche **2229**). Paris: Gallimard.

Duffell, M. 1991. 'The Romance hendecasyllable: an exercise in comparative metrics.' 2 vols. Ph.D. thesis, Queen Mary and Westfield College, University of London. 2 vols.

Duggan, Hoyt. 1986a. 'The shape of the b-verse in Middle English alliterative poetry'. *Speculum* **61**. 564–92.

1986b. 'Alliterative patterning as a basis for emendation in Middle English alliterative poetry'. *Studies in the Age of Chaucer* **8**. 73–105.

1987. 'Notes towards a theory of Langland's meter'. *Yearbook of Langland Studies* **1**. 41–70.

1988a. 'Libertine scribes and maidenly editors: the text and meter of *Pearl*.' Paper presented at the 23rd International Congress on Medieval Studies, Kalamazoo, Mich.

1988b. 'Final -*e* and the rhythmic structure of the b-verse in Middle English alliterative poetry'. *Modern Philology* **85**. 119–45.

1988c. 'The evidential basis for Old English metrics'. *Studies in Philology* **85**. 145–63.

1990a. 'Langland's dialect and final -*e*'. *Studies in the Age of Chaucer* **12**. 157–91.

1990b. 'Stress assignment in Middle English alliterative poetry'. *Journal of English and Germanic Philology* **91**. 309– 29.

1990c. 'Scribal self-correction and editorial theory'. *Neuphilologische Mitteilungen* **91**. 215–27.

Duggan, Hoyt, & Thorlac Turville-Petre, eds. 1989. *The Wars of Alexander*. EETS, 2nd ser., **10**. Oxford: Oxford University Press.

Dunn, Charles W. 1960. *The foundling and the werewolf: a literary–historical study of 'Guillaume de Palerne'*. (University of Toronto Department of English Studies and Texts 8). Toronto and London: University of Toronto Press.

Elwert, W. Theodor. 1965. *Traité de versification française*. Paris: Klincksieck.

Emerson, Oliver F. 1921. 'Imperfect lines in *Pearl* and the rimed parts of *Sir Gawain and the Green Knight*'. *Modern Philology* **19**. 131–41.

1922. 'Some notes on *The Pearl*'. *PMLA* **37**. 52–93.

1927. 'More notes on *The Pearl*'. *PMLA* **42**. 807–31.

Ende, F. Von. 1973. *The prosody of the 'Pearl' poet: a technical analysis of the poems in MS. Cotton Nero A.x.* Digest of Abstracts International **A** **3065-6**.

Evans, G. Blakemore. 1974. *The Riverside Shakespeare*. Boston: Houghton Mifflin.

Fein, S. G. 1989. '*Haue mercy of me* (Psalm 51): an unedited alliterative poem from the London Thornton manuscript.' *Modern Philology* **86**. 223-41.

Fisiak, J., ed. 1990. *Historical linguistics and philology*. (Trends in Linguistics. Studies and Monographs **46**). Berlin and New York: Mouton de Gruyter.

Foulet, A., & M. B. Speer. 1979. *On editing Old French texts*. Lawrence: Regents Press of Kansas.

Fox, D., ed. 1968. *The testament of Cresseid*. London: Nelson.

Franck, J. 1894. 'Rhythmik des Alliterationsverses'. *Zeitschrift für deutsches Altertum* **38**. 225-50.

Freeman, D. C., ed. 1968. *Linguistics and literary style*. New York: Holt.

Froissart, Jehan. *See* McGregor.

Fry, D. K. 1967. 'Old English formulas and systems'. *English Studies* **48**. 194-204.

Fulk, R. D. 1992. *A history of Old English meter*. Philadelphia: University of Pennsylvania Press.

Fuller, John. 1972. *The sonnet*. (Critical Idiom Series **26**). London: Methuen.

Furnivall, F. J., ed. 1868. '*The Canterbury Tales*': *a six-text print in parallel columns*, vol. 1: '*The General Prologue*'. London: Trubner.

Fussell, Paul. 1979. *Poetic meter and poetic form*. 2nd edn. (1st edn 1965). New York: Random House.

Garcilaso de la Vega. *See* Rivers.

Gardner, H. 1949. *The art of T. S. Eliot*. London: Cresset.

Giegerich, H. J. 1985. *Metrical phonology and phonological structure: German and English*. Cambridge: Cambridge University Press.

  1986. *A relational model of German syllable structure*. (Series A. Paper 159) Duisburg: LAUDT.

  1992. *English phonology: an introduction*. Cambridge: Cambridge University Press.

Gollancz, *Sir* I., ed. 1921. *Pearl*. London: Chatto & Windus.

Gordon, E. V., ed. 1953. *Pearl*. Oxford: Clarendon Press.

Gordon, Ian A. 1966. *The movement of English prose*. London: Longman.

Gower, John. 1899. *The complete works of John Gower: French works*. Ed. G. C. Macaulay. Oxford: Clarendon Press.

Granson, Oton de. 1936. In *La poésie française en Catalogue du XIIIe siècle à la fin du XVe*, ed. Amadeu Pagès. (Bibliothèque Méridionale, 1st ser., **23**). Toulouse: Edouard Privat, 176-244.

Graves, R., ed. 1957. *English and Scottish ballads*. London: Heinemann.

Gross, H. 1979. *The structure of verse: modern essays on prosody*. 2nd edn. New York: Echo Press.

Guest, E. 1838. *A history of English rhythms*. London: George Bell & Sons. (New edn 1882, ed. W. W. Skeat).

Guthrie, S. R. 1988a. 'Babcock's curve and the problem of Chaucer's final -e'. *English Studies* **89**. 386–95.

1988b. 'Prosody and the study of Chaucer: a generative reply to Halle-Keyser'. *Chaucer Review* **23**. 30–49.

Hall, J., ed. 1920. *Selections from early Middle English 1130–1250*. 2 vols. Oxford: Clarendon Press.

Halle, M., & S. J. Keyser. 1966. 'Chaucer and the study of prosody'. *College English* **28**. 187–219.

1971. *English stress: its form, its growth, and its role in verse*. New York: Harper & Row.

Hayes, B. 1982. 'Extrametricality and English stress'. *Linguistic Inquiry* **13**. 227–76.

1983. 'A grid-based theory of English meter.' *Linguistic Inquiry* **14**. 357–94.

1984. 'The phonology of rhythm in English'. *Linguistic Inquiry* **15**. 33–74.

1988. 'Metrics and phonological theory'. In Frederick J. Newmeyer, ed., *Linguistics: the Cambridge survey*, vol. 2. Cambridge: Cambridge University Press, 220–50.

1989. 'The prosodic hierarchy in meter'. In P. Kiparsky & G. Youmans, eds., *Phonetics and phonology*, vol. 1: *Rhythm and meter*. San Diego: Academic Press, 201–60.

Henryson, Robert. *See* Fox, D.

Heusler, Andreas. 1891. 'Zur geschichten der altdeutschen Verskunst'. *Germanische Abhandlungen* **8**. 1–159.

1925–9. 'Deutsche Versgeschichte, mit Einschluß des altenglischen und altnordischen Stabreimverses'. In H. Paul, ed., *Pauls Grundriß der germanischen Philologie*, vol. 8. Berlin: Walter de Gruyter.

Hieatt, Constance. 1989. 'A brief guide to the scansion of Old English poetry'. *Old English Newsletter* **23**. 33–5.

Hogg, Richard, & C. B. McCully. 1987. *Metrical phonology: a coursebook*. Cambridge: Cambridge University Press.

Hollowell, Ida M. 1982. 'On Old English verse rhythm'. *English Studies* **63**. 385–93.

Holt, R., ed. 1878. *The Ormulum*. 2 vols. Oxford: Clarendon Press.

Homer. *See* Stanford.

Hooper, W., ed. 1969. *Selected literary essays* [C. S. Lewis]. Cambridge: Cambridge University Press.

Hoover, D. L. 1985. *A new theory of Old English meter*. New York: Peter Lang.

Hoepffner, E., ed. 1908–21. *Oeuvres* [Guillaume de Machaut]. 3 vols. (Société des anciens textes français **57**). Paris: Firmin Didot.

Howell, A. G. Ferrers, trans. 1973. *De vulgari eloquentia* [Dante Alighieri]. London: Rebel Press.

Hrushovski, Benjamin. 1960. 'On free rhythms in modern poetry.' In Sebeok, ed. 173–90.

Hutcheson, Rand. 1995. *Old English poetic metre*. Cambridge: D. S. Brewer.

Jakobson, R. 1963. 'On the so-called vowel alliteration in Germanic verse'. *Zeitschrift für Phonetik, Sprachwissenschaft und Kommunikationsforschung* **16**. 85–92.

   1987. 'Linguistics and poetics'. In Krystyna Pomorska & S. Rudy, eds., *Roman Jakobson: language in literature*. Cambridge, Mass.: Belknap Press of Harvard University Press, 62–94. *See also* Sebeok, ed., 350–77.

Jasinski, M. 1970. *Histoire du sonnet en France*. 2nd edn. Geneva: Slatkine.

Jefferson, J. A. 1987. 'The Hoccleve holographs and Hoccleve's metrical practice'. In D. Pearsall, ed., *Manuscripts and texts: editorial problems in later Middle English literature*. Cambridge: D. S. Brewer, 95–109.

Jespersen, O. 1913. 'Notes on metre'. In *Linguistica: selected papers in English, French and German*. Copenhagen: Levin & Munksgaard, 249–74.

Jordan, Richard. *See* Crook.

Kahn, D. 1980. *Syllable-based generalizations in English phonology*. New York: Garland.

Kaluza, M. 1881. 'Das mittelenglische Gedicht *William of Palerne* und seine französische Quelle'. *Englische Studien* **4**. 196–287.

   1911. *A short history of English versification*, trans. A. C. Dunstan. New York: Macmillan.

Kane, G. 1981. 'Music "neither unpleasant nor monotonous"'. In P. L. Heyworth, ed., *Medieval studies for J. A. W. Bennett*. Oxford: Oxford University Press, 43–63.

Kane, G., & E. T. Donaldson, eds. 1975. *Will's vision of Piers Plowman and do-well, do-better and do-best: 'Piers Plowman': the B version*. London: Athlone Press. (Rev. edn. 1988. Athlone Press and University of California Press, Berkeley.)

Kean, P. M. 1967. *'The Pearl': an interpretation*. London: Routledge & Kegan Paul.

Kelly, M. H., & D. C. Rubin. 1988. 'Natural rhythmic patterns in English verse: evidence from child counting-out rhymes'. *Journal of Memory and Language* **27**. 718–40.

Kemble, J. M. 1833 (2nd edn. 1835). *The Anglo-Saxon poems of 'Beowulf', 'The Travellers Song' and 'the Battle of Finnsburh'*. London: William Pickering.

Kendall, C.B. 1983. 'The metrical grammar of *Beowulf*: displacement'. *Speculum* **58**. 1–30.

1991. *The metrical grammar of 'Beowulf'*. (Cambridge Studies in Anglo-Saxon England **5**). Cambridge: Cambridge University Press.

Ker, W.P. 1898. 'Analogies between English and Spanish verse (arte mayor)'. *Transactions of the Philological Society*. 113–28.

1966. *Form and style in poetry*. New York: Russell & Russell.

Keyser, S.J. 1969a. 'Old English prosody'. *College English* **30**. 331–65.

1969b. 'Reply.' *College English* **31**. 71–4.

Keyser, S.J., & W. O'Neil. 1985. *Rule generalization and optionality in language change*. Dordrecht: Foris.

Kiparsky, P. 1975. 'Stress, syntax and meter'. *Language* **51**. 576–615.

1977. 'The rhythmic structure of English verse'. *Linguistic Inquiry* **8**. 189–247.

1989. 'Sprung rhythm'. In Kiparsky & Youmans, eds., 305–40.

Kiparsky, P., & G. Youmans, eds. 1989. *Phonetics and phonology*, vol. 1: *Rhythm and meter*. San Diego: Academic Press.

Klaeber, F., ed. 1950. *'Beowulf' and 'The Fight at Finnsburg'*. 3rd edn. Boston: Heath. (1st edn. 1922).

Koelb, C. 1979. 'The iambic pentameter revisited'. *Neophilologus* **63**. 321–9.

Kuhn, H. 1933. 'Zur Wortsellung und -betonung im Altgermanischen'. *Beiträge zur Geschichte der deutschen Sprache und Literatur* **57**. 1–109.

Kurylowicz, J. 1979. 'Linguistic fundamentals of the meter of *Beowulf*.' In M.A. Jazayery, E.C. Polomé & W. Winter, eds., *Linguistic and literary studies in honor of Archibald A. Hill*. The Hague: Mouton, 111–19.

Lachmann, K. 1876. 'Über althochdeutsche Betonung und Verskunst'. *Kleine Schriften* **1**. 358–406.

Laing, M. 1988. 'Dialectal analysis and linguistically composite texts in Middle English'. *Speculum* **63**. 83–103.

ed. 1989. *Middle English dialectology*. Aberdeen: Aberdeen University Press.

Lanier, S. 1909. *The science of English verse*. New York: Scribner.

Lass, R. 1987. *The shape of English*. London: Dent.

Lavaud, R., & G. Machicot, eds. 1950. *Poème sur Boèce (fragment): le plus ancien texte littéraire occitan*. Trans. the editors. Toulouse: Institut d'Études Occitanes.

Lawton, D., ed. 1982. *Middle English alliterative poetry and its literary background*. Woodbridge, Suffolk: D.S. Brewer.

Lehiste, Ilse. 1977. 'Isochrony reconsidered'. *Journal of Phonetics* **5**. 253–63.

Lehmann, W.P. 1956. *The development of Germanic verse form*. Austin: University of Texas Press.

Lehnert, M. 1953. *Sprachform und Sprachfunktion im 'Orrmulum' (um 1200): die Deklination*. (Suppl. 1 to *Zeitschrift für Anglistik und Amerikanistik*). Berlin: Deutscher Verlag der Wissenschaften.

Lentini, Giacomo da. 1965. *Sonetti della scuola Siciliana*. Ed. Edoardo Sanguineti. 2nd edn. Turin: Einaudi, 15–40.

Leonard, W. E. 1916. '*Beowulf* and the Niebelungen couplet'. *University of Wisconsin Studies in Language and Literature* 1. 99–152.

1929. 'Four footnotes to papers on Germanic metrics'. In Kemp Malone, ed., *Studies in English philology: a miscellany in honor of Frederick Klaeber*. Minneapolis: University of Minnesota Press, 1–13.

Le Page, R. B. 1957. 'A rhythmical framework for the five types'. *English and Germanic Studies* 6. 92–103.

Lewis, C. S. 1939. 'The fifteenth-century heroic line'. *Essays and Studies* 24. 28–41.

1969. *Selected literary essays*. Ed. Walter Hooper. Cambridge: Cambridge University Press.

Liberman, Mark. 1975. 'The intonational system of English.' Ph.D. thesis, Massachusetts Institute of Technology.

Liberman, Mark, & A. Prince. 1977. 'On stress and linguistic rhythm'. *Linguistic Inquiry* 8. 249–336.

Longnon, A., ed. 1932. *Oeuvres*. 4th edn. rev. Lucien Foulet. Paris: Champion.

Lotz, J. 1960. 'Metric typology'. In Sebeok, ed., 135–48.

Lucas, P. J. 1987. 'Some aspects of the interaction between verse grammar and metre in Old English poetry'. *Studia Neophilologica* 59. 145–75.

Luecke, J.-M. 1978. *Measuring Old English rhythm*. (Literary Monographs Series 9). Madison: University of Wisconsin Press.

Luick, K. 1891. 'Zur a.e. und altsächsischen Metrik (Schwellvers und Normalvers, Alliteration und Versrhythmus)'. *Beiträge der Geschichte der deutschen Sprache und Literatur* 15. 441–54.

1914–40. *Historische Grammatik der englischen Sprache*. 2 vols. Stuttgart: Bernhard Tauchnitz. (Repr. 1964 with additional material by Friedrich Wild & Herbert Koziol.)

Macaulay, G. C., ed. 1899. *The complete works of John Gower: French works*. Oxford: Clarendon Press.

Machaut, Guillaume de. 1908–21. *Oeuvres*. Ed. E. Hoepffner. 3 vols. (Société des anciens textes français 57). Paris: Firmin Didot.

Magnuson, K., & F. G. Ryder. 1970. 'The study of English prosody: an alternative proposal'. *College English* 31. 789–820.

Magoun, F. P. 1953. 'The oral-formulaic character of Anglo-Saxon narrative poetry'. *Speculum* 28. 446–65.

Maling, J. 1971. 'Sentence stress in Old English'. *Linguistic Inquiry* 2. 379–99.

Malof, J. 1964. 'The native rhythm of English meters'. *Texas Studies in Literature and Language* 5. 580–94.

1970. *A manual of English meters*. Bloomington and London: Indiana University Press.

Marchand, H. 1969. *Categories and types of present-day English word-formation*. Munich: Beck'sche Verlagshandlung.

Marot, Clément. 1966. *Oeuvres complètes*, vol. 4: *Oeuvres diverses*. Ed. C.A. Mayer. London: Athlone Press.

Marti, M., ed. 1970. *Opere minore in volgare*, vol. 2: *Filostrato etc.* Milan: Rizzoli.

Matonis, A.T.E. 1981. 'Middle English alliterative poetry'. In Benskin & Samuels, eds., 341–54.

　1984. 'A re-examination of the Middle English alliterative long line'. *Modern Philology* **81**. 339–60.

　1988. 'The Harley lyrics: English and Welsh convergences'. *Modern Philology* **86**. 1–21.

Mayer, C.A., ed. 1966. *Oeuvres complètes* [Clément Marot], vol 4: *Oeuvres diverses*. London: Athlone Press.

McCully, C.B. 1988. 'The phonology of English rhythm and metre, with special reference to Old English.' Ph.D. thesis, University of Manchester.

　1991. 'Non-linear phonology and Elizabethan prosody'. *Transactions of the Philological Society* **89**. 1–35.

　1992. 'The phonology of resolution in Old English word-stress and metre'. In Fran Coman, ed., *Evidence for Old English*. (Edinburgh Studies in English Language 2). Edinburgh: John Donald, 117–41.

McCully, C.B., & R.M. Hogg. 1990. 'An account of Old English stress'. *Journal of Linguistics* **26**. 315–39.

　1994. 'Dialect variation and historical metrics'. *Diachronica* **11**. 13–34.

McGregor, R.R., Jun., ed. 1975. *The lyric poems of Jehan Froissart*. (North Carolina Studies in the Romance Languages and Literatures **143**). Chapel Hill: University of North Carolina.

McIntosh, A. 1949. 'Wulfstan's prose'. *Proceedings of the British Academy* **35**. 109–42.

　1982. 'Early Middle English alliterative verse'. In D. Lawton, ed., *Middle English alliterative poetry and its literary background*. Woodbridge, Suffolk: D.S. Brewer, 20–33.

Meunier, J.M., ed. 1933. *'La vie de Saint Alexis': poème française du XIe siécle*. Paris: Droz.

Micha, A., ed. 1990. *'Guillaume de Palerne': roman du XIII siècle*. (Textes littéraire français **384**). Genève: Droz.

Michelant, H., ed. 1876. *Guillaume de Palerne*. (Société des anciens textes français). Paris: Firmin Didot.

Miller, G.A. 1956. 'The magical number seven plus or minus two'. *Psychological Review* **63**. 81–97.

Minkova, D. 1984a. 'Early Middle English metrical elision and schwa deletion'. In N.F. Blake & C. Jones, eds., *English historical linguistics: studies in development*. Sheffield: CECTAL, 56–66.

1984b. 'On the hierarchy of factors causing schwa loss in Middle English'. *Neuphilologische Mitteilungen* **80**. 445–54.

1985. 'The prosodic character of early schwa deletion in English'. In A. G. Ramat et al., eds., *Papers from the 7th International Conference on Historical Linguistics*. Amsterdam: John Benjamins, 445–59.

1990. 'Adjectival inflexion relics and speech rhythm in late Middle and early Modern English'. In S. Adamson et al., eds., *Papers from the 5th International Conference on English Historical Linguistics*. Amsterdam: John Benjamins, 313–37.

1991. *The history of final vowels in English*. Berlin: Mouton de Gruyter.

1992. 'Verse structure in the Middle English *Genesis* and *Exodus*'. *Journal of English and Germanic Philology* **91**. 157–79.

Minkova, D., & Robert P. Stockwell. 1994. 'Syllable weight, prosody, and meter in Old English'. *Diachronica* **11**. 35–64.

Mitchell, B. 1985. *Old English syntax*. 2 vols. Oxford: Oxford University Press.

Monteverdi, A. 1963. 'Storia dell' iscrizione ferrarese del 1135'. *Memorie della Accademia die Lincei*. Cl. di scienze mor. stor. e fil., ser. 8, **11**, fasc. 2. 101–38.

Moorman, C., ed. 1977. *The works of the 'Gawain'-poet*. Jackson; University Press of Mississippi.

1986. *The 'Pearl' poet*. New York: Twayne.

Morse, R., ed. 1975. *Saint Erkenwald*. Cambridge: D. S. Brewer.

Mossé, F. 1952. *A handbook of Middle English*. Baltimore: Johns Hopkins University Press.

Nakao, T. 1977. *The prosodic phonology of late Middle English*. Tokyo: Shinozaki Shorin.

Nist, J. 1964. 'The word-group cadence: basis of English metrics'. *Linguistics* **6**. 73–82.

Northup, C. S. 1897. 'A study of the metrical structure of the Middle English poem *The Pearl*'. *PMLA* **12**. 326–40.

Oakden, J. P. 1930–5. *Alliterative poetry in Middle English*. 2 vols. Manchester: Manchester University Press. (Reprinted in 1 vol., Hamden, Conn.: Archon Books, 1968).

Obst, W. 1987. *Der Rhythmus des 'Beowulf': eine Akzent- und Takttheorie*. (Anglistische Forshungen **187**). Heidelberg: Carl Winter.

O'Loughlin, J. L. N. 1935. 'The Middle English alliterative *Morte Arthure*'. *Medium Ævum* **4**. 153–68.

Omond, T. S. 1907. *A study of metre*. London: De La More Press.

Opland, J. 1980. *Anglo-Saxon oral poetry*. New Haven and London: Yale University Press.

O'Rahilly, C., ed. and trans. 1949. *'Eachtra Uilliam': an Irish version of 'William of Palerne'*. Dublin: Dublin Institute for Advanced Studies.

Orleans, Charles D'. *See* Champion, Purcell.

Osberg, R.H. 1984. 'Alliterative technique in the lyrics of MS Harley 2253'. *Modern Philology* **82**. 125–55.

Osgood, C.G., ed. 1906. *'The Pearl': a Middle English poem*. Boston: Heath.

Parkes, M.B. 1983. 'On the presumed date of the manuscript of the *Ormulum*: Oxford, Bodleian Library, MS Junius 1'. In E.G. Stanley & D. Gray, eds., *Five hundred years of words and sounds: a festschrift for Eric Dobson*. Cambridge: D.S. Brewer, 115–28.

Partridge, A.C. 1982. *A companion to Old and Middle English studies*. London: Andre Deutsch.

Paul, H., ed. 1891–3. *Grundriß der germanischen Philologie*. 3 vols. Strassburg: Karl Trubner.
    ed. 1925–9. *Grundriß der germanischen Philologie, unter Mitwirkung zahlreichen Fachgelehrter*. Berlin: Walter de Gruyter.

Pearsall, D. 1977. *Old and Middle English poetry*. London: Routledge.

Petrarch. *See* Vianello.

Petrocchi, G., ed. 1975. *La 'Commedia' secondo l'antica volgata* [Dante Alighieri]. 2nd edn. Turin: Einaudi.

Pighi, G.B. 1970. *Studi di ritmica e metrica*. Turin: Bottega d'Erasmo.

Pomorska, K., & S. Rudy, eds. 1987. *Language in literature*. Cambridge, Mass., and London: Belknap Press of Harvard University Press.

Pope, J.C. 1942. *The rhythm of 'Beowulf'*. New Haven: Yale University Press.
    1966. *The rhythm of 'Beowulf'*. Rev. edn. New Haven: Yale University Press.

Pope, Mildred K. 1934. *From Latin to modern French*. Manchester: Manchester University Press.

Preminger, A., with F.J. Wernke & O.B. Hardison, eds. 1975. *Princeton encyclopaedia of poetry and poetics*. London: Macmillan.

Prince, A. 1989. 'Metrical forms'. In Kiparsky & Youmans, eds., 45–81.

Pulgram, E. 1964. 'Prosodic systems: French'. *Lingua* **13**. 125–44.

Purcell, Sally, ed. 1973. *Selected poems of Charles of Orleans*. Cheadle, Cheshire: Carcanet.

Pyle, F. 1973. 'Chaucer's prosody'. *Medium Ævum* **42**. 47–56.

Quirk, R. 1963. 'Poetic language and Old English metre'. In A. Brown & P. Foote, eds., *Early English and Norse studies presented to Hugh Smith in honour of his sixtieth birthday*. London: Methuen, 150–71.

Reinhard, M. 1976. *On the semantic relevance of the alliterative collocations in 'Beowulf'*. Bern: A. Francke.

Renoir, A., & A. Hernandez, eds. 1982. *Approaches to Beowulfian scansion: four essays*. (Old English Colloquium Series 1). Department of English, University of California, Berkeley.

Rivers, E.L., ed. 1972. *Poesias castellanas completas*. (Clásicos Castalia **6**). Madrid: Castalia.

Robinson, F.C. 1985. *'Beowulf' and the appositive style*. Knoxville: University of Tennessee Press.

Robinson, Ian. 1971. *Chaucer's prosody*. Cambridge: Cambridge University Press.

Ronsard, Pierre de. *See* Schmidt, Albert-M.

Rosenthal, F. 1878. 'Die alliterierende englische Langzeile im 14. Jahrhundert'. *Anglia* **1**. 414–59.

Russom, G. 1987. *Old English meter and linguistic theory*. Cambridge: Cambridge University Press.

Saavedra Molina, J. 1946. 'Tres grandes metros: el endecasilabo'. *Anales de la Universidad de Chile* **104**. 63–122.

Saint-Gelais, Mellin de. 1873. *Oeuvres complètes*. Ed.Prosper Blanchemain. 2nd edn, rev. 3 vols. Paris: P. Daffis.

Saintsbury, G. 1961. *A history of English prosody*. 2nd edn. New York: Russell & Russell.

Samuels, M.L. 1972. 'Chaucerian final -e'. *Notes & Queries* **217**. 445–8.

1985. 'Langland's dialect'. *Medium Ævum* **54**. 232–47.

1988. 'Dialect and grammar'. In J. Alford, ed., *A companion to 'Piers Plowman'*. Berkeley and Los Angeles: University of California Press, 201–21.

Sanguineti, E., ed. 1965. *Sonetti della scuola Siciliana*. 2nd edn. Turin: Einaudi.

Sapora, R. 1977. *A theory of Middle English alliterative meter*. (Speculum Monographs **1**). Cambridge, Mass.: Medieval Academy of America, 83–114.

Savage, H.L. 1956. 'Review of Gordon's *Pearl*'. *Modern Language Notes* **71**. 124–9.

Schipper, J. 1910. *A history of English versification*. Oxford: Clarendon Press.

Schlerman, B.J. 1989. *The meters of John Webster*. New York: Peter Lang.

Schmidt, A.V.C. 1987. *The clerkly maker: Langland's poetic art*. Cambridge: D.S. Brewer.

Schmidt, Albert-M., ed. 1964. *Les amours* [Ronsard] 2 vols. (Le livre de poche **1242, 1243**). Paris: Gallimard.

Schumacher, K. 1914. *Studien über das Stabreim in der mittelenglischen Alliterationsdichtung*. (Bonner Studien zur englischen Philologie **11**). Bonn: Peter Hanstein.

Scott, C. 1980. *French verse-art: a study*. Cambridge: Cambridge University Press.

Sebeok, T.A., ed. 1960. *Style in language*. Cambridge, Mass.: MIT Press.

See, K. von. 1967. *Germanische Verskunst*. (Sammlung Metzler **67**). Stuttgart: Metzler.

Selkirk, E.O. 1984. *Phonology and syntax: the relation between sound and structure*. Cambridge, Mass.: MIT Press.

Shippey, T.A. 1972. *Old English verse*. London: Hutchinson.

Sievers, E. 1885. 'Zur Rhythmik des germanischen Alliterationsverses'. *Beiträge zur Geschichte der deutschen Sprache und Literatur* **10**. 209–314, 451–545.

1893. *Altgermanische Metrik*. Halle: Niemeyer.

Simms, N. T., ed. 1973. *William of Palerne*. Norwood, Pa.: Norwood Editions.

Simpson, P. 1943. 'The rhyming of stressed and unstressed syllables in Elizabethan verse'. *Modern Language Review* **38**. 127–9.

Smithers, G. V., ed. 1952. *Kyng Alisaunder*. (EETS, old ser., **227**). Oxford: Oxford University Press.

1983. 'The scansion of *Havelok* and the use of ME *-en* and *-e* in *Havelok* and by Chaucer'. In D. Gray & E. G. Stanley, eds., *Middle English studies presented to Norman Davis in honour of his seventieth birthday*. Oxford: Clarendon Press, 195– 234.

ed. 1987. *Havelok*. Oxford: Clarendon Press.

Sonnenschein, E. A. 1925. *What is rhythm?* Oxford: Basil Blackwell.

Southworth, J. G. 1954. *Verses of cadence*. Oxford: Basil Blackwell.

1962. *The prosody of Chaucer and his followers*. Oxford: Basil Blackwell.

Speght, T., ed. 1602. *The workes of ovr ancient and learned English poet, Geoffrey Chaucer*. London: Adam Islip.

Spurgeon, C. F. E. 1925. *Five hundred years of Chaucer criticism and allusion: 1357–1900*. 3 vols. Cambridge: Cambridge University Press.

Standop, E. 1975. 'Metric theory gone astray: a critique of the Halle–Keyser theory'. *Language and Style* **8**. 60–77.

Stanford, W. B., ed. 1964. *The Odyssey*. 2nd edn. London: Macmillan.

Stanley, E. G. 1988. 'Rhymes in English medieval verse: from Old English to Middle English'. In E. Kennedy, R. Waldron & J. S. Wittig, eds., *Medieval English studies presented to George Kane*. Wolfeboro, N.H.: D. S. Brewer, 19–55.

Steele, Joshua. 1775. *An essay towards establishing the melody and measure of speech*. Facs. edn. Menston: Scolar Press.

Stevenson, C. L. 1970. 'The rhythm of English verse'. *Journal of Aesthetics and Art Criticism* **28**. 327–44.

Stevick, R. D. 1975. *'Beowulf': an edition with manuscript spacing notation and graphotactic analyses*. New York and London: Garland.

Stewart, G. R. 1930. *The technique of English verse*. New York: Holt.

Stockwell, R. P. & D. Minkova. 1989. 'Kuhn's Laws and verb-second: on Kendall's theory of syntactic displacement in *Beowulf*'. Manuscript, University of California at Los Angeles.

Strang, B. M. H. 1970. *A history of English*. London: Methuen.

Sumera, M. 1970. 'The temporal tradition in the study of verse structure'. *Linguistics* **62**. 44–65.

Suphi, M. 1985. 'Non-linear analyses in English historical phonology'. Ph.D. thesis, University of Edinburgh.

1988. 'Old English stress assignment'. *Lingua* **75**. 171–202.

Suzuki, S. 1985. 'Syllable structure in OE poetry'. *Lingua* **67**. 97– 119.

Sweet, H. 1879. 'On the laws of stress in compounds, in English'. *Transactions of the Philological Society*. 4–6.

Tarlinskaja, M. 1973. 'The syllabic structure and meter of English verse from the thirteenth through the nineteenth centuries'. *Language and Style* **6**. 249–72.

1974a. 'Meter and rhythm of pre-Chaucerian rhymed verse'. *Linguistics* **121**. 65–87.

1974b. 'K voprosu o sredneangliyskom slovesnom udarenii (na materiale stiha XII–XVII vv.' [Word stress in Middle English (based on verse material XII–XVII centuries]. *Sbornik naucnih trudov Moskovskogo gosudarstvennogo pedagogiceskogo instituta inostrannyh jazykov imeni Morisa Toreza Vypusk* **81**. 104–41.

1976a. 'The accentual structure and meter of English verse (13–19th centuries)'. *Linguistics* **169**. 41–58.

1976b. *English verse: theory and history*. The Hague: Mouton.

1989. 'General and particular aspects of meter: literatures, epochs, poets'. In Kiparsky & Youmans, eds., 121–54.

Tasso, Torquato. *See* de Bendittis.

Tatlock, J. S. P., & A. G. Kennedy. 1963. *A concordance to the complete works of Geoffrey Chaucer and to the 'Romaunt of the Rose'*. Gloucester, Mass.: Peter Smith.

Thomas, W. 1904. *Le décasyllable roman et sa fortune en Europe: essai de métrique comparée*. With a preface by A. Beljame. (Travaux et mémoires de l'Université de Lille, n.s. 1, Droit, lettres, fasc. 4). Lille: Lille University Press.

Thompson, J. 1961. *The founding of English metre*. New York: Routledge & Kegan Paul. (2nd edn. 1966)

Tolkien, J. R. R., ed. 1975. *'Sir Gawain and the Green Knight', 'Pearl', and 'Sir Orfeo'*. London: Allen & Unwin.

Tolkien, J. R. R., & E. V. Gordon, eds. 1967. *Sir Gawain and the Green Knight*. 2nd rev. edn. Oxford: Clarendon Press.

Trigg, S., ed. 1990. *Wynnere and wastoure*. (EETS, 2nd ser., **297**). London: Oxford University Press.

Turville-Petre, T. 1977. *The alliterative revival*. Cambridge: D. S. Brewer.

1980. 'Emendation on grounds of alliteration in *The Wars of Alexander*'. *English Studies* **61**. 302–17.

1987. 'Editing *The Wars of Alexander*'. In D. Pearsall, ed., *Manuscripts and texts: editorial problems in later Middle English literature*. Cambridge: D. S. Brewer, 143–60.

ed. 1989. *Alliterative poetry of the later Middle Ages*. London: Routledge.

Tyrwhitt, T., ed. 1822. *The Canterbury Tales*. 5 vols. London: W. Pickering.

Vantuono, W., ed. 1984. *The 'Pearl' poems: an omnibus edition*. 2 vols. New York: Garland.

Vega, Garcilaso de la. 1972. *Poesías castellanas completas*. Ed. Elias L. Rivers. (Clásico Castalia **6**). Madrid: Castalia.

Vianello, N., ed. 1966. *Il cansoniere* [Petrarch]. Basiano: Bietti.

Vinaver, E. 1939. 'Principles of textual emendation'. In *Studies in French language and medieval literature presented to Professor Mildred K. Pope*. Manchester: Manchester University Press, 351–69.

Visch, E.A.M. 1989. 'A metrical theory of rhythmic stress phenomena'. Doctoral diss., Utrecht University.

Watson, G.G., ed. 1967–8. *John Dryden: Of dramatic poesy, and other critical essays*. London: Dent.

Weismiller, E.R. 1989. 'Triple threats to duple rhythm'. In Kiparsky & Youmans, eds., 261–90.

Wexler, P.J. 1966. 'Distich and sentence in Corneille and Racine'. In R. Fowler, ed., *Essays on style and language*. London: Routledge, 100–17.

Whitman, F.H.A. 1993. *A comparative study of Old English meter*. Toronto: University of Toronto Press.

Williams, M. 1967. *The 'Pearl' poet: his complete works*. New York: Random House.

Wimsatt, W.K. 1970. 'The rule and the norm: Halle and Keyser on Chaucer's metre'. *College English* **31**. 774–88.

Wimsatt, W.K., & M.C. Beardsley. 1959. 'The concept of meter: an exercise in abstraction'. *PMLA* **74**. 585–98.

Windeatt, B.A. 1977. '"Most conservatyf the soun": Chaucer's *Troilus* metre'. *Poetica* (Tokyo) **8**. 44–60.

ed. 1984. *Troilus and Criseyde*. London: Longman.

Winters, Y. 1947. *In defense of reason*. Denver: University of Denver Press.

1957. *The function of criticism: problems and exercises*. Chicago: Swallow; London: Routledge & Kegan Paul.

1967. *Forms of discovery: critical and historical essays on the form of the short poem in English*. Chicago: Swallow.

Wittgenstein, L. 1958. *The blue and brown books*. New York: Harper & Row.

Woods, S. 1985. *Natural emphasis: English versification from Chaucer to Dryden*. San Marino, Calif.: Huntington Library.

Wrenn, C.L., ed. 1973. *Beowulf, with the Finnesburg Fragment*. 3rd edn., rev. by W.F. Bolton. London: Harrap.

Wright, J., & E.M. Wright. 1928. *An elementary Middle English grammar*. 2nd edn. Oxford: Oxford University Press.

Youmans, G. 1982. 'Hamlet's testimony on Kiparsky's theory of meter'. *Neophilologus* **66**. 490–503.

1983. 'Generative tests for generative meter'. *Language* **59**. 67–92.

1989. 'Milton's meter'. In Kiparsky & Youmans, eds., 341–79.

Index